KINGDOM *PURSUIT*

Exploring the Many Facets
of Missions

Joint General Editors Dr. Carl D. Chaplin and Sue Harris

**DISCIPLESHIP
MINISTRIES**

© 2017 Committee on Discipleship Ministries
1700 North Brown Road, Suite 102
Lawrenceville, Georgia 30043
Bookstore: 1-800-283-1357
678-825-1100
www.pcacdm.org

Unless otherwise indicated, all quotations from Scripture are from the English Standard Version of the Bible, copyright © 2001 by Crossway Bibles, a division of Good News Publishers.

ISBN: 978-1-944964-15-3

"How refreshing to read essays from God's harvest workers who serve on the front lines of The Great Commission. These compositions are powerful testimonies of missionaries, who not only have their ears to the ground, but whom the Lord has utilized as the very instruments of transformational change and kingdom labor that brings glory to Christ. Their captivating stories in Kingdom Pursuit inspire me toward greater engagement and intentionality of global missions. Kingdom Pursuit makes me want to love and serve my Lord."

—Alexander Jun, Ph.D., Moderator of the 45th General Assembly, Presbyterian Church in America

My experience working in the world of Christian missions has shown me two important realities. First, God is at work in the world in unprecedented ways. The Church has never grown faster than at the present time. The second is that so many in the Church have no knowledge or understanding of how dynamic God's kingdom work is around the world. Kingdom Pursuit can be an antidote to encourage your heart for missions, and is a wonderful invitation for churches and individuals to answer the call from the Lord of the Harvest to get involved in the task of worldwide evangelism. If you love missions, are part of the mission team of your church, or need a resource to open up the world of missions, Kingdom Pursuit will prove to be a great resource.

—Dr. Paul Kooistra, former Coordinator of PCA Mission to World, and President of Covenant Seminary, PCA

When Jesus commissioned his followers to "make disciples," he called them to pursue actively a kingdom against which the gates of hell would not prevail . . . a kingdom that would have no end . . . a kingdom made up of people from every tribe, tongue, and nation.

A healthy discipleship ministry cultivates a mindset that looks beyond the walls of the local church to embrace what God is doing around the world. Kingdom Pursuit is a valuable tool for those who seek to build such a ministry. The short essays will equip and encourage you to maintain focus on God's kingdom purposes. I rejoice at how God has used many of the authors to shape my thinking about ministry over the years, especially in a world that is increasingly global in its mindset. Though each writer addresses a specific international context, the gospel principles are transcendent. ANY church leader who desires to see the good news spread to the ends of the earth will benefit from the insights of Kingdom Pursuit.

—Dr. Stephen T. Estock, Coordinator, PCA Discipleship Ministries

Kingdom Pursuit draws from wisdom granted by God's Spirit through decades of missionary service at MTW. The authors call themselves and others to engage new challenges as the Gospel of the Kingdom is proclaimed in our day. Rooted in Scripture and tested by practical experience, Kingdom Pursuit is valuable reading for everyone called to serve the mission of the church --and that's all of us.

—Richard Pratt, President and Founder of Third Millennium Ministries

If you are looking for a one-stop resource that covers virtually every top-level issue related to the global mission of God, I don't know if there is a more helpful resource anywhere than Kingdom Pursuit. Combining literally hundreds of years in missions experience, the writers cover crucial subjects like the global refugee crisis, human slavery and trafficking, the essentials of cultural intelligence and ethnic diversity, sustainable funding, healthy compassion practices, and more—fusing the "deed" ministry of Christ with the "word" ministry of Christ. As a ministry leader, I am deeply grateful for this effort to produce Kingdom Pursuit, and I trust that you will be also.

—Scott Sauls, senior pastor of Christ Presbyterian Church in Nashville, Tennessee and author of *Befriend* and *From Weakness to Strength*

Contents

Dedication

First and foremost this book is dedicated to the Lord of the Harvest, our Lord Jesus Christ. He is the one we serve and the one who gives each person the strength, desire and joy to serve Him as a missionary in places far from their place of birth. This book is dedicated to the thousands of Mission to the World missionaries who are serving or who have served around the world. It is dedicated to those who will serve in the future. Each one is a testimony to obedience to Christ and the Holy Spirit's call on their life. Each missionary serves like the Apostle Paul "in weakness and in fear and much trembling, and [their] speech and [their] message were not in plausible words of wisdom, but in demonstration of the Spirit and of power, so that [people's] faith might not rest in the wisdom of men but in the power of God." (1 Cor. 2:3-5)

It is our desire that many will gain valuable insights about missionary work and a better understanding about the many tasks of missions like the many facets of a diamond. It is our hope that many will learn about the joys, the privileges, and the opportunities encountered by those who give of themselves to serve Christ in a place that is not their home.

Truly may the glory of God be spread and more people come to worship Him as this book helps people serve him better and understand the work of missions in ways they haven't before.

Acknowledgements

This book would not have been possible without the collected contributions of missionaries and mission leaders from around the world. We thank all 40 authors who submitted articles. Only 28 of those articles are able to be included in the printed version of this book because of book size limitations. If an ebook is published later, we hope to include more of the articles in it. We give thanks to those missionaries who have gone before us and serve with us, and to the national partners that have contributed to the collected knowledge, insights and blessings of our mission efforts.

We thank Melissa Kelley who edited all the articles for style and grammar. We thank her for her recommendations of changes and improvements to each article. Also, her writing skills show up in the two articles she wrote based on interviews with the authors (*Developing Flawed Servants into Thriving Leaders* by Bill Goodman and *From Church Planting to "Human Planting"* by Turgay Üçal).

Daniel Simmons put his creative skills to work to design the cover with the one chosen being only one of many he created. Amy Glass, Director of MTW Marketing and Communications, and her team gave good suggestions about the book title and the publishing process. Thanks to you all.

Stephen Estock, Coordinator of Christian Discipleship Ministries (CDM), provided knowledge, guidance and planning to get this book published. We thank Stephen and all the CDM staff who worked on this book project.

A special thanks to Brian Deringer who had the idea for this book, who requested and obtained funding from MTW for the book project, and who provided valuable direction and encouragement along the way in the five year process. Former MTW Coordinator, Paul Kooistra, and current Coordinator, Lloyd Kim, are thanked because of their godly leadership and for seeing the value of having this book published.

The missionaries of Mission to the World, PCA, have thousands of years of combined knowledge, insights, and experience about missions. Only some of that is reflected in the excellent articles of this book.

—*Joint General Editors Dr. Carl D. Chaplin and Sue Harris*

In this book you will read practical guidance on many facets of missions by men and women who have many years of ministry in missions. You will grasp in these pages that mission work involves mercy ministry, leadership development, serving with people from different cultural, social and economic backgrounds, and seeking to show the love of Christ to those who reject you and God's Word all for Christ and building his church. You will hear missionaries speak from their life experiences gained through struggles, joys, tears and elation seeing God move in people's hearts. More than filling your heads with knowledge, the writers will inspire you, sharpen you, and challenge you to engage with them in kingdom advancement to see God praised as people come to personally know Jesus Christ as their savior.

Foreword

by Dr. Michael Oh, Global Executive Director
CEO, Lausanne Movement & MTW Missionary

Before I began leading the Lausanne Movement, I was a missionary with MTW. In fact, I still am.

My transition in March 2013 involved passing on my day-to-day leadership duties of CBI Japan, which I had founded in the city of Nagoya.

So I write this foreword with great admiration of the ministry of MTW globally and a great appreciation for the blessing of being a part of it.

The stories in this book portray so many of the multi-dimensioned blessings of MTW that I have experienced personally: gospel-centeredness, a grace base, commitment to theological education, an emphasis on church planting and commitment to partnership with national leadership, to name a few.

I see those dimensions beautifully captured in this volume.

The breadth and depth and richness of thought and experience is really quite remarkable considering that these are the words of leaders from a single mission agency reflecting the work of a single mission agency. It is certainly reason to give thanks and also to pause for a moment or even an hour to pray for the more than 600 long-term wonderful missionaries and over 100 two-year MTW missionaries serving around the world.

I also see, with much joy, a number of mission strategies very much in line with, and perhaps even influenced by, the Lausanne Movement, including unreached people groups (UPGs), oral preference learners, integral mission, disability concerns, and the Bible's grand narrative of mission.

I see the way that biblically-based and research-based prophetic calls and strategies from the first, second, and third Lausanne Congresses in Switzerland, the Philippines, and South Africa in 1974, 1989, and 2010 and the subsequent Lausanne Covenant, Manila Manifesto, and Cape Town Commitment are echoed in these pages.

It makes me deeply grateful and moves me again to ask you to pray for the Lausanne Movement and for my leadership along with the leadership of our global leaders, including the author of chapter 16 of this volume, Dr. Victor Nakah, who serves as regional director for

EPSA (English & Portuguese Speaking Africa) for Lausanne and now MTW's International Director for Africa.

The ideas and stories captured in this book were sown and harvested with many tears and much hardship. They deserve to be heard and studied.

I trust and pray that the fruit of this volume will include many more missionaries being raised up for the mission field that is white for harvest, many more missionaries inspired, informed, and encouraged, and many more senders who will faithfully and biblically mobilize all the blessings that they have received from the Lord for His global Kingdom efforts.

> *Come labor on . . .*
> *who dares stand idle on the harvest plain . . .*
> *while all around . . .*
> *waves the golden grain?*

Introduction

by Brian Deringer

You may have heard that missions shouldn't be that complicated.

Some might say, "After all, we live in a globally-connected world where crossing cultures is no longer important. Don't most people speak English now?" "And why spend so much money to send missionaries when your dollars go further supporting indigenous leadership?" In fact, you may have heard that much of what is done in missions actually encumbers the coming of Christ's kingdom. Why not focus on missions at home and let others do the same?

But it's not that simple. Do you wonder if there might be more to missions than short-term trips and writing checks? Would you like to be better informed about the difficulties and complexities of international ministry? Do you want to examine what sets missions apart, even in this global age?

With these questions in mind, Mission to the World commissioned a series of essays from its missionaries and partners to inspire readers to think more deeply about missions. What resulted is this book, *Kingdom Pursuit*. In it, we hear from veteran missionaries and national leaders worldwide who reveal the necessity of having called, trained, and competent workers. These 28 essays explore how missionaries and local leadership strive together to make great impact for the kingdom, and how to avoid being a stumbling block for the gospel.

Each article addresses a critical topic such as mercy ministry, leadership development, mutual accountability, working with refugees, and more. But one common thread runs through these articles—a passionate desire to see His kingdom come.

We hope this book will spark conversations on missions committees, with donors, and in the missionary community. It might motivate you to pray, to dialog in concrete ways with the missionaries you support, to give, or to go!

Are you ready to dig in? Let's begin by hearing from a missionary to Germany, Eowyn Stoddard, as she addresses a challenge currently before the Church in Europe. History is being made because of the movement of refugees across the continent. How will, or rather, how should the Church respond? And why?

SECTION 1

Compassion and Justice

1

Ministry in the Midst of the Refugee Crisis

by Eowyn Stoddard

"Today, we are making history! Today, we are walking in the footsteps of Bonhoeffer and the confessing church whose motto it was that the church must always be the church for others."[1]

So said Stephen Beck, an ordained PCA pastor, church planter, and professor, discussing the new challenges facing the German church in an era of immigration. Beck joined more than 180 church leaders for a conference in February 2016 to discuss how recent immigration trends are impacting the church and to find ways to work together.

More than one million refugees have streamed into Germany since 2015—and with a German population of 80 million, this means almost one out of every 80 people is now a refugee! This statistic will change the face of Germany forever. We will all be affected in some form or another. The challenge that lies ahead for the church is immense.

But first, a bit of context. In 1934, the German state church was restructured and the Frankfurt churches received a new bishop who was a puppet of the Nazi party. The church's theology was changed to exclude the Old Testament and Jesus' Jewishness, and non-German members were dismissed. The former pastor of the Matthäus Church, Karl Veidt, a member of the confessing church like Dietrich Bonhoeffer, was arrested and tortured by the Gestapo. Eventually, the Nazis imposed a speaking ban and Matthäus Church was bombed along with the rest of Frankfurt. Similarly, under the rising pressure of Nazism, which excluded more and more people from the church, Bonhoeffer himself was faced with the "German Christian" question. He concluded that there is no such thing as a German Christian. He was a Christian first, and a German second. This idea of being a Christian first is very Pauline. Bohhoeffer, like Paul, understood that the church of Christ was a new body, one made of radically different members. There is no Jew, no Greek when it comes to church. Hitler wanted the German church to believe that it was for the Arian. It was the only way to justify the chopping off of many of its members.

Without this understanding of the church being for others, we will not be able to see the immigrant, the refugee, the foreigner in our midst as an important part of "us." It is a constant challenge to cast off fear and embrace God's plan of salvation which includes the nations. The influx of refugees into Germany is causing some logistical nightmares. Some churches are distancing themselves, rationalizing that reaching out to them is not their job. Others are embracing the challenge at great cost. It is a messy, heart-wrenching, potentially dangerous business, but the blessing that ensues is not to be overlooked. It is the opportunity that God is giving his church right here, right now. Never in the history of the world have so many Muslims been free to explore who Jesus is. Great numbers of them are coming to faith across Europe. This is God's doing! This has been his plan all along.

A biblical theological understanding of the Scriptures and the climactic multi-ethnic goal of history has huge implications for how we view the foreigners in our midst.

GOD'S TIDAL WAVE

A biblical theological understanding of the Scriptures and the climactic multi-ethnic goal of history has huge implications for how we view the foreigners in our midst. (See appendix on "A Biblical Theology of the Foreigner."[2]) Do we see them as a problem? A crisis? Or is this the church's opportunity to love her neighbors and extend the message of the gospel to them, seeing them as part of the fulfillment of God's plan for this earth?

Much fear surrounds the issue of refugees in Germany and in the

West in general. Will they bring terrorism with them? Will they destroy German culture or other host cultures? Will they integrate? Certainly, the answers to these questions are unclear. However, in God's kingdom fear is never to be the driving force. The driving force is the power of the gospel. But some would say, what about religious fanatics? We must remember that religious fanaticism has never been a problem for God. The Apostle Paul had himself been a religious fanatic, persecuting and killing Christians. God alone was able to reach him, by revealing Himself to him directly and stripping him of his previous life and animosity toward Christ and His followers. The believers who first heard the news about Saul's conversion were justifiably suspicious and fearful. What if this was just a ploy, a tactic to infiltrate their ranks? As it turns out, God sometimes handpicks some of His greatest enemies to use them as His most powerful servants. In fact, we find this very same Paul preaching the following at the Areopagus in Acts 17:24-27:

> *"The God who made the world and everything in it, being Lord of heaven and earth, does not live in temples made by man, nor is he served by human hands, as though he needed anything, since he himself gives to all mankind life and breath and everything. And he made from one man every nation of mankind to live on all the face of the earth, having determined allotted periods and the boundaries of their dwelling place, that they should seek God, in the hope that they might feel their way toward him and find him. Yet he is actually not far from each one of us."*

Paul believed that God is the maker of all nations and the mover of peoples. God is sovereign over history and appoints boundaries and dwelling places for men. There is no denying that our world is in flux and God is moving people en masse. For what purpose, one might ask? The answer is clear, according to Paul: God moves people so that they may find Him! God is not far from any of us, but sometimes our cultural context does not allow us to see Him clearly. Until we move. At that point, our world and our preconceived notions are shattered. We start to see certain things with more clarity. An example here in Germany is the freedom Chinese students have to explore Christianity for the first time, outside of their native culture and free from expectations or constraints. Refugees fleeing their homelands (not all necessarily because of persecution) are reaching our shores searching for a better earthly life. The best thing that could happen to them would be to have an encounter with the risen Lord, who would Himself become their light and their life.

FROM CURSE TO BLESSING

God is doing a new thing! Germans and German Christians in particular have always felt great shame about the past. Germany had been a curse to the nations through her systematized murderous plan to annihilate anyone who did not fit the Aryan bill. Our fellow missionary, Tammie Matlack, who has a passion for intercessory prayer, recalls that German intercessors have been praying for years that God would allow Germany to bless the nations once more, for a chance to reverse the curse. In 1989, the wall that separated East and West Germans fell, creating a new, united Germany. Christians knew that this bloodless revolution was a gift from God wrought through prayer. Not a shot had been fired, not a life lost. The peaceful revolution started out as a prayer meeting that got so large, it overflowed into the streets. The wall of separation fell. Many thought that God would bring about a revival so great that Germany would become a blessing to the nations by sending out thousands of missionaries to the ends of the earth. This has not happened . . . at least not in such scope. But little did we know that God had a much better plan up His sleeve, namely to bring the nations to Germany for healing.

People from all over the world are flooding to Germany from places that cannot normally be reached for the gospel. Now these people are free to explore the Christian faith without repercussions. Missiologically, we are entering a new phase. The German missiologist Engelmann, who also spoke at the Frankfurt conference, identified three phases of spreading the gospel. The first wave was sending missionaries out to continents unknown. The second big wave was attempting to reach the unreached people groups in the 10/40 window. Now, the third wave is the reverse of the second: peoples from closed nations are streaming out of their countries and coming to the West. The advantage of this phase is the simplicity of being a missionary. All one needs to be a missionary is a change in perspective! One need not travel halfway across the world to meet someone from Syria or Afghanistan. They are on our doorstep and many of them come with great openness to the gospel.

We are already hearing testimonies of men, women, and children finding the Lord Jesus after being disillusioned with their religion. Some have seen the horrors of ISIS and are turning their backs on their religious upbringing when they experience the love of Christ from Christians at refugee camps. Some are having revelations of Jesus in their dreams. Others are eager to study what the Bible says. Recently, some teammates and I heard testimonies of people of Islamic background wanting to become followers of Jesus after only three meetings of Bible study! God is doing an amazing work in this country right now and our MTW teams are eager to join what God is doing.

All of our church-planting projects are asking similar questions: What will this mean for our churches? How do we convince our people that we have a calling and an opportunity here? Does it mean every church plant must have refugees as a target group? How do we get to know and reach refugees with God's love? What can the church offer that the government cannot? How can we deal with massive logistical challenges like language barriers, funding, or helping refugees with multi-faceted needs? What about the German friends to whom we also want to be faithful? Can we adapt? Redouble our prayer efforts? Set aside other agendas? We are hearing that time is a key factor in reaching refugees. Are we willing to sacrifice large amounts of time to build new relationships?

RECONSIDERING MERCY MINISTRY

This new opportunity ought to prompt us to reconsider ministries of mercy. There are, of course, differing opinions as to what this means. Some proponents of the social gospel would argue that meeting the physical and social needs of refugees is enough. However, we believe that mercy ministry should be holistic. Ideally, we are trying to consider all facets of human need: physical, emotional, social, practical, and spiritual. The reality is, however, that whether or not a person responds to the gospel, the church should still minister to the person's other facets of need. Our example is Jesus Himself who healed and fed multitudes regardless of whether they responded to His message. There will be people who take advantage of the church's generosity, who will only want a certain measure of help. We must trust God that He is the One drawing people to Himself. We cannot know in advance who God's elect children are, so we are called to treat all with equal respect and love, simply because it is the right thing to do. At the same time, however, the church has a unique call to preach the gospel. This is where each church must ask the question to what extent it should attempt to meet all needs (which can be all-consuming) and to what extent it can work together with other organizations that meet physical needs, so that it can focus specifically on spiritual needs. The church can be a blessing in the one area the government cannot address, and that is the unique calling of gospel ministry.

One need not travel halfway across the world to meet someone from Syria or Afghanistan. They are on our doorstep and many come with great openness to the gospel.

CONCERNS OF SUSTAINABILITY AND ASSIMILATION

Even in the face of such a great opportunity, we ought to remain cautious to not start programs that will collapse if we or our money leave. We must ensure that national partners are in the driver's seat and that the core ministry team is filled mostly with nationals. We can assist with manpower, ideas, and even gather one-time financial gifts that will go directly to the refugee ministry. However, we ought not to place ourselves in positions we cannot leave without great detriment to the ministry. The goal of such a ministry ought to be the assimilation of the refugee in society and in the church. Paul described the church as a body made up of Jews and Greeks, slaves and free men, men, women, and children. Our task is not done when we have fed the refugees and preached Christ to them. Our strategy ought to be driven by the end goal of history when people from all tribes, tongues, and nations will worship God together. We ought to be praying and striving for this reality to start on this side of glory, here and now in our churches. Wouldn't it be an amazing testimony to God's power to bring people together if refugees became believers, were discipled in Christian growth, and emerged as part of the leadership of this new kind of church? This would truly take the church to the next level of living out the reality of the picture described for us in Revelation.

THINKING OF REFUGEE MINISTRY?

The following ideas are by no means exhaustive. Much of what we are doing is learning by trial and error. So, here are a few things to think and pray about and possibly act upon as you consider whether you or your church might be called to reach out to refugees.

Start with prayer:
- Pray in reliance that God's Spirit would lead you and all your efforts. He must **open the doors** and pave the way for you.
- If your ministry is going to be productive, you will need **relationships with key people** involved. Pray for local believers who are able and willing to invest time and energy in this new endeavor. Pray for contacts with government officials, refugee home coordinators, and especially for good relationships with refugees.
- You will need to pray for **protection**. The enemy does not want you infringing on his domain and he may let you know it through spiritual opposition. Pray that Satan and his legions would be bound and that you would be given free access to develop what God has put on your heart.
- Pray for **new DNA in your church** or church-plant. Pray that God gives to all involved a heart of compassion and friendship for outsiders. Pray they wouldn't be driven by fear but motivated by love and the hope and power of the gospel.

Prepare:
- **Teach and preach redemptive historical theology of the inclusion of the foreigner.** Show your congregation how they could be a part of God's plan to include the foreigner in His kingdom.
- **Count the cost.** Do you have the manpower, the long-term perspective, the time, and the resources to start such a ministry? If not, return to step one and pray.
- **Brainstorm** with your church group about what you can offer specifically. What are the gifts of the group? What resources do you have? What connections and relationships do you have?
- **Ask local government what their needs are** and what the church can offer that the government cannot. You might discover some overlap with what your group can offer.
- **Network with other churches in the area.** The needs of an area are too great for just one church to meet. Visit other refugee ministries and learn how others are doing it, what is working well, and why. Collaborate with others in local mercy ministries.
- **Collect a list of resources** like good language classes, Bibles in foreign languages, and evangelistic materials.[3] Do not reinvent the wheel. For example, if good language classes are offered somewhere, utilize the resource. Don't feel like you must reproduce it.

- **Don't insist that things happen within the church building.** Maybe you need to meet at the local refugee center or a home.
- **Get training,** including intercultural training, evangelism for Muslim background people, etc.

Our strategy ought to be driven by the end goal of history when people from all tribes, tongues, and nations will worship God together. We ought to be praying and striving for this reality to start here and now in our churches.

How to Start:

- Because this area of involvement is so huge and you will quickly come to your limits, it is important to **develop a vision** with the nationals who are working alongside you. Ask questions like: "What is the goal of this ministry?" "What would success look like?" "We'd call the job done when ... " "How does this ministry fit into our bigger church-planting strategy?" Dream big but let it be concrete.
- Make sure to **develop a simple, yet clear strategy** leading to a course of action and, if possible, the steps indicating in which order you want to proceed. This will be essential because there are a multitude of needs and it is easy to lose focus.
- **Recruit.** Don't do anything alone. You will need a team of people who will work together, support and complement one another, and pray together.
- **Raise awareness and funds.** Communicate with those supporting you in prayer and financially and give them opportunities to help in practical ways.
- **Start small.** With the information gathered in the steps above, decide what your focus will be. Do one thing well. Keep learning, growing, and expanding only as God provides opportunities and resources.
- **Be a friend.** Refugees need more than just practical aid. They want relationship and friendship. Learn about their culture, have them over for a meal, and include them in activities.
- **Start talking with refugees about God right away.** In their cultures,

talking about God is normal. The refugees are often shocked that no one in the West talks to them about God.

• **Include refugees.** Once you know some refugees well enough, include them in your refugee task force or outreach. They will have much to offer (language, cultural background knowledge, relationships, shared experiences). Expect to learn from them. Don't always put yourself in the giving role. Make sure they are able to make significant contributions.

CONCLUSION

Despite all the difficulties and unanswered questions, one thing is sure: The face of missions in Germany (and in Europe at large) is changing forever. In Germany, this is our new reality. God has moved a mass of people to live within our borders. We can either stand on the shore of disbelief and stay paralyzed with fear, or we can hop on the tidal wave God has created and see how far it will carry us. As we move forward in confidence that our sovereign Lord has prepared these times, His sheep, and the good works we are to walk in, we see that He is bringing a new harvest of Christ-followers who will turn this world on its head. Is it scary? Yes! Will it cost us? Yes! Do we feel like it is an impossible task? Yes! But we must remind ourselves that God often loves to move in impossible situations, to open up Red Seas and barren wombs, to feed thousands with just a few loaves and fish, and make God's enemies into His closest friends as far as the curse is found. He is the God of all impossibilities so that He might get all the glory.

Eowyn grew up an MK in France and sensed the Lord's call to missions in her late teens. She pursued a BA degree in German and an MA in theological education. She and her husband, David, (MTW Europe International Director) have been working in church-planting in Berlin, Germany since 2001. Refugee ministry is a new development for them both and a response of the local church plant to the influx of refugees in the area.

APPENDIX

A Biblical Theology of the Foreigner

Beck, in his talk in Frankfurt, explained God's mission of redemption through the lens of the foreigner. I would propose that our understanding of the church's mission will be only as deep as our grasp of biblical theology. Following is a review of this theology as seen in Scripture.

Abraham was not a Jew by birth. He was a Gentile, called out by God to be the recipient of God's covenant promise. "Go from your country and your kindred and your father's house to the land that I will show you. And I will make of you a great nation, and I will bless you and make your name great, so that you will be a blessing. I will bless those who bless you, and him who dishonors you I will curse, and in you all the families of the earth shall be blessed" (Genesis 12:1-3). Abraham had to leave his homeland and became a sojourner, a nomad, wandering from place to place. "By faith Abraham obeyed when he was called to go out to a place that he was to receive as an inheritance. And he went out, not knowing where he was going. By faith he went to live in the land of promise, as in a foreign land, living in tents with Isaac and Jacob, heirs with him of the same promise. For he was looking forward to the city that has foundations, whose designer and builder is God" (Hebrews 11:8-10). The writer of Hebrews interprets Abraham's wanderings as his act of obedient faith. The father of the faith was a wanderer by God's sovereign choice.

Moses, too, was an exile, a Hebrew slave in an Egyptian Pharaoh's household. God called Moses to wander in the desert and lead His people out of slavery into the Promised Land. Moses received God's law in which His provision for the foreigner was legislated (Deuteronomy 10:18-19). The Israelites were to treat the foreigner well because they too had been foreigners in another land (Numbers 15:14-16).

It is clear that God Himself was willing to wander with His people and dwell in a tent just as they did. God's presence went ahead of the Israelites in the form of a pillar of cloud and fire to show them the way.

In the Mosaic Law there were provisions for foreigners "joining in," but what the prophets foretold must have boggled their minds because they prophesied about "going out" into all the nations. One day God's Spirit would reach all nations. But how? Ezekiel describes the living water flowing from the temple to the ends of the earth bringing life wherever it flowed (Isaiah 11:9 and Habakkuk 2:14). One day the whole earth would be filled with God's glory (Philippians 2:5-8). This is an extension of the Abrahamic Covenant in its scope.

The full, universal knowledge of the Lord was revealed in the person of Christ. Being in very nature God, He left His heavenly home to become a foreigner on earth (Matthew 2:14-15). The perfect Israelite was exiled to Egypt so that He could lead the new exodus out of slavery to sin and death through His own death (Matthew 15). Jesus dwelt among men but knew He had no permanent home on earth. Jesus explained to the disciples, "Foxes have holes, and birds of the air have nests, but the Son of Man has nowhere to lay his head" (Luke 9:58).

He was in the world, and the world was made through Him, yet the world did not know Him. "He came to his own, and his own people did not receive him" (John 1:10-11). He was rejected by His own people. During His ministry, Jesus indicated by His actions that salvation was not going to be for Jews alone. He interacted with a Canaanite woman and healed her daughter (Luke 7), praised the faith of a Roman centurion above that of the Jews, and cast demons out of a Gadarene man (Mark 5). He died as a common thief. Through His resurrection, He is the head of a new humanity, one not based on race, religion, or land, rather on the resurrection power of the Spirit who can make all things new, including a new people of God, bought by the blood of Christ.

The following passage may not seem relevant at first glance, but it is the most important proclamation one could make about the universality of the salvation applied to humankind:

> *"Thus it is written, 'The first man Adam became a living being,' and the last Adam became a life-giving spirit. But it is not the spiritual that is first but the natural, and then the spiritual. The first man was from the earth, a man of dust; the second man is from heaven. As was the man of dust, so also are those who are of the dust, and as is the man of heaven, so also are those who are of heaven. Just as we have borne the image of the man of dust, we shall also bear the image of the man of heaven. I tell you this, brothers: flesh and blood cannot inherit the kingdom of God, nor does the perishable inherit the imperishable."* (1 Corinthians 15:45-50)

These verses reference the new identity that Christ-followers possess because of their spiritual union with the Man of heaven. All humans derive from Adam. In Christ, however, a new race of man is formed, one which has been created by the Spirit and given new life and a new identity. They shall not return to dust—rather, their home destination is heaven, regardless of where they are from here on earth. This means Christians are all foreigners on a heaven-bound journey.

God's kingdom continued to expand after Pentecost, when the Spirit came in power on all flesh, and foreigners heard the message of the gospel in their own language. The mission Christ gave His followers was to go into all the world proclaiming His message (Matthew 28:18-20). And so, through their travels, they brought the gospel to other distant places. The reversal of Babel had begun and the gospel was set on a course of expansion throughout the world (Acts 1:8).

The Apostle Paul was charged with the task of developing and explaining a theology of Gentile inclusion, the great mystery hidden in the Old Testament and finally revealed in the New (Colossians 1:25-27). Paul describes how Christ's work toppled the wall that separated Jews and non-Jews (Ephesians 2:11-16).

Peter, who first struggled with Gentile inclusion, later addressed the mixed group of scattered believers as elect exiles, and encouraged them to live as sojourners. Whether Jew or Gentile, what binds them together is their common identity as bought with the precious blood of Christ. This world is not their ultimate home, hence they must live as pilgrims on a journey. Where the church has done this, she has stayed on her toes—vibrant, strong, and on the move for God's mission. Where the church has gotten comfortable, compromised with the world, and made it her home, she has lost her edge and gotten stuck in the quagmire of complacency.

God's Word and the promise of the gospel—because it is combined with His powerful presence—will continue to bear fruit to the ends of the earth until Christ comes back in the fullness of time. Then, on that day, all of God's people will stand before His throne, including the symbolic multitude of stars in the sky and sand on the shore promised to Abraham.

God will honor His Son on that last day by giving Him His treasured possession, fulfilling the prophecy of Psalm 2: "The LORD said to me, 'You are my Son; today I have begotten you. Ask of me, and I will make the nations your heritage, and the ends of the earth your possession'" (Psalm 2:7-8). Christ gave up His heavenly home to receive the inheritance that is the people that God would give Him from every nation. The people given to Christ will respond in grateful adoration:

"And they sang a new song, saying, 'Worthy are you to take the scroll and to open its seals, for you were slain, and by your blood you ransomed people for God from every tribe and language and people and nation'" (Revelation 5:9).

---

1   Dietrich Bonhoeffer, *Letters and Papers from Prison* (Touchstone: 1997), 382. "The Church is the Church only when it exists for others ... not dominating, but helping and serving. It must tell men of every calling what it means to live for Christ, to exist for others."

2   See Appendix at the end on "A Biblical Theology of the Foreigner."

3   Wycliffe Bible translator materials on language learning are a good start if one must do it oneself, otherwise there may be language classes offered at the refugee homes that can be supplemented with tutoring for language practice.

   A good introduction to the Bible from a Muslim background perspective is the Al Massira class. It features redemptive historical theology and shows how Christ was at work in the Old Testament, preempting many typical objections to the trustworthiness of the Bible, the divinity of Christ, and the Trinity. It calls for a decision to follow Christ at the end.

2

Walking With The Refugee: Church Planting Among Syrians In The Middle East

by P. C. (name withheld for security reasons)

No fewer than 65 million humans in the world today have run away from their homes in search of safety, and about one third of these have crossed national borders to do so. People fleeing war and persecution are not a new phenomenon. What is new in our modern era is the sudden and enormous scope of such peoples.

It is important to note that the vast majority of refugees, nearly two-thirds, live in cities and not in camps. This is not a short-term crisis. For those forced to flee, the average wait before returning home is 17 years. This means that not only is the displacement problem bigger than ever, it also isn't going away anytime soon.

The long-term presence of refugees is one of the great opportunities for the church in our time—building the kingdom among strangers and exiles. As we address this opportunity here, first we will share our context and journey—among Syrians in the Middle East—and ways we are processing and responding to the crisis. Then we will examine the refugee crisis from a biblical, theological perspective. Finally, we will address four aspects of ministry to Syrian refugees in the Middle East which I believe are important for any team or church to consider. These four areas are: acting and speaking the gospel together, church planting, seeking partnership, and personal considerations for workers. Our intention is not to be exhaustive, but rather to begin a conversation among those bringing the gospel to refugees.

JOURNEY TO THE MIDDLE EAST

Since 2014, Syrians have made up the largest share—approximately 14 million—of displaced people worldwide. This tragedy is the culmination of five years of revolution and civil war. The brutality of the conflict, made most notorious by the group naming itself Islamic State (ISIS), has had devastating effects on the civilian population and infrastructure. The latest United Nations (UN) registration figures record 5 million displaced persons outside Syria and many more are unregistered. One in four persons in Lebanon are a refugee from Syria and Jordan estimates 1.4 million Syrians are within their borders, more than double the UN registered number of 650,000.

Walking through downtown Beirut, one sees a myriad of young Syrian men and children trying to find work. The crisis is visible in the northern villages of Jordan where schools are swollen beyond capacity with the addition of Syrian children. In Zaatari refugee camp, thousands of shops line the main street—ironically dubbed the Champs-Élysées—selling goods to its 80,000 residents. Twenty-five refugee camps dot the landscape of southern Turkey, housing more than 280,000 Syrians while 2.5 million more reside in Turkey's cities and countryside.

For five years, Syria's neighbors have borne the brunt of the crisis. Now they are tightening their borders and reducing relief spending. This, along with military escalations by the so-called Islamic State (ISIS) in Syria and Iraq, has contributed to a second mass exodus of refugees from the region. One million Syrians have claimed asylum in Europe and, in the process, overwhelmed the borders and immigration systems across that continent. While migrants from many countries make up the influx, the largest share is Syrians.

Despite the high numbers heading to Europe, the vast majority of Syrian refugees are still in the Middle East, spread among Turkey, Lebanon, Jordan, and other Arab nations. This article focuses on engaging the Syrian refugee still in the Middle East, but it can be adapted and applied to any refugee destination.

AN UNEXPECTED CRISIS

I must admit that the refugee crisis of the Middle East took me by surprise. Six years ago, my wife and I were making plans to learn Arabic and relocate to Syria to see churches planted among unreached Syrian Muslims. Little did we know that we would be thrust into a refugee ministry in a neighboring country along Syria's border. Now our focus is loving Syrians through tangible relief projects and introducing them to Jesus. In fact, we are convinced that the Syrian conflict has brought a pivotal opportunity for the spreading of the gospel and the birth of the church among this unreached people group. We pray to see a movement of churches that plant churches among Syrians in partnership with the regional body of Christ.

We rejoice at many new articles, conferences, and trainings that are emerging to help the church serve refugees and pray for increased awareness of the strangers and displaced among us. Our unique focus in this article is on the cross-cultural worker that is going to the Middle East. I write to those called by the Lord to go to those places where there is no church—or a very small one—that are receiving refugees. I write to workers who are leaving their homes and cultures to acculturate to the norms of the refugee.

We are convinced the Syrian conflict has brought a pivotal opportunity for the spreading of the gospel and the birth of the church among this unreached people group.

Today, many refugees come from some of the least reached people groups in the world. Therefore, reaching them with the gospel is a unique and strategic priority for the church. In the case of Syrians, there are at least two reasons I believe the church should also prioritize reaching them in the Middle East. First, the vast majority of Syrian refugees remain in the bordering nations to Syria. It is logistically easier to reach a people group when they are concentrated in a particular area. Second, Syrians who remain within the region typically maintain more active connections back into Syria and may be more likely to return home in the future than those who immigrate to the West. These Syrians could play a significant role for church planting movements extending back into Syria.

SEEING THE REFUGEE

There are many lenses through which to view a refugee crisis. We can look at it politically—citing the political realities that have caused the crisis and the debate in Europe among national leaders dealing with the refugee influx. The international political system has failed to bring peace to Syria and to keep civilians from the line of fire from both sides of the conflict. News media often focus on the political side, covering peace conferences, policy changes, security realities, and the impact on elections. Refugees are generalized—for good or ill—and often described en masse as a social or political factor among many. In this way, the refugee is sometimes dehumanized and reduced to a statistic in need of a policy response.

We can view the refugee crisis economically; the material poverty of many refugees is easily communicated in visual media. We see the economic impact of the crisis in the scarce jobs of Jordan and Lebanon. We see Greece's public spending strained by the needs of migrants arriving on its shores. Emergency relief organizations have sprung into action with a call for donations from around the world. Arriving refugees need food, housing, clothing, and basic living supplies—all of which come through the channels of their host countries' economies. Eventually, refugees need permanent housing, education, and jobs—which all impact local markets.

Finally, we see the humanitarian side of the refugee problem. Today, we estimate that over 500,000 have died inside Syria since the start of the war. As fellow humans, we want to empathize with the experiences of our refugee neighbors. We want safety and a future for our children; surely, the refugee wants the same for her children. We watch human rights groups daily update their records, keeping track of abuses and war crimes in hopes that international prosecutors will later bring justice to the criminals.

All of these perspectives provide a glimpse of the refugee. As Christians we must go a step further and ask the question—how should a follower of Christ view the refugee? How might we view the crisis biblically or spiritually? What theological resources in Scripture and what examples in the history of God's redemptive work do we have for understanding and responding to the refugee? Let us begin to answer by looking to Christ himself.

JESUS THE REFUGEE

Jesus was a refugee His entire life. Matthew's gospel records His flight to Egypt and ensuing return to Israel after Herod died. What we may overlook, however, is that Jesus' family wanted to return to Judea—their ancestral homeland (Matthew 2:22). Out of fear of Herod's son on the throne and again warned in a dream, Joseph did not return there but rather took his family to the far north of the country, to Galilee. Jesus grew up in a displaced family.

This is paramount to our response to the refugee—that God sent His Son into our world and His Son was a refugee. He was acquainted with the life of a sojourner and stranger; He knew persecution and exile. In fact, Jesus' many returns to His ancestral home of Judea eventually brought His death on the cross. When believers are brought into Christ's life, death, and resurrection, they are sharers in His experience as a persecuted sojourner. Jesus Himself said to those who would follow Him, "Foxes have holes, and birds of the air have nests, but the Son of Man has nowhere to lay his head" (Matthew 8:20). It is as though Jesus says to the refugee: "I have walked this road before. I've slept in temporary lodging; I've known exile and persecution. I've experienced death. I identify with you."

We love the stranger because Christ loved us when we were strangers from God. ~ Ephesians 2:12, 19

Jesus' compassion and love for the refugee empowers our service for the refugee. We love the stranger because Christ loves the stranger. We love the stranger because Christ loved us when we were strangers from God (Ephesians 2:12, 19).

The theme of exile and the stranger is a significant motif for God's people historically. In fact, a theology of displacement runs throughout Scripture to describe God's nation. Abraham was called by the Lord to live as a foreigner in Canaan and his sojourns to Egypt only exacerbated his experience as an outsider. Moses led a nation of exiles out of Egypt, traveling in foreign territory for decades until finally entering the Promised Land. Even after the Israelites settled in what would become their ancestral lands, the Lord declared they would continue to be "strangers and sojourners" with Him (Leviticus 25:23). Even in the golden age of God's settled people, they are still identifying as strangers.

God's people had experienced slavery and exile and thus the Lord in turn commanded them to treat the stranger among them with compassion. The Hebrew Bible pronounces judgment for those in Israel who "oppress the hired worker in his wages, the widow and the fatherless, [and] who thrust aside the sojourner" (Malachi 3:5). All of these circumstances are widely represented among today's refugees.

In the New Testament, the writer of Hebrews traces our spiritual lineage and asserts that our forebears "acknowledged that they were strangers and exiles on the earth" (Hebrews 11:13). The Apostle Peter gives us what is perhaps the most developed theology of God's displaced people. Addressed to the "elect exiles of the Dispersion," Peter celebrates the work of God to save His people and give them an unshakeable inheritance in Christ (1 Peter 1:1-4). He calls them "a chosen race, a royal priesthood, a holy nation, a people for his own possession," and then he addresses them as "sojourners and exiles" (1 Peter 2:9,11).

As followers of Jesus, we are God's chosen people *and* we are exiles and strangers awaiting a future and heavenly inheritance. Displacement is an essential part of our identity in Christ as we live in this world. This is especially challenging to those of us who do not *feel* like "strangers and exiles." The words of Scripture are an indictment of the comfortable to examine their hearts and their obedience.

We come from a spiritual lineage of refugees and strangers in this world. Scripture and the example of our Lord Jesus gives us ample resources to love and walk with the refugee. Let us run forward to meet the refugee. Let us take risks to walk alongside and share in their experience. Let us be Jesus to them as He Himself walks beside them.

PRACTICAL CONSIDERATIONS

Living and Speaking the Gospel

The material needs of refugees are often overwhelming. This is one of the first realities that strike the worker among displaced peoples. Suddenly, sharing the gospel and hope of eternal glory can seem secondary or, worse, an unethical abuse of vulnerable people.

I advocate for the twin approach that responds to all the sufferings of the refugee. I am convinced that gospel demonstration (through acts of mercy and meeting felt needs) and gospel proclamation (through diverse means of witness, discipleship, and church planting) must go together in the church's mission among refugees.

Speaking to this issue, John Piper urged the Lausanne Congress at Cape Town to affirm, "we Christians care about all suffering, especially eternal suffering." He went on to say, "I hope we can say that. But if we feel resistant to saying 'especially eternal suffering,' or if we feel resistant to saying 'we care about all suffering in this age,' then either we have a defective view of hell or a defective heart."

Expanding on this subject ahead of the Cape Town conference, Christopher J. H. Wright writes, "the gospel as a whole, true to the Bible as a whole, shows us God's heart for His broken, suffering, wicked world. For the last and the least (socially, culturally, and economically) as well as the lost (spiritually)—not that these can be separated, since human beings are whole persons." Wright concludes with a call to "communicate all that makes the gospel staggeringly comprehensive good news."

As followers of Jesus, we are God's chosen people and we are exiles and strangers awaiting a future and heavenly inheritance. Displacement is an essential part of our identity in Christ as we live in this world.

I believe this comprehensive, gospel-based approach must be reflected in the church's response to displaced peoples. However, this does not mean that each worker equally balances both of these ministries; each one is uniquely gifted and called to particular works. We need people gifted in relief and development—passionately mobilizing resources, assessing and prioritizing physical needs and local assets, and setting up distribution systems that work. And we need the evangelists, the pastors, the relationally-wired people who drink cups of tea, meet dozens of people, and study the Scriptures to share with the refugee the glory and grace of Christ. Yes, we need church planters and spiritual leaders to be in the thick of humanitarian disasters.

Ministries of both gospel demonstration and gospel proclamation can be interwoven, mutually supporting, and shared by the same church or mission team. Often, mercy ministry provides a platform and entrance for sharing the gospel. Even in restricted access countries, this can provide "face time" with the people God is calling the church to reach. Sometimes the church's willingness to help in times and places where others will not can lead the way in our witness. When a church operates a relief and development project with integrity and fairness, Christ's gospel is adorned and made visible to people who may not have experienced it before. I cannot count the number of times Syrian Muslims in our country have remarked at how much the Christians have helped them, often while feeling neglected by their own brethren.

Because we preach and live the gospel of Christ's kingdom, we have a mandate to think big about possibilities for mercy ministry. We are compelled by kingdom ethics to seek justice, promote reconciliation, provide trauma counseling, pray for healing, and do a myriad of other creative and redemptive works that help restore a torn-down people. The possibilities are great for long-term, creative work and many skills and personalities will be needed. We must not simply follow the news headlines, but rather lead the way in bringing the kingdom in its fullness.

Church Planting among Refugees

In our country, we long to see churches planted with the DNA to go and plant more churches. We want to play a part in building a disciple-making, church-planting movement among Syrians which eventually stretches back into Syria. A refugee crisis changes things—including some of the dynamics of church planting. We will look at three areas that we believe are uniquely affected when seeking a church planting movement among refugees: gaining access, discovering networks, and reproducing.

Gaining Access. The Syrian refugee crisis has brought an explosion of missionary access to this unreached people group. As time passes, however, the circumstances and needs of refugees will change, and more creative avenues of access will be needed. Most of the emergency relief needs of Syrians have passed. Fewer refugees need food packages, clothing, emergency shelter, and other basic supplies. Except for the small trickle of new arrivals from Syria, the humanitarian response has already largely shifted from relief to development. What they increasingly need is education, job training, expanded healthcare, community development, and wider economic opportunities.

With increased development comes greater partnership and mutuality between the foreign worker and the refugee. There will be fewer "handouts" and more opportunities to work together to rebuild and improve livelihoods. Thus, I believe the future of access to refugees will be characterized by going deeper with fewer. In terms of evangelism, the wide net that we cast today (through large relief and distribution projects) will eventually shrink. As the net shrinks, we will be spending less time trying to find spiritually open and hungry people and more time discipling the ones God has given us.

The crisis has been joined with an unprecedented level of openness to hearing the gospel. By this, I mean a willingness by Syrians to welcome a Christian worker into their home, respectfully listen to the gospel message, and even engage in Bible study. I do not necessarily mean a hunger for the spiritual truths of the gospel, nor do I mean a large number of salvation experiences. Those two phenomena are still decidedly rare, despite increased access. There is also much false openness because many simply want the aid and have little interest in the gospel. One of the most challenging tasks for long-term workers is discerning genuine gospel openness as opposed to desire for aid. Early in a relationship, it is often impossible to tell the difference.

We are compelled by kingdom ethics to seek justice, promote reconciliation, provide trauma counseling, pray for healing, and do a myriad of other creative and redemptive works that help restore a torn-down people.

Yet, it has never been easier to visit a Syrian's home, share the gospel freely, pray with a family in Jesus' name, and start a home Bible study. These things are happening every day and the worker need only decide how many hours in her week she wishes to spend in these activities and they will be filled. Never before have so many Syrians heard the gospel.

One possible reason for this openness comes from a diminished confidence we have observed among Syrians in their religious heritage. Radical Islamist groups such as ISIS have shocked the region and struck at the staying power in people's lives of the majority religion. Syrians are asking new questions of their traditions and have been less skeptical of the Christian tradition. This has translated into greater openness to listening and fewer attempts to proselytize Christian workers themselves.

The location of access has also shifted. In the Middle East, public spaces are the domain of men. Women's social activities are kept primarily to the home. Before the war, reaching Syrian men meant being out in the street, at the market, in coffee shops, or on a university campus. Now men are more accessible in the home. Sitting at home and having little to do, men have even started helping with the domestic needs of their families—something uncommon in the past. Home visits and activities are now much more mixed in gender than ever before. This means workers commonly meet and talk with a whole Syrian family together. Bible studies are often with whole families. In fact, this has been our preference—reaching whole families together—since decisions are rarely made without consulting with one's family. Our prayer is that families will come to faith and continue to meet, worship together, and reach out to other families.

The mass displacement of Syrians has meant a Christian worker has more access to different kinds of people. Before the war, ministry often meant focusing on one set of society, like students, one's immediate neighbors, businessmen, or the poor. Now he can visit a wide range of people from many backgrounds since they have fled their old neighborhoods and live in close proximity to each other. People who never would have associated before now find themselves together in similar circumstances. This will slowly change with time as people resettle and re-establish norms, but for now there is a unique opportunity for the church planter to access many different kinds of people in one place.

Discovering Networks. The war in Syria, now in its sixth year, has completely shaken that nation. Towns have formed militias and fought the government. Neighbors have turned on neighbors. Large swaths of land were emptied of most of its people when radical groups moved in. In short, the social fabric of Syrian society has been shattered. People are away from their old normal and have lost past connections. When community is destroyed, how does the church planter identify the networks of his target people? How does the church planter do this when the refugees themselves may not be aware of who their community is now?

Community is slowly re-forming among refugees. I believe this gives the church planter two tasks: the first is to discover networks, and the second is to partner to create them. I learned of an example of the first task from a colleague in our country. After learning that many Syrians in their neighborhood were not receiving sufficient medical care, he asked a local refugee family to host a clinic in their home. The family invited everyone in their network whom they knew needed medical care, and then provided tea and an open space for the clinic. A team of foreign doctors came for two days and treated dozens of people, many of whom had not seen a doctor for years. As a result, the worker helped provide a felt need and, in the process, discovered a whole network of Syrians connected to each other.

The second task—partnering with the refugee to create community—can take many forms: teenagers attending an English class, ladies forming a knitting group, or men on a construction project. Anything that gets people together and forms new connections creates community within which the gospel can penetrate. I know of a men's workout group among refugees that meets every week to exercise and then discuss a Scripture passage. These men are sharing within the group some of the deepest burdens on their hearts and, in the process, forging new community.

When relatives, neighbors, and work connections have all been lost, it is the privilege of the church planter to discover the remaining natural networks that exist among refugees, and to build new social bonds for the gospel to take root and churches to emerge.

Reproducing Discipleship Methods. There is much discussion within the mission community on reproducibility in our discipleship and church planting methods. On one level, I believe most agree that those we evangelize and disciple must be able to do the same for others in time. Often the point of disagreement, as missiologist Jackson Wu points out, is not reproducibility itself, but rather the variable of time. The question that we must answer is: how quickly should someone be able to reproduce what you invest in them?

Reproduction is essential to apostolic church planting among an unreached people group. I encourage church-planting teams to consider the factor of time in their methodology. The task of discipling a believer from a Muslim background is a long and irregular journey in which many foundations must be laid and others dismantled by the gospel of Christ. Months and possibly years of spiritual growth and life-on-life mentoring are needed to prepare the believer for some aspects of ministry. However, equipping the believer to begin sharing with his family and network right away can be beneficial in many circumstances and thus reproduce the ministry of the church planter almost immediately. For longer-term success, however, more time may be needed to "test and prove" a new believer in the faith and prevent serious heresies from emerging in their theology before he or she takes on the task of church planting (1 Timothy 3:10). I argue that we should be open to a variety of tools and timetables for discipling new believers.

The medium of communication is also important to reproducibility. Syrians, for example, have a culture of oral preference. While most can read and write, they prefer receiving information via listening and viewing and not by reading. Moreover, written Arabic is very different from spoken Arabic. Only the well-educated can function fluently in written Arabic. To communicate on a heart level with Syrians, we must use oral methods. Recordings of Scripture and stories paraphrased into Syrian dialect, videos, music, and face-to-face interactions are all effective communication avenues.

The technology we use to share the gospel and disciple the believer must be in line with the technology possessed by the refugee. Syrians, for example, generally do not have many books, except for a copy of the Quran. They also do not have DVD players, computers, or CD players. What they do have are basic-level smartphones. Social media, mp3 recordings, video files, and Scripture apps are all effective means of sharing spiritual content with Syrians. We have found that audio and video files shared via Bluetooth, social media, or on a micro SD card can then be passed along to a refugee's whole family and wider network.

Finally, reproduction can seem frustrated when refugees relocate or leave the country. In the past, the worker in the Middle East could assume that his time was limited and eventually he would leave his target people group. Now it is much more likely the refugee will leave the worker's location before the worker does. A colleague encouraged me explaining we must not be discouraged when people leave, though we have invested so much time and effort in them. We do not know the fruit God will bring through them in the places they go. Rather, we let it be a reason for urgency to invest in the ones God has given us since we do not know how long we have with them. We are hearing reports from colleagues in Europe and the U.S. who are seeing the fruit of previous ministry to Syrians who arrive from the Middle East.

Let us consider our methodologies and timetables, our means of communication and the technology we use so that the work of discipleship and church planting is reproducible among the refugees our Lord is calling to Himself.

SEEKING PARTNERSHIP

The refugee phenomenon of our time is too big for any single church or organization to handle. This alone is a strong case for partnership across the global church and across denominational lines. We must work together to tackle such a deep and wide crisis. Christ's church is as widely dispersed around the world as the refugees themselves and, I believe, is therefore uniquely positioned to respond to the crisis.

When the first 40 families crossed into our area from Syria, a local church near the border with a few dozen members was quick to respond with food packages, household items, and home visits ministering to the refugees. As the number of refugees grew, that local church's ministry grew. Eventually, worldwide partnerships formed both with large, Christian NGOs and secular ones, distributing approximately $1 million a year in aid to no less than 5,000 families. The U.N. then moved in and the international community worked alongside the national government to serve the scores of refugees that came.

Already the presence of Syrians in our country is becoming the new normal. There will come a day when the global relief and development community will reduce its presence and the established churches will remain. If we are to have long-term impact in planting churches and seeking long-term prosperity, healing, and even reconciliation, then partnership with the local, established church is paramount.

The task of discipling a believer from a Muslim background is a long and irregular journey in which many foundations must be laid and others dismantled by the gospel of Christ.

Partnership with the local church can be a long and challenging journey and is not always successful. Partnership requires humility for both partners—the local church and the cross-cultural ministry team. We need much listening, learning and unlearning. We need a rhythm of extending mutual grace and forgiveness, accepting some ambiguity and disagreement, and a constant seeking of mutual roles and goals. Ultimately, partnership is a work of God's grace as we let our shared identity in Christ and missional calling unify us.

I believe we are called to a partnership of mutual listening and learning. The Latin American theologian and missionary J. Samuel Escobar, describes it this way: "This partnering, unlike the global franchising of evangelistic strategies developed in North America or Europe, begins in a truly global dialogue about how to announce the whole gospel, how to become a whole church, and how to understand what God is already doing in the whole world today." As on the global scale, the local partnership must be characterized by humility, listening, and the mutual sharing of what we each bring to the table.

Not only does the global church have the privilege to partner together, we also have the opportunity to partner with the humanitarian sector in the refugee crisis. As God's transformative agent in the world, the church is called to influence and often lead in works of mercy. This gospel of the kingdom which Christ has inaugurated gives the church a unique position to lead the way on matters of mercy, forgiveness and reconciliation, caring for the outcast and orphan, exercising justice following war atrocities, and for setting the agenda for rebuilding a people. When the Syrian war eventually ends and national healing and rebuilding begin, which we earnestly pray will be soon, the church within and outside Syria must be ready to help and even lead. We should encourage our teams and churches to advocate for kingdom ethics and priorities in government policies, in the humanitarian sector, and in our own local neighborhoods as we respond to the crisis.

Finally, we have the opportunity to partner with the refugee himself. His knowledge, networks, and unique assets—however limited they may seem—are very important for successful outcomes in relief and long-term development. The refugee's assets and desires are crucial to applying aid where needed and keeping the development of the community sustainable long after foreign resources have moved on.

The example of the in-home medical clinic mentioned earlier is a great example of partnering with refugees. The refugee family hosted the clinic in their home, invited everyone in their network, and provided the refreshments. This family felt empowered as an active partner, rather than a passive receiver, in helping their own community and identifying where the needs were. Also, the ministry team was able to follow up by visiting each family that attended. Not only was there potential for following up on needs for a future clinic, the team gained access to a network of connected people among whom they could follow up to see who desired spiritual ministry.

PERSONAL CONSIDERATIONS FOR WORKERS AMONG REFUGEES IN THE MIDDLE EAST

We are praying for scores of new workers called by the Lord Jesus into His harvest among the Syrian people and other unreached people groups in the Middle East. In many ways, the work among displaced people from Syria and other neighboring conflict zones is only beginning. Therefore, we want to conclude with practical considerations for teams and workers in the Middle East refugee context. These are gleaned from experience and conversations with many field colleagues; it is by no means exhaustive.

For the cross-cultural worker among Syrians, Arabic is essential; the vast majority of Syrians speak only Arabic and sometimes a limited amount of French. In Southern Turkey, for example, much relief work is under way by Christian workers but follow-up has been limited because workers there do not typically learn Arabic, only Turkish. Gaining a working fluency in the Syrian dialect of Arabic is a must for long-term, effective church planters. The typical expat worker in the Middle East should set aside her first two years in country exclusively for Arabic study and cultural learning.

Another outcome of this reversal of roles is that the cross-cultural worker among Syrians usually experiences an exhausting demand on his time and resources. Many relationships with Syrians can feel one-sided as the refugee friend is often trying to extract help of some kind. While understandable given the circumstances, it is also emotionally, spiritually, and physically draining on the worker. Agreed guidelines for giving to refugees are another helpful safeguard for members. There is the challenge of economic disparity. We encourage any new worker to begin considering her lifestyle before coming to the field and to seek out resources and conversations with colleagues on living among refugees.

Finally, a strong sense of calling is paramount for anyone serving among Syrians in the Middle East. We believe God is calling all kinds of people and in different life stages—singles and married couples, families with children, businesspeople, laypeople, second-career people—into this work. We each bring our unique gifts and backgrounds to the task of bringing the gospel to unreached, Syrian refugees.

The author is a graduate of Gordon-Conwell Theological Seminary and a teaching elder in the PCA. Having spent over 10 years ministering to Arabic-speaking peoples, he longs to see a thriving church planted among the least reached in the Arab World. He and his wife have two children and live in a Middle Eastern city.

i   "Figures at a Glance," *United Nations High Commissioner for Refugees (UNHCR)*, accessed 13 November 2016, http://www.unhcr.org.uk/about-us/key-facts-and-figures.html. All of these are known as displaced persons, including those internally displaced within their home country. The international system designates those who cross national boundaries as refugees.

ii   Ibid.

iii "Migration, Refugees, and Displacement," *United Nations Development Programme (UNDP)*, accessed 13 November 2016, http://www.undp.org/content/undp/en/home/ourwork/sustainable-development/development-planning-and-inclusive-sustainable-growth/migration-refugees-and-displacement.html.

iv   "Figures at a Glance," *UNHCR*.

v   Mohammad Ghazal, "Population stands at around 9.5 million, including 2.9 million guests," *The Jordan Times*, 30 January, 2016, http://www.jordantimes.com/news/local/population-stands-around-95-million-including-29-million-guests.

vi   "Turkey: Refugee Crisis," *European Commission Humanitarian Aid and Civil Protection*, accessed 13 November 2016, http://ec.europa.eu/echo/files/aid/countries/factsheets/turkey_syrian_crisis_en.pdf.

vii This is common for a number of displaced and unreached people groups today. For example, Iraqi refugees from ISIS-held areas have fled in large numbers to other parts of Iraq, Turkey, and Jordan. Another example is the situation of Yemeni refugees, most of whom are internally displaced. Sizable numbers have also settled across the Red Sea in Djibouti, only twenty miles from the Yemeni coast.

viii Anne Barnard, "Death Toll from War in Syria Now 470,000, Group Finds," *New York Times*, February 11, 2016, http://www.nytimes.com/2016/02/12/world/middleeast/death-toll-from-war-in-syria-now-470000-group-finds.html?_r=0.

ix   John Piper, "Making Known the Manifold Wisdom of God through Prison and Prayer," *Third Lausanne Congress for World Evangelization*, October 10, 2010, http://www.desiringgod.org/messages/making-known-the-manifold-wisdom-of-god-through-prison-and-prayer.

x   Christopher J.H. Wright, "Whole Gospel, Whole Church, Whole World," *Christianity Today* 53, no. 10 (2009), http://www.christianitytoday.com/ct/2009/october/index.html.

xi   Jackson Wu, "Reproducibility: Idol or Necessity in Modern Missions?" *Patheos* (blog), March 7, 2013, http://www.patheos.com/blogs/jacksonwu/2013/03/07/reproducibility-idol-or-necessity-in-modern-missions/.

xii J. Samuel Escobar, "Unity and Partnership in the Global Church," *Christianity Today*, September 21, 2009, http://www.christianitytoday.com/ct/2009/septemberweb-only/response1.html?start=2.

xiii We recommend Jonathan Bonk, *Missions and Money: Affluence as a Missionary Problem* (New York: Orbis, 2007).

xiv I write as one learning and stumbling in what it means to love and make disciples among Syrians. In some small way, I hope to inform and inspire workers preparing to come to the region and contribute to the wider conversation among teams of church planters. I owe much gratitude to colleagues for their thoughts, time given for interviews, and their fellowship in the task. This article would not have been possible without their help.

3

Moved by Compassion:
Why Charity Works

by Andrew Warren

Thirteen years ago, in 1993, my wife Bev and I started a ministry to people dying of AIDS in Addis Ababa, Ethiopia. This was before life-giving antiretroviral drugs extended people's lives for years or decades. In those early days we sat beside, or often on, the beds of people wasting away with AIDS. We shared the gospel, held their hands, provided the best care we could, loved them, and often buried the "least of these." We didn't have a strategy. We didn't have a model. All we had was a deep sense of sorrow and compassion for people for whom no one else cared.

These beautiful people, made in God's image, were like the man on the road to Jericho who fell among robbers. They needed a Good Samaritan to pick them up, bind their wounds, and give them care. They needed compassion exhibited in concrete ways to relieve their suffering.

I have been asked if it wouldn't be more productive to teach people how to avoid getting HIV. Isn't prevention better than treatment? I have been asked if we weren't creating dependency by doing what is sometimes disparagingly called "charity." I have even been asked if it is right to treat people who are sick with a disease that is often associated with sinful behavior. (Fortunately, not often.)

We didn't act out of ignorance, but consciously chose to do "charity." We were in the middle of what seemed to be a crisis of biblical proportions. AIDS was on track to wipe out a generation in Africa and leave many countries vulnerable to collapse. In parts of Africa villages were left with only the elderly and children. People were dying, sometimes on the street in front of our office. Creating dependency wasn't a risk or an issue. Every corner had a billboard with a condom ad or an AIDS-prevention message. What wasn't happening was care for the sick and dying.

EVALUATING SUCCESS

In the past 13 years we have cared for 1,300 AIDS-affected families. In the early days before treatment started, 120 people died. And since then, eight years ago, we have helped these surviving families in many ways. Most now are healthy, many have responded to the gospel, families have been reconciled and most—more than 75 percent—are now self-supporting and living without any help. Any development organization would be thrilled with this track record.

Why did the project succeed? God provided graciously. He provided co-workers who shared a vision and knew the community and culture. He provided money adequate for our needs, opened doors with government officials, and connected us with HIV/AIDS experts.

It also worked because compassion drove us—not a church-planting strategy or a way to get entry to the country—but a need that drew out a response of deep sorrow over brokenness, pain, and suffering.

It worked because we responded, as much as we were able, with generosity. We didn't limit what we would do. If someone needed food, we brought it. If they needed a ride to the hospital, we took them. They responded to our generosity with openness. We gave generously because of God's generosity to us in Christ through the gospel. People recognized that they mattered to us as individuals and not just as numbers to report to a donor. We weren't just another NGO doing a project or people doing a job. We communicated in many ways that we saw them as being made in God's image and that they mattered to us because of that. We loved them, and they responded to that love. We often hear, "You are my family."

It worked because we showed up every day. We showed up in the middle of the night. People found us at 3 p.m. or 3 a.m. if they needed us. We sat on their beds, held their hands, and put our arms around them. We set up shop in the community, had our office there, and the door was open with someone there to talk or pray. We lived close by and spent our days walking through the neighborhood, and we became part of the community.

Another reason it worked is because we created interdependent relationships rather than one-way or dependent relationships. As our beneficiaries' health improved, we employed them to care for others who were still sick. They became a part of the team. We worked with government officials as partners, not adversaries, seeking their opinions, asking for help, and giving credit for their contributions. Our team—Ethiopians and missionaries—worked in partnerships acknowledging each other's gifts and importance.

We also had a clear understanding of who we wanted to serve, which defined our criteria for selecting people as beneficiaries. We wanted to help the sickest and poorest people in our city. Having a realistic understanding of what it means to be poor is an important factor in serving effectively. Sometimes poverty gets defined as a state of mind rather than a state of being. In other words, poverty is seen as a poor self-image or a misunderstanding of your relationship to God. It becomes less about not having enough to eat, or adequate health care, or shelter, and more about not seeing who you should be and what resources God has already placed at your disposal. This can shift blame, or some part of it, onto the poor person, and it also spreads out who can be included.

Randy Nabors in his book *Merciful* says,

> "I am, of course, amazed at justifications I have heard from the non-poor to spiritualize this word (poor), as if God didn't care about the physical realities of suffering, hunger, homelessness, exposure, sickness, and alienation." [1]
>
> "There are those who teach that the poor, whether in the West or in other parts of the world, don't really need our money and probably don't need us either. Instead, they say, what they need are learned techniques, changes in values, maybe training in self-organization. While I can agree with some of the concerns, I am faced with the reality this is not primarily what Jesus teaches when talking about mercy." [2]

MEASURING IMPACT

Setting benchmarks for progress and then measuring that progress also contributed to our success. Just hoping that you are making an impact isn't enough. In our ministry we wanted to extend and improve the lives of people with HIV/AIDS. This meant measuring mortality and morbidity. In other words, how many people died and how often people were sick. We measured these by our annual mortality rate, the percentage of people in the project who died in a year, and by tracking people's CD4 counts, a measure of a person's immune system. We continued to refine this and add other measurements, like our graduation rate, when people become self-sufficient and leave the ministry. All of these tell us if we are making progress toward our goals.

Setting goals and measuring impact allows you to do something else important and that is to change and adapt. If you can see that something isn't working, then you can change. Doing this requires collecting and using good data.

When we set goals and track our progress, it allows us to develop and maintain an important organizational practice. This is sometimes called the cycle of adaptation. First, we listen, observe, learn, and make an initial assessment of the need and the situation. Second, we experiment and innovate, or act based on our assessment. Third, we evaluate and learn what works and also what failed. Fourth, we modify our actions and plans based on what we learned. This is a cycle that we need to intentionally and continuously practice.

This is also important for fundraising. When we ask someone to support our project, we have an obligation to do what we say and then show that we have made the impact we promised. We must be people of integrity and not promise what we can't deliver or promise an outcome and not measure our progress to see if we have kept our word.

Setting goals and measuring impact allows you to do something else important and that is to change and adapt. If you can see that something isn't working, then you can change.

CHARITY OVER DEVELOPMENT

A final factor in the project's impact came from our desire to respond biblically. Who does the Bible repeatedly tell us to help? Widows, orphans, prisoners, the sick and hungry, the "least of these." And the example it gives is one of selfless sacrifice for people who cannot help themselves. It is also a demonstration of the gospel. We are generous because God is generous to us in Christ. Timothy Keller's book *Generous Justice* is a great resource on this topic.[3] We treat people the way we would like to be treated.

We don't exploit people in order to raise money by portraying them as helpless victims needing rescue. We treat them as unique individuals created in God's image and deserving the same love and respect that we want.

So, did we create unhealthy dependency? Is what we have done unsustainable and its impact short-lived? (As missionaries, who live off the generosity of others, we must be careful about denouncing the dependency of others. If dependency is intrinsically bad then we are in trouble.)

Instead of stepping over, walking past, or closing our eyes and hearts to "the least of these," we are called to be Good Samaritans. "I desire mercy and not sacrifice . . . " (Matthew 9:13).

We didn't teach people to fish or start a microfinance program. We broke almost every rule of good development and best practice, but didn't create unhealthy dependency. Almost everyone has become self-sufficient. How? We made a choice to do charity rather than development.

Some people have postulated a continuum with relief (or charity) on one end and development on the other, with rehabilitation in the middle. The assertion is that it may sometimes be necessary to do charity, but that it is preferable to move along the continuum toward development, where long-term improvement happens.

We in the West have a cultural bias toward development. Unfortunately, development's track record is poor. We are problem solvers with a deep-seated conviction that every problem has an answer and that fixing poverty is not fundamentally different from fixing a broken toaster—diagnose the problem, buy the right part, install it correctly, and move on to the next problem.

Poverty has not responded well to this approach. Even in the rare situation where improvements happened, the link between those improvements and development activities is tenuous. Questioning development's efficacy is no longer an individual, or even minority, opinion. Todd J. Moss in his book *African Development* says:

> *"The international donors in particular are prone to a continuously evolving mea culpa with hubris, what might be called the 'yes, but now*

we have it right' syndrome. A recurring theme in the progression of development thinking is that past strategies had mistakenly overlooked some crucial aspect, but the missing link has now been identified and everything can be fixed this time around." [4]

Some other reasons for skepticism about development strategies include the problems of complexity and personal freedom. Both the places we work and the people we serve are unique and complex. It is naïve to think that something that works in one place will work in the same way in another. There is also a growing school of thought that I resonate with that says that development happens as personal freedom grows. The poor are often very good at improving their lives when given freedom to choose and an environment that protects their freedoms. They are also often quick adopters of new technologies, and when they have access to resources they will use them effectively. When development organizations arrive with a prepackaged plan and a we-know-best attitude they often short-circuit indigenous systems, discourage creativity, and retard progress. New York University economist William Easterly, in his book *The Tyranny of Experts*, says, "The global double standard of rights for the rich and not for the poor is very much alive in the technocratic worldview of development."[5]

Another problem with development is its historical and philosophical underpinnings. Development focuses on political units, nations, or at the lowest level, communities. Development also has utopian roots, envisioning "… humanity moving toward a common future of modernity and mass consumption."[6] Even when development's goals are more modest, the individual is often forgotten or even harmed in order to accomplish a "greater" good.

"By contrast, charity sees poverty and inequality as persistent qualities of a fallen world, unlikely to be completely resolved through human action," Scherz writes. Charity focuses on the individual, and is also a three-way transaction between the recipient, the giver, and God.

"… givers of charity often conceive of the worldly effects of their gifts and their own ability to change the future in far more limited terms. Charity also differs from both humanitarianism and development in the roles that religious injunctions and divine exchange play in motivating the charitable gift. The people described in this book who made charitable gifts thought of these gifts as offerings to God made as

acts of supplication, as thanksgiving for blessings received, and, most profoundly, as thanksgiving for the unrepayable gift of salvation." [7]

My last and largest reason for preferring charity to development is the biblical example. Proverbs 3:27-28 says, "Do not withhold good from those who deserve it, when it is in your power to act. Do not say to your neighbor, 'Come back later; I'll give it tomorrow,' when you have it with you."

Randy Nabors in *Merciful* expounds on these verses.

> *"It is right and good to build development strategies, but it is wrong to use that as an excuse to deny immediate help to our neighbors. In that case, the Good Samaritan might be still working to create a 'Traveler's Aide' so everything could be done decently and in order,' while the poor man who was beaten dies of his wounds. ... We don't want to stop hearing the cry of the poor and lose passion for rapid and effective response. We don't want our hearts to become calloused and have our attitudes become cynical while we build strategies to help the poor for the long term."*

Instead of stepping over, walking past, or closing our eyes and hearts to "the least of these," we are called to be Good Samaritans. "I desire mercy and not sacrifice ..." (Matthew 9:13).

"It is also important to remember that most of the teaching we receive from Jesus about how we deal with the poor has more to do with our heart, and our immediate response to the poor, than about what is the best organized program for them—or for us."[8]

Andrew Warren has been a missionary with MTW since 1982 and has served in Kenya, Hungary and Ethiopia. He is the MTW Ethiopia Country Director and the founder and Executive Director of Ethiopia ACT. ACT is a multi-cultural team that is actively loving the "least of these" of Addis Ababa, by working to bring reconciliation in all areas of life, resulting in Gospel-centered churches, transformed lives and communities.

1   Randy Nabors, *Merciful* (CreateSpace Independent Publishing Platform: 2015), 264.

2   Nabors, Merciful, 167.

3   Timothy Keller, *Generous Justice* (New York: Penguin Books, 2012).

4   Todd J. Moss, *African Development* (Boulder: Lynne Rienner Publishers, 2011).

5   William Easterly, *The Tyranny of Experts: Economists, Dictators, and the Forgotten Rights of the Poor* (Basic Books, 2014).

6   China Scherz, *Having People, Having Heart: Charity, Sustainable Development, and Problems of Dependence in Central Uganda* (Chicago: University of Chicago Press, 2014), 5.

7   Scherz, *Having People, Having Heart*, 6.

8   Nabors, *Merciful*, 304.

4

Mercy of Jesus Shared in Obedience

by Mike Pettengill

On the outskirts of a poor third-world city in Honduras, in the middle of a remote village, on the edge of a dense jungle, sits a medical clinic. The name of the clinic, Tree Of Life, originates from Revelation 22:2 which reads, "through the middle of the street of the city; also, on either side of the river, the *tree of life* with its twelve kinds of fruit, yielding its fruit each month. The leaves of the tree were for the healing of the nations." This clinic helps heal 3,500 patients a year. A typical patient at this clinic earns $75 per week and lives in a one-room, dirt-floor shack. On average, the clinic takes in $2 per patient and spends nearly $20 per patient. The clinic will never be self-supporting and was never intended to be. Patients are cried with, prayed for, provided health education, and loved.

On the one-year anniversary of the Tree Of Life medical clinic, hundreds from the community gathered to celebrate the great blessings the clinic had provided their families. Moments before the speeches began, a tiny old woman, a frequent visitor to the clinic, walked up to the missionary who runs the clinic. "Young lady," she said in a near whisper, "may I say something to everyone about the clinic?" Every well-organized, type-A fiber in this Western missionary's body screamed "no," but she gave the old woman permission. Not knowing if the old lady had positive or negative things to say, the missionary invited her to address the crowd. The quiet woman, hunched over from living too many hard years, shuffled to the front. The crowd grew respectfully quiet. The old-woman said only, "I come to this clinic because Jesus is here."

The glory of Jesus Christ. That is why the Tree of Life medical clinic was opened. That is why the clinic treats patients. That is why the clinic will continue to operate even though it loses money. The Tree of Life medical clinic provides desperately poor people with the grace, mercy, and justice that can only be found in Jesus Christ.

That is our job as Christians. We are to provide the mercy of Jesus Christ to others so they see Him more clearly. Justice for those in need is eternally significant to Jesus Christ. When we serve others, we worship God. We should serve the needy as Christ served us; giving everything and expecting nothing in return.

THE NEED FOR MERCY

Man's pain and man's suffering originates from man's sin. Everything God made was good (Genesis 1:31). The first man was tempted and sinned in a perfectly voluntary act. The contagion of sin spread throughout man and left no part of our being untouched. Man became utterly corrupt (Genesis 6:5, Romans 7:18). Paul tells us that by one man, death entered the world and passed on to all men (Romans 5:12). Sin causes man to turn against God and to turn against each other. With the addition of sin in our existence we have pain, sickness, death, suffering, poverty, racism, injustice, corruption, theft, starvation, and other means of creating distance between us and our Creator.

The need for God's grace, mercy, and justice in the world are a direct result of the fall of man. Now, as a result, we are all needy recipients of the blessings provided by the Lord. The birth, death, and resurrection of Jesus Christ were mandated by the sin of man. Through Christ alone is our sinful heart reconciled to God.

We should serve the needy as Christ served us;
giving everything and expecting nothing in return.

DISPENSING MERCY

It is our sin that created a need for the mercy of Christ. It is also our hands which are called upon to disseminate God's love. Scripture commands disciples of Christ to show His mercy and justice to each other and to the lost. We are vessels for which His good work is poured out on others (2 Timothy 2:21). When we serve the poor, the widows, and the orphans in Christ's name, they receive mercy, Christ receives glory, and we comprehend justice. When we were poor, lost, and destitute, the Lord shared His mercy with us so we could share His mercy with the poor, lost, and impoverished. Tim Keller said, "Because Jesus served you in such a radical way, you have a joyful need to serve."

Christ's disciples are called to dispense God's mercy and justice, not so we can be observed or glorified, but so that our Father can be glorified. Any action of mercy that elevates us as the provider is sinful. The dispenser of grace must always be seen as Christ. Those suffering must never see us as anything other than a willing vessel. The disciples of Christ are called to give food to the hungry, drink to the thirsty, welcome strangers, clothe the naked, visit the sick and imprisoned (Matthew 25:31-40). Those who do not do these things will be eternally punished (Matthew 25:41-46). Serving the needy provides evidence we are disciples of Christ and have a truly altered heart. The love of Christ in our hearts compels us to show mercy to others, as we too have been shown mercy.

SCRIPTURE SCREAMS MERCY

The term "mercy" (or merciful) appears more than 200 times in the ESV. Of course a majority of the mercy in Scripture refers to God's great mercy toward man. However, many occurrences of mercy relate to the actions we, as disciples of Christ, are to show to others so God can receive glory. The word "mercy" appears in Scripture (in all its Greek and Hebrew forms) more often than the words grace, justice, tithe, Sabbath, pray, church, baptism, and preach. Indeed mercy has great significance to our Lord. David Platt reminds us, "The Bible informs us, compels us to care for the poor, to love the outcast, to serve the needy."

Our thankfulness for God's mercy creates a strange conflict in our heart. We naturally desire to serve and comfort ourselves, but our new heart screams for us to show mercy to others. We feel a strange urge to show our love for Christ by showing His love to others. Micah 6:8 says, "He has told you, O man, what is good; and what does the LORD require of you but to do justice, and to love kindness, and to walk humbly with your God?" Charles Spurgeon wrote of this verse, "The prophet does not say, 'to do mercy,' but to 'love' it, to take a delight in it, to find great pleasure in the forgiveness of injuries, in the helping of the poor, in the cheering of the sick, in the teaching of the ignorant, in the winning back of sinners to the ways of God."

James teaches that our faith is not real if it only results in wisdom and a warm heart and not in deeds of service. James 1:27 says, "Religion that is pure and undefiled before God, the Father, is this: to visit orphans and widows in their affliction, and to keep oneself unstained from the world." R.C. Sproul says of this verse that widows and orphans "are not to be neglected, but are to be honored, respected, and helped whenever help is needed."

Our thankfulness for God's mercy creates a strange conflict in our heart. We naturally desire to serve and comfort ourselves, but our new heart screams for us to show mercy to others. We feel a strange urge to show our love for Christ by showing His love to others.

WICKED WITHHOLD MERCY

Scripture tells us that it is the wicked, not the disciple of Christ, who withholds mercy. The Bible says believers are instructed to not withhold good (Proverbs 3:27) and that no mercy is found in the wicked (Proverbs 21:10). In fact, in much of the OT we see that mercy is withheld from those whom the Lord wishes to punish or eliminate. Withholding mercy is how the wicked are destroyed (Deuteronomy 7:2, Deuteronomy 28:49-50). Those who are marked by the Lord for destruction are to receive no mercy (Joshua 11:20).

A disciple of Christ is merciful to others and a wicked man shows no mercy (Psalm 112). James 4:17 also tells us that if we know the right thing and don't do it, sin is in us. 1 John 3:17 goes as far as to question our dedication to the Lord if we withhold from the needy. "But if anyone has the world's goods and sees his brother in need, yet closes his heart against him, how does God's love abide in him?" Tim Keller echoed this theme when he said, "If you look down at the poor and stay aloof from their suffering, you have not really understood or experienced God's grace."

CREATING DEPENDENCY

Many well-intentioned Christians have elevated the concern over creating dependency above our biblical mandate to share the grace, mercy, and justice of Christ with others. The concern lies in the belief that our dissemination of physical goods to the sick and poor can create a dependency upon the giver of the gifts. The belief is that it is more important to help the poor provide for themselves and to restore their dignity. The concern is if we provide for the destitute, they will never learn to provide for themselves.

The belief in not creating dependency is supported by many solid economic, philosophical, and political viewpoints. Unfortunately, there is very little biblical reasoning to withhold mercy and justice to the poor and sick. When Christ walked the earth, He sought to create dependency on Him. Christ never withheld his physical or eternal healing based on a fear of dependency. Never once did Christ say to the blind, paralytic, or leper, "Wait, I am concerned that if I heal you, you might become dependent upon my grace and mercy." He desired to have his followers dependent upon that which only He could provide.

It is not our place to determine who gets mercy and who does not. And, it is not our place to determine why some receive mercy and some do not. Our job as disciples of Christ is to dispense God's mercy and justice to all who need it. We have not been entrusted by God to determine who is and who is not worthy. Christians dispense grace and mercy and let the Lord sort out who is lazy and who is industrious. All mercy comes from the Lord. Mercy, grace, and justice bring glory to God. Choosing to withhold mercy from an individual is consciously deciding not to glorify God.

MERCY FOR GLORY

Disciples of Christ have been selected to disseminate God's mercy to bring Him greater glory. When you give dignity, mercy, love, justice, charity, and respect to others, you are letting them see Christ in your words and actions. True justice and mercy is filled with the grace of God and is radical and offensive to the world. It is a radical concept in today's world to do justice for the needy when it is clear that there is no ability for them to repay you. A.W. Tozer said, "How utterly terrible is the current idea that Christians can serve God at their own convenience."

Feeding the poor, clothing the hungry, serving the sick—these are not natural actions that flow from the human heart. It is unnatural for us to provide justice for the poor and homeless. The justice we dispense is an echo of the grace and mercy God gave us. The desire to serve grows from the grace of Jesus Christ in us. We provide a voice and aid to the poor and oppressed so they can receive the justice found only in Christ's love.

It is not our place to determine who gets mercy and who does not. Our job as disciples of Christ is to dispense God's mercy and justice to all who need it.

Mercy given separate from God's glory is sinful. Those who serve the needy and do not have Christ's glory at the center of their purpose are doing so to glorify themselves or their belief system. Disease, poverty, and starvation are blessings if they help point us toward our greater need for Jesus. Only true mercy comes from Christ and only Christ produces true mercy.

MERCY ME

Pray the God of mercy will give you opportunities to provide justice to the oppressed and grace for the broken. Serving others isn't imparting our views, imposing our will, or forcing our culture on others. It is sharing the joy and mercy of a perfect love. Answering God's command to share His mercy and love with the poor is a pleasure too few enjoy and too many disregard. Augustine implored us, "So give to the poor; I'm begging you, I'm warning you, I'm commanding you, I'm ordering you."

Poverty and injustice are conditions brought on by sin. Not all the poor are lazy and not all the rich are industrious. Many of us have been blessed with material and financial abundance by God, not because we are good or special, but so that we can serve the needy. The rich and the poor were not meant to be separated by wealth—rather unified, in God's glory, by the love and resources He gave us all. Tim Keller said, "If it is the gospel that is moving us, our giving to the poor will be significant, remarkable, and sacrificial."

MERCY SHARED

There was a young man who was well known and not well trusted in an extremely poor community in rural Honduras. The teenage boy was known as a liar and a thief throughout the community and he had done little to show me otherwise. He had periodically run with gangs and was seldom up to any good. Nearly every time I saw him he would approach me and ask for something: money, medicine, food, shoes. I just didn't trust the kid. I was certain he wanted to scam me and sell my well-intentioned gifts for drugs or alcohol. Countless times I told him no and countless times he cursed me and threatened me.

Disciples of Christ are to pour out unending love, grace, and mercy on others because we first received unending love, grace, and mercy from God.

One day I decided to give in, not due to my benevolent heart or out of a desire to glorify God. I wanted to give him a few items so I could catch him in his lies and have grounds to never trust him again. I decided to provide him with a box of food and a new pair of shoes. The boy received the blessings, thanked me and ran off. I had already prearranged that another boy would follow him and report back to me how the kid had squandered my gifts. Within an hour my stoolpigeon reported back to me. The boy had indeed sold the shoes, but to buy food. He then took the now overflowing box of food and transported it on his bike to several houses. House after house he delivered food to a sick aunt, a widowed grandmother, a 14-year-old pregnant sister, and kept none for himself. Immediately my heart was flooded with Genesis 50:20, "As for you, you meant evil against me, but God meant it for good, to bring it about that many people should be kept alive, as they are today." In this story I was the one committing evil, and the young thug was God's distributor of grace and mercy. My mistrust had kept God's blessings from dozens of individuals. God used the true pure heart that day.

Disciples of Christ are to pour out unending love, grace, and mercy on others because we first received unending love, grace, and mercy from

God. Daily we should pray, "Dear Lord, allow me to see the poor with your eyes, love the orphan with your heart, and serve the widow with my hands." Daily we should seek to glorify the Lord by serving those in need.

Mike and his wife, Erin, have been fulltime missionaries with MTW since 2007. For seven years Mike served as Team Leader for a church planting and medical/mercy ministry in La Ceiba, Honduras. Mike and Erin served with MTW in Equatorial Guinea as a seminary professor and mentor to pastors for 2 years. In the Summer 2017, Mike became the new director of MTW's West Coast Hub. His new job is to promote missions, recruit missionaries, and mentor them from churches in California, Arizona, and Nevada. Mike attended Reformed Theological Seminary and has written one book.

5

The Truth about Anti-Trafficking Ministry

by Katherine Long

Over this past decade, "Anti-Trafficking" has become a buzz word in the churches around America. People are dying to hear the amazing stories of what God is doing through His people in the fight against injustice around the world. As a missionary and an advocate in anti-trafficking, I meet with churches and individuals to raise support and awareness of this issue. When I or someone else reveals that front lines are not only in "those poor places" but also right here in America, all too often churches/individuals become paralyzed in disbelief and fear. As I traveled, I began noticing that I was hearing the same fears over and over again regarding the work I do in justice ministries. "What do justice ministries have to do with church planting? What role does the church play in justice? Where do we even start? Isn't it dangerous?" There are so many questions that come up when the Lord stirs in your heart to act. Unfortunately, there is no answer book nor instruction manual for how to begin that I can give to an individual or a church body. But I hope that by addressing these six most common fears/concerns, the Church will not only see that justice ministries are biblical, but they are also life giving for your church and for you.

"It feels so overwhelmingly big! I wouldn't even know where to start!"

This is the number one fear I hear when people feel moved but are paralyzed by the sheer enormity of the sex trade.

Stop and Pray. It is so easy to see a need and to try and fix it. Yes, the Lord wants to use us, but we need to remember that as Americans, we can think we are helping, but in reality we are hurting. So stop for a bit, and give to the Lord your desires to go into new territory. Ask the Lord to reveal to you what He wants you to do or not do. "Likewise the Spirit helps us in our weakness. For we do not know what to pray for as we ought, but the Spirit himself intercedes for us with groanings too deep for words" (Romans 8:26). This verse gives us the freedom to not know how to start or what to pray for, because the Spirit knows what we need to pray. Is there someone or someplace specific that He wants you to pray for? Ask the Lord to open your eyes to see people the way He sees them. Ask Him to reveal to you the people who are ostracized from the community, whether it be family outcasts, homeless, youth, or even people who are hidden from your sight. The Lord will respond. How do I know this? Because He is the God of mercy and justice; our God is the God of action. "Truly I tell you, whatever you did for one of the least of these brothers and sisters of mine, you did for me" (Matthew 25:40).

"When we hear Christ talk about the poor, the blind, the oppressed, we often think of someone else. The important thing for us to remember is that these stories are about us.

The Three E's. When speaking to churches, IJM (International Justice Mission) uses the three E's to help churches get involved: encounter, explore, engage. "Encounter" means reading God's Word about justice and studying His heart toward those who suffer. We read His Word about the poor, the meek, and the suffering and it is easy to think that God is talking about a specific people group. "Oh those poor people over there, I can't imagine." The Bible is filled with suffering and we see how He responds to them. We must remember that it is not an "us" vs. "them." Stephanie Hubach of MNA says it like this, "When we hear Christ talk about the poor, the blind, the oppressed, we often think of someone else. The important thing for us to remember is that these stories are about us. It keeps us from operating under a position of superiority. It's not that we are whole and they are broken, the message of the gospel is that He is whole and we are broken." So, as you read your Bible, ask the Lord to reveal to you His heart for the poor and needy, and for yourself.

"Explore" means seeing what is out there already. Start reading firsthand accounts of trafficking victims, refugees, and biographies of abolitionists. Invite guest speakers to teach your Sunday school class. Learn who is doing what in your community and find out if there is something missing or if there are multiple organizations doing the same thing and ask why. For example, in your exploring you may find that there are many aftercare homes for victims of human trafficking and yet there are no prevention programs in any of the schools where most of the at-risk youth attend. That is a hole in the system. Do some research on what is already being done around the world and in your city. God is already at work—find out where and join in!

"Engage" means to go out and do. The process of the three E's can take years, and it should take years. Prayer, research, networking, financing—all of these things are ongoing. Be patient and remember that it is okay for things to move slowly. The Lord's perfect timing is often slow in this field, so be patient, trust in His timing, but be ready.

One of my favorite things about my job is seeing many denominations come together to address the issue of human trafficking. When engaging, try to engage with existing programs and organizations. There is no need to have multiple organizations in one town doing the exact same thing. Chances are, the group that is doing something is doing it well but in desperate need of people's resources, prayer, and financial resources. Join forces and prove to the young women we serve that we are united together as the body of Christ to serve and protect them. Just because some of our theology or liturgy does not match does not mean that we should not join hands and be a united front against the problem of trafficking. I have been working with different denominations for the last five years, and no matter what our beliefs are, we all believe in the sovereignty of God and that we cannot heal any of these women: it is up to the Holy Spirit to lead and guide us and them. How beautiful it is to see the Body unite for such a cause.

MINISTRY UP CLOSE

"Engaging" can look like short-term missions trips or internships in our country or in other countries. Short-term work has had a stigma in the past of being unhelpful and sometimes even damaging to the work on the ground. Though this can sometimes be true, we have actually seen short-term teams and interns do amazing things for justice ministries. Short term or long term, what is important is coming with an attitude to serve. Feel free to send people from your churches as long as they are well informed and ready to serve the team on the ground even if it means cleaning toilets instead of "rescuing women." One thing that short-term teams can do is come with resources that the team on the ground is lacking, such as housing supplies, outreach supplies, finances, and training materials. We have seen some amazing things happen with partnerships with stateside churches. A word of warning—sometimes going to visit programs or organizations can be frustrating for supporting churches because you pray for the work, you help fund the work, and so when you arrive you want to see the program in action but you will not be able to. There is a reason for this. It is not that you or your church team are untrustworthy, it is simply to keep the outreach team or program safe and it helps prevent us from treating the women like they are an exhibit in a zoo. Respect the rules that the team keeps in place for the protection of yourselves and the participants. Remember, it is not an "us" vs. "them" but a "we." We must always protect the anonymity of these young women and never use their stories as marketing tools without their consent. They have already been exploited and are working through that trauma; we never want to exploit them again.

Another challenge to ministry is our own perception of what we have to offer. When people start thinking about engaging, sometimes they are paralyzed by the lack of skills they bring to the table. They think that because they aren't counselors, pastors, or nurses they can't serve. This is not true. Every justice ministry needs accountants, doctors, police officers, job skills trainers, artists, mothers, fathers, construction workers, and lawyers.

For example, in Bulgaria it takes a huge group of people working together in order to get a little girl away from her orphanage and into a brothel in Amsterdam. Recruiters, orphanage directors, border police, and brothel owners must create an organized machine to get girls to the streets and brothels. If we are going to address the issue of trafficking then we must have a large network of people devoted to helping these young women walk away from exploitation toward safety and personal recovery. How amazing would it look to not only see police and social workers trained in anti-trafficking, but also see an entire community of teachers, nurses, hair stylists, mechanics, truck drivers, etc. all trained in spotting trafficking and knowing how to help the woman as she transitions back into society?

◇◇

No little boy wakes up and decides to pimp.
No little girl wakes up and decides to prostitute.
It takes years of recruiting, manipulation, and
resources to implant this idea into a child's head.

◇◇

RAISING OUR AWARENESS

Often people hear about trafficking and they want to engage by building homes and starting outreaches. This is wonderful and very needed, of course, but as you are writing checks to these projects, why not also consider what is going on in your community. Imagine a river where ministry workers are at the base of the river pulling trafficking survivors out of the water and bringing them to a shelter. But who is at the top of the river preventing the young women and boys from falling in? This is where churches can play a key role in addressing the issue of trafficking. Anti-trafficking prevention ministry is simply discipling the next generation. No little boy wakes up and decides to pimp. No little girl wakes up and decides to prostitute. It takes years of recruiting, manipulation, and resources to implant this idea into a child's head. If no one else is in their life to ask them hard questions, caring for them and pursuing them, what do you think is going to happen?

Not only is it important for the church to be discipling the next generation, it is also important for the church to be a safe place for people struggling with pornography and sex addictions. According to Covenant Eyes' website, 9 out of 10 boys and 6 out of 10 girls are exposed to pornography before the age of 18, and 64% of Christian men and 15% of Christian women watch porn at least once a month. This statistic is alarmingly high. As disturbing as it is to discuss, we must also address sexual abuse in our churches and create safe places for victims as well as perpetrators to find healing. One in five girls and one in twenty boys is a victim of child sexual abuse, and statistically, abusers themselves come from a past of sexual abuse. It is a horrible cycle of abuse that can be prevented if we can make the church a safe place and not a place of shame. If the church does not start talking about these issues, who do you think the next generation will go to for guidance? The media? Their friends? We must address these issues in the church and stop ignoring it because it is an "inappropriate" topic. If this many people are affected, then this topic is actually very appropriate and relevant.

In *Stopping the Traffick*, Ian De Villiers writes, "Christians can see abuse as being too ugly or unbelievable for Christians to engage with. In practice, there is a widespread Christian discomfort when it comes to thinking about sex outside of marriage beyond simply seeing it as immoral: anybody involved is tainted at best, more likely stigmatized; open discussion is censored. The more conservative the community, the harder it is to talk about sex without stigma and judgment. But where victims of sexual exploitation may be coerced rather than forced, and where guilt and fear are common, judgmental attitudes cannot be helpful."[1]

"I can't imagine doing what you do; it seems so messy and disturbing."

Let's be honest here, this is a normal and honest reaction that one feels when hearing about the horror that is the sex trade. It is dark, it is disturbing that it happens, but what we must remember is that it is not new. Prostitution and exploitation are throughout the entire Bible. Jesus Himself is from a lineage with women who prostituted and were exploited. The fact is, it started with the Fall.

"Humans have a fundamental, created need for intimacy. Dominion has been given, but it can be turned to evil—seeking to be like God, seeking power over others. It becomes clear that sexual exploitation is one of the ultimate ways in which the creation pattern is destroyed: from 'helper' to 'dominated,' from intimacy to used. Relationship is broken; the image of God shattered. Healing and re-creation cannot come easily or lightly."[2]

We live in a fallen, broken world of the "already but not yet." Murder, rape, and exploitation are happening and will continue to happen until Jesus Christ comes back. They just will. They can happen to us and from us at any moment. We have no way of truly protecting ourselves from these events, "only by the grace of God do we go." The true question is, "What are we going to do about it?" Are we going to sit back and let it happen to those "poor, sad" people, or are we going to be safe, healing places for hurting people to join us because we realize that we too are in recovery? "For all have sinned and fall short of the glory of God, and are justified by his grace as a gift, through the redemption that is in Christ Jesus" (Romans 3:23-24). Unless we realize that we are all broken, we are all messy, we are all in need of a doctor, our churches will never be a place of healing and compassion. When the Holy Spirit reveals to us the true nature of our sin, we won't see trafficking as simply "messy and disturbing;" we will want to go out into the world and tell them the Good News that our God lives and our God restores. We will want to bring people to the feet of Jesus. For only there is the true source of healing and restoration.

When the Holy Spirit reveals to us the true nature of our sin, we won't see trafficking as simply "messy and disturbing;" we will want to go out into the world and tell them the Good News that our God lives and our God restores.

Just as when you first believed and the Holy Spirit gave you a new heart, now ask Him to give you new eyes, that you may see people around you the way that He sees them. "Create in me a clean heart, oh God, and renew a right spirit within me" (Psalm 51:10). Remember that though Jesus was perfect, His community was not. He hung out with the messiest of all messes—tax collectors, prostitutes, and fishermen. The forgotten, the outcasts of society were His community. We need not worry about bringing messy people into our communities. Yes, it will inch you out of your comfort zone, but ultimately you will see Jesus shine even brighter in you and through you.

"These rich pictures [of Jesus' community] are about living together in vibrant and strong relationships. It worked for Jesus in a community of all sorts of people. Could a local church become an inclusive, healing community offered to those who need safety and healing? And could such a community stand as both a testimony against and an alternative for those who would abuse power?"[3] May our churches be a place for healing as well as prevention of the abuse of power.

"It seems so dangerous doing what you do. Isn't there risk?"

If I wanted to answer this question bluntly and without compassion, I could just list Bible verses and leave it at that. But the truth is, it's not as easy as that. It is one thing to read Bible verses and it is another to live it out in our daily lives. Let's consider these verses: "I have been crucified with Christ; and it is no longer I who live, but Christ lives in me; and the life which I now live in the flesh I live by faith in the Son of God, who loved me and gave Himself up for me" (Galatians 2:20). And Luke 9:23-24, "And He was saying to them all, "If anyone wishes to come after Me, he must deny himself, and take up his cross daily and follow Me. For whoever wishes to save his life will lose it, but whoever loses his life for My sake, he is the one who will save it." Let's pause and ask ourselves, "What does that actually mean to me?"

MY PERSONAL STORY

It was Christmas time, and my sister and I had come home from college. We were getting ready to enjoy the Andrew Peterson concert "Behold, the Lamb of God" that was performing at our home church. I was in the middle of switching majors at the time, in between jobs, and feeling pretty unsure about everything in my future. I wanted to do missions but God kept saying "no, not yet" and I was left feeling useless and defeated. As I was thinking about all of these things Sara Groves walked across the stage toward her piano. She began playing and my soul rested and bathed in her beautiful lyrics. Then she paused to introduce her next song. "This song is called 'When the Saints.' It was written for and dedicated to a trafficking survivor and leader who inspires me." All of a sudden, I was not resting; I sat upright and she had my full attention.

"Trafficking survivor?" I thought. "What is a trafficking survivor?" As Sara began explaining this young woman's journey from darkness to leadership, I wept. I wept for this young woman. I wept for my naiveté. I wept for the thousands, no millions, of people I have never thought about. Sitting next to my sister, I imagined what I would do if she was taken or coerced by someone and was gone forever. I quickly answered, just as an elder sister would, "I would stop at nothing to find her!" And then I closed my eyes and heard the Lord say, *"These young ones missing are your sisters and brothers. You must go and seek out my lost sheep."*

I remember sitting in the pew thinking about all of the risks. Death. Abduction. Loss of limbs. Loss of family. Loneliness in a foreign country.

Dysentery. You name it, I was thinking about it. And then a peace came over me and I heard, *"Katherine, I have taken care of you thus far. Yes it will be too much of a burden for you to carry, but you need not fear. For my yoke is easy and the burden is light. You cannot carry this burden, I will."* In that moment my fears subsided. I am not saying they went away forever ... but they were quieted.

Instead of focusing on whatever circumstance or trial I am in, the Lord reminds me to focus on Him and He will make my paths straight. And if I die doing His will, the only thing that can happen is that I will wake up with Him in Glory.

> *No guilt in life, no fear in death,*
> *This is the power of Christ in me;*
> *From life's first cry to final breath.*
> *Jesus commands my destiny.*
> *No power of hell, no scheme of man,*
> *Can ever pluck me from His hand;*
> *Till He returns or calls me home,*
> *Here in the power of Christ I'll stand.*
> —"In Christ Alone," by Keith Getty and Stuart Townend

Jim Martin writes, "Learning about the nature of injustice-related suffering in our world is often challenging because it requires something more of churches: courage. Privileged cultures around the world usually choose to isolate themselves from the suffering of the poor and vulnerable, once they have achieved a level of affluence that permits it. But Christians who take the Scriptures seriously find in them a mandate. They find that like the Samaritan in Jesus' story, God is calling them to draw near to suffering, to see and to be moved with compassion. This first step is simple, but risky. It requires a willingness to learn about, pray for, and engage (in small but significant ways) in the suffering of the world's vulnerable."[4]

"Why should the church care? How is it consistent with our call to plant churches?"

I am a missionary and part of a church-planting team. So I am often asked, "How does an anti-trafficking ministry fit in with our call to church planting?" Before I was asked this the first time I had never thought about it. To me, it seemed like a natural part of church planting. It seemed like a perfect fit for my church-planting team's model of community development and mercy ministry. But when asked I did not have a clear answer for them. So I began praying and asking others what their answers would be. Is this even something that church-planting teams should be a part of? As I was asking a colleague, he turned to me with a confused expression and simply said, "Katherine, you do realize that you are simply evangelizing and discipling? You not only are going out to an outreached people group, but you are also equipping the saints to go and serve. Ministry to trafficked and prostituted women is a ministry of mercy, evangelism, and discipling."

What we have found is that anti-trafficking ministries—whether in prevention, intervention, or rehabilitation—are a fertile ground for the gospel. When someone has been beaten to nothingness, oppressed until they have no value, they will eventually cry out to their Creator for help.

The fact of the matter is, most of the women we meet on the streets are tightly controlled. They will never be able to leave. One out of 100 may be able to find a way out and we won't stop praying for that number to increase, but we go into this ministry with the understanding that even with their freedom, these young women are lost. What they need, what the pimps need, what the users need, what their children need is a Savior. So when we go and give hot coffee and biscuits to these women, we come as the hands of Jesus and we speak His word on the road so they can hear our love and His love for them. What we have found is that anti-trafficking ministries—whether in prevention, intervention, or rehabilitation—are a fertile ground for the gospel. When someone has been beaten to nothingness, oppressed until they have no value, they will eventually cry out to their Creator for help. So when they come out of the life, who do they run to? We have a saying in the anti-trafficking community that the easy part of the job is getting a girl out of prostitution, the hard part is placing them in new, healthier communities. These survivors need Christian healing communities because they were dead, then they were rescued by God, and now they must deal with the fact that they believe in a God that, for some reason, allowed so much evil to happen to them and their loved ones. These are difficult questions and this is where the Church is so vitally important! Good theology, open arms, and loving and patient service are healing balm for these young ones.

Jim Martin writes, "What we've found, counterintuitively, is that the places of violent oppression and abuse that may seem utterly God-forsaken are in fact the places where we have most deeply experienced the presence and power of God. The call to the work of justice is therefore not God sending His church 'out' to a place where God cannot be found. Rather, God is inviting us 'in' to the place where He is already at work. Our good God is offering what many of us so deeply desire in our churches. In the work of justice, God is beckoning us to come and experience His profound love for us and for the vulnerable of this world. The call to fight against injustice is a call to deep discipleship."[5] Anti-trafficking and justice ministries are frightening and dirty at times, but those moments do not even compare to the moments of seeing someone see their value for the first time. The Glory of God completely outweighs the horrors of evil that we see in this ministry.

"I want to do something but all I can think of is the hurt in my past, and I hear the lies that I am not good enough or whole enough to serve."

This is a serious response from people when I speak. Whenever I speak in front of large groups, typically two to three people will come up to me with tears in their eyes because while describing anti-trafficking ministry in Bulgaria, I have described their own life. They are looking for help and a safe healing community where they can soak in the Lord's all-consuming and non-judgmental love and healing mercy.

What we must remember is that we are all in recovery from past hurts and abuse, whether from sins done to us or sins we have done ourselves. We all search for intimacy in other things besides the Lord, and every time we are left with emptiness. No matter what your story, God is the God of redeeming stories. The Bible is full of redemption! Take Joseph for example, he was sold by his own family, enslaved, sexually desired by a powerful woman and when he refused he was thrown away and imprisoned. But the Lord used all of those things to bring glory to Himself and to save His people from starvation. Geneses 50:19 says,

" . . . you meant evil against me, but God meant it for good, to bring it about that many people should be kept alive, as they are today."

Anti-trafficking and justice ministries are frightening and dirty at times, but those moments do not even compare to the moments of seeing someone see their value for the first time. The Glory of God completely out ways the horrors of evil that we see in this ministry.

However, even though we are all broken, if you desire to work in anti-trafficking and yet you have not gone through a recovery program or you are not involved in an accountability group, I would recommend waiting. Burnout is very real, and if you have not dealt with your own past, it is not wise to work with the trauma of others. But there is hope! The Lord loves to use people who have gone through trauma to serve those who are in trauma, this is one way he brings about redemption! Some of the most amazing anti-trafficking organizations are lead and run by survivors. Our God is the God of name changing, He is the God of redemption, He is the God who saves.

If you have gone through recovery yourself and want to serve but are afraid, ask the Lord to give you a partner who will encourage you as you start this process. The harvest is ripe but the laborers are few! We need help, and you may be the perfect person for this ministry. Do not listen to the lies that seek to shame you and keep you quiet. Just as the Lord freed you physically, ask the Lord to free you emotionally so that He can use your story to bring you peace, help others find peace, and to bring glory to Himself.

"Prostitution is the oldest profession in the history of the world! It will never go away!"

This statement is not inaccurate because prostitution, in itself, has been going on for thousands of years. But I do have two problems with it.

1. It is not a profession. No little girl wakes up and thinks to herself, 'When I grow up I want to be a prostitute.' What actually happens is that prostitution finds these young girls and then manipulates their minds into thinking they are not good for anything besides the sale of sex. If prostitution is a profession then why does it only involve women who have no other choices? Why is it allowed to have bosses that rape and violate on a daily basis? If it is a profession then we should allow job shadowing and trainings. But there are none. If it is a profession, it is an extremely dangerous profession that has the life expectancy of seven years once entering into it. Prostitution is not a profession, and should never be called one.

2. The attitude behind this statement denotes a tone of surrender. It's always been there so therefore it always will be there. I would love to wake up in the world and know that there is no more prostitution, abuse, and exploitation. And one day I will! Isaiah 25:8 says, "He will swallow up death forever; and the Lord God will wipe away tears from all faces." But until that time, exploitation and abuse will be a part of this world. Does that mean that we give up on those who fall victims to it? No! It means that we protect, try to prevent, and keep our arms open to the ones who have fallen into this trap. Just as Christ never stops pursuing us, we are never to stop standing up for those who cannot stand for themselves.

I know that this ministry brings up shame, fears, and concerns. I know that the stories that are heard can leave one feeling defeated and helpless. But I can honestly say that through this ministry I have seen God perform miracles, in me and around me. Dan Allender once said "The reason we love working in this field of darkness is because, in such darkness, our God shines the brightest." This statement is so very true. For the last five years I have been working in anti-trafficking ministries in the United States and Bulgaria. I work hands-on with women and children who are ostracized from the community, the government, and sometimes even their own families. I admit that this job is difficult, dark, and often I am left feeling helpless. It is not easy seeing the things that my team and I have seen. Secondary trauma is a real thing and I have two counselors to prove it. But, after leaving that Andrew Peterson concert with my family in 2009, I was what William Wilberforce called an "incurable fanatic." At that time, I found very little anti-trafficking work in America and so I moved my research to organizations working abroad and found Daughters of Bulgaria. Then I did not see much happening in my home country, but today, I see the American church moving toward justice ministries and it causes me to weep with joy. May we be congregations, nay, may we, the One Church Body, be a body that protects, stands up for, feeds, clothes, prays for, and learns from each other. May we, followers of Christ, not focus on our fears and shame, but fix our eyes on Jesus. May we imitate Him as He was on Earth, stepping into brokenness, loving others more than ourselves and giving all the praise and glory to our Heavenly Father.

Hebrews 12:1-3: *"Therefore, since we are surrounded by such a great cloud of witnesses, let us throw off everything that hinders and the sin that so easily entangles. And let us run with perseverance the race marked out for us, fixing our eyes on Jesus, the pioneer and perfecter of faith. For the joy set before him he endured the cross, scorning its shame, and sat down at the right hand of the throne of God. Consider him who endured such opposition from sinners, so that you will not grow weary and lose heart."*

Katherine is from Birmingham, Alabama and is a missionary to Bulgaria with Mission to the World. She lives in the capitol, Sofia, and is involved in church planting and anti-trafficking ministries. She has served with MTW since 2007 and in Bulgaria since 2012.

---

1   Glenn Miles and Christa Foster Crawford, *Stopping the Traffick: A Christian Response to Sexual Exploitation and Trafficking* (Eugene, Oregon: Wipf and Stock, 2014), 31.

2   Miles and Crawford, *Stopping the Traffick*, 33.

3   Miles and Crawford, *Stopping the Traffick*, 37.

4   Miles and Crawford, *Stopping the Traffick*, 44.

5   Miles and Crawford, *Stopping the Traffick*, 43.

6

Ministry of Compassion to Those with Special Needs

by John Alex Rug

Recently, a friend from a church in the United States wrote me about a family in Africa with two young children born with disabilities. I responded that the resources I knew of were in the United States or in Chile, but what the parents of these special needs children desperately needed more than anything were people right there in Africa who could disciple them with respect to the children's circumstances. Worse than the actual physical disability is all the spiritual and emotional baggage that can accompany it.

When Jesus and His disciples came across a blind man (John 9:1), they asked Jesus, "Rabbi, who sinned, this man or his parents, that he was born blind (John 9:2)?"

There is a lot of baggage that can accompany a disability and Jesus confronted it (John 9:3). Jesus had compassion, yes. But not pity! For the man to go and wash in the pool of Siloam (John 9:7), he had to get help. As a blind person I appreciate that this might have been difficult to get. How many prying questions did he answer on the way to the pool of Siloam? Who would help someone who was considered beyond the reach of God's kingdom? Compassion, but no pity. Jesus didn't overprotect him. (This passage and teaching recently resulted in the salvation of an Ethiopian woman I visited. God's Word is powerful.)

CHALLENGE AND TEACHING OF THE MIRACLES
One might draw the conclusion that it is too frustrating to know how to minister to those with disabilities. It would be easier if we could

just heal them all or ignore them altogether. The problem is that Jesus didn't do either.

The doctrinal controversy over the miracles of Christ and especially over the matter of miracles today has obscured the fact that we are all called to act in the spirit of the miracles. If we do, we will be showing that Jesus is the Messiah and that God has a heart of compassion. How can we do this? We act in the spirit of the miracles by reducing the effects of disabilities, in Jesus' name.

We are all called to act in the spirit of the miracles. If we do, we will be showing that Jesus is the Messiah and that God has a heart of compassion. How can we do this? We act in the spirit of the miracles by reducing the effects of disabilities, in Jesus' name.

Traditionally, the body of Christ has struggled with miracle-related issues: Jesus was always successful in performing miracles. Christians cannot say the same thing in these days. Is this due to lack of faith on the part of the one to be healed, or the one praying? Is this because God has ceased to do miracles? Does He want to heal everybody today? Like it or not, the person with a disability often finds himself at the center of this controversy. He may be accused of not having enough faith or even of being demon possessed. He might be encouraged to refrain from praying for healing since, according to some, God does not do miracles now.

In John 5:1ff, Jesus heals a paralytic on one of the five colonnades surrounding the pool of Bethesda. Most everyone there had a disability of some sort and was hoping for healing from the waters of that pool. It is interesting to note that Jesus did not heal everybody. It is also helpful to realize that the man he healed likely had no faith. In verses 8-15, we see that the man used Jesus' words to excuse his own "sabbath breaking" actions and showed himself to be an ungrateful scoundrel, not a man of faith. Though faithless, he was healed. Others who had faith among the crowd at Bethesda were passed over. (Revisit the Exodus 4:10-12 passage to see that God did not heal Moses of his speech disability, at least at that time.) Yet a significant portion of Christ's church continues to oppress people with disabilities, in effect, running them out of the church due to "lack of faith."

I for one am not prepared to assert that all miracles have ceased because I would be forced to discount all the testimony of fellow believers to the contrary. What does characterize miracles is the fact that they are rare. For this reason so many people still have disabilities. A person with disabilities must recognize the sovereignty of God as he or she confronts the question, "Will Jesus heal me this side of the grave?" (God's sovereignty also has everything to do with what the Lord chooses or doesn't choose to have happen by modern medicine.) I have seen many tears shed over this matter.

If we lay aside the controversy over the miracles, we are still left with the question: What is the practical value of the miracles of Jesus for those with disabilities? While others who seemingly have nothing at stake may engage in theological controversy, running off those who are not healed or showing them indifference, the Church ought to be wrestling with this question. Since "all Scripture is God-breathed and is useful for teaching, rebuking, correcting, and training in righteousness," we must recognize that God wishes to bless His people through the miracle accounts in His Word. While it is a tremendous blessing that they show Christ to be the Messiah and that God has a compassionate heart, I am convinced there is a simple practical application: Reducing the effects of disabilities in Jesus' name is in keeping with the spirit of the miracles and brings glory to His name.

THE GOLDEN RULE

Jesus calls us to love our neighbor as ourselves (Matthew 19:19, 22:39). This command even crops up in the context of God's generosity in answering prayer (Matthew 6:12): "So in everything, do to others what you would have them do to you, for this sums up the Law and the Prophets." Jesus is the good Neighbor, having gone to great lengths to address our tremendous disability of sin in His perfect all-sufficient work of salvation of His Church. But I fear we neutralize His command in favor of being apathetic.

Example: Two people come to a complicated intersection, one is sighted and the other blind. The sighted person might reason: "I have no need of help crossing this street. Therefore, I need not help my blind neighbor." What he ought to do is to put himself in the place of his neighbor even as Jesus did. But this requires a certain knowledge of what his neighbor might be confronting—an inability to see the light and to judge the traffic due to the many phases of the light cycle. He has to ask himself, "If I were in his shoes, would I want help?" He could at least ask if the blind person needed assistance.

On a much grander scale, we must learn how we might help our neighbor. His needs and abilities might well be different from our own. This affects how individuals and congregations can reach out to people with a wide variety of disabilities as well as other marginalized people.

One restaurant owner refused our offer to put his menu into Braille at no cost to him because he had stairs up into his place of business. While stairs may present a bit of a challenge to a blind person, they do not stop him from using them. The man did not understand the difference between lack of sight and the need for a wheelchair.

A person wrongly guides a blind person by taking his arm and propelling him forward. Instead, he should offer him his arm or shoulder. The blind person has no need of someone watching his feet. But he might need a shoulder to guide him. If he should stumble, he has the other person's shoulder to help steady himself. These are simple examples of taking the time to place ourselves in our neighbor's shoes.

MADE IN GOD'S IMAGE:
THE PRACTICAL SIGNIFICANCE

In the Westminster Shorter Catechism, question 10 asks, "How did God create man?" The answer it provides is: "God created man, male and female, after his own image, in knowledge, righteousness, and holiness, with dominion over the creatures" (Genesis 1:27-28, Colossians 3:10, and Ephesians 4:24). As pointed out earlier, being made in God's image gives men and women dignity. We might describe sin as man lending dignity to that which displeases God, and refusing to lend dignity to that which pleases Him.

All of this becomes immensely important to a person with disabilities because society tends to treat him without dignity. This denial of dignity can include abandonment by family, overprotection, prejudice, and much more.

But the Lord Jesus saw things differently and reached out to all kinds of marginalized people. Regardless of what society might say, God insists we are image bearers. A newly-blinded person in a highly-classist society might well be reluctant to use a cane in public, not wanting to be considered a beggar. Such a person must know that as one made in God's likeness, he lends dignity to the use of the cane, and he should see himself as God does. This will help free him to move about more easily.

SELF ESTEEM AND CHRIST'S ESTEEM

For the person with disabilities who comes to know Jesus, he or she has the advantage of experiencing Christ's esteem. Often those with disabilities have a low self esteem. But the knowledge that Jesus shed His blood for me is overwhelming and deals with the self esteem issue. If we are part of God's people, we are "heirs of God and coheirs with Christ" (Romans 8:17). While our salvation is for God's glory, it is also undeniably for our good.

We will more easily relate to those with disabilities if we recognize them as normal in a world that has been abnormal since its plunge into sin, misery, and death.

RENEWAL AND INCLUSION

As God's people we must be a blessing to the place where we live. The Lord commanded the Jewish exiles in Babylonia (Jeremiah 29:7): "Also, seek the peace and prosperity of the city to which I have carried you into exile. Pray to the Lord for it, because if it prospers, you too will prosper."

If we are to seek the well-being of the city in which we find ourselves, then we must include and integrate into our church plant those with disabilities—those elements of society who are naturally excluded. Clearly, God's people should be at the forefront of this, and His Church should be spearheading this as part of its overall mission.

We will more easily relate to those with disabilities if we recognize them as normal in a world that has been abnormal since its plunge into sin, misery, and death.[1] But how does all of this work out in practice?

PRACTICAL APPLICATION

Years ago, I personally witnessed activity among Cuban churches that was the result of some 54 denominations working together on the matter. They have camps for the blind, for the deaf, and people with other disabilities. What is striking is that these people are part of congregations that have actively sought them out in Jesus' name. The Cuban context doesn't allow for some activities that can be brought forward elsewhere. But the cooperation between churches and the actual outreach among those with disabilities is what makes the ministry in that country truly remarkable.

There is a growing interest in the Presbyterian Church in America in reaching out to people with disabilities. Stephanie Hubach works with Mission to North America along with others to encourage local churches to get involved. I personally know of four PCA congregations with significant ministries to the deaf, the intellectually challenged, people with Down Syndrome, and others. These are encouraging signs!

There is also a growing involvement on the part of Mission to the World in reaching those with disabilities. I am grateful that the 1984 Committee of MTW showed no reservations about sending me, a blind man (and my family), to Chile as a missionary. But at that time, targeting people with disabilities was the last thing on my mind, something God saw fit to change.

It is really the Church that must adopt Jesus' heartfelt concern for the marginalized, including those with disabilities, and promote the spread of the gospel, addressing spiritual, emotional, and physical concerns even as He did.

There are MTW missionaries cooperating with the Isaiah 55 Ministries in Reynosa, Mexico, in a significant work among the deaf. Isaiah 55 and MTW, together with a wonderful Mexican staff, are impacting the lives of some 60 deaf students. I have had the privilege of ministering among them on brief occasions.

We began an MTW Ministry to the blind in Viña del Mar, Chile, in 2004. The ministry gained foundation status in 2013. As such, the CEMIPRE Foundation ministers to people with disabilities, especially the blind and visually impaired. This work might be divided into two parts: the rehabilitation of people with disabilities and the sharing of hope with them. We teach Braille, computer, English, Bible studies, folklore workshops, and much more in which we address the spiritual, physical, and emotional aspects of the lives to which we minister.

Recently I was working with a woman who had just lost her sight. She was contemplating suicide. I took her out to experience the plants and flowers on the property. She exclaimed at one point, "What a beautiful flower!" When I asked her how she knew that when she was completely blind, she said, "I felt it." "Ah, if you can feel beauty," I said, "doesn't it make sense to stick around and see what God has for you in this life?" This was just the beginning of the hope side of the equation.

People with all kinds of backgrounds come to the Foundation. They know we will not force feed them Christianity (as that is counter productive). However, they also know that we seek to base what we do on the Scriptures and will unashamedly communicate the gospel of Jesus Christ to them. We are also concerned that believers find their way into the church plant or another sound congregation near their homes.

With so few Christians and churches actively reaching out to those with disabilities, we view CEMIPRE as a prophetic ministry, calling God's people to take into account the very ones Jesus was not willing to ignore.

With MTW's encouragement, I have taken opportunities to share the vision of Jesus for those with disabilities in several different countries, keenly aware the outworking of that vision may look different from place to place.

It is my conviction that the CEMIPRE Foundation must gain endowments as well as local financial support. Its utility in the church-planting community must continue beyond my years of ministry. But ultimately, the goal is to enlist God's church to take up this work. After all, it is the Church that has the guarantee that the gates of hell will not prevail against it (Matthew 16:18). It is really the Church that must adopt Jesus' heartfelt concern for the marginalized, including those with disabilities, and promote the spread of the gospel, addressing spiritual, emotional, and physical concerns even as He did. As this happens, more and more will hear the kingdom call to that final banquet!

The Rugs have served as church planters in Chile since 1986. Currently, they are working with the National Presbyterian church-planting effort in the city of Valparaíso. In order to facilitate a church-planting movement that includes reaching those with disabilities, a largely unreached and overlooked group of people seldom found in church, the Rugs minister to them, their relatives, and friends through a resource center for the disabled (the CEMIPRE Foundation).

Note: John is blind. When it comes to working with people with disabilities, his experience has mostly been with the blind, though he has had limited opportunity to work with the deaf and those with other challenges. The fact that his examples tend to have more to do with blindness is not to negate the importance of thinking more globally, in terms of people with a vast array of disabilities.

ADDENDUM

What Scripture Says about Disabilities

While we may have access to many resources online and elsewhere, the most basic and compelling one is, of course, the Bible.[2]

Genesis 1:26-27: God made mankind in His own image. In a word, this gave men and women a dignity that is meant to glorify God. Mankind is the viceroy in God's creation. This image-bearing quality of man was distorted but not lost with the fall of our race into sin and misery. However, it is important to recognize that people with disabilities are made no less in God's image than others. When talking with a newly-blinded person, there is a greater openness to the biblical doctrine of creation once he or she understands that a person is made no less in God's image after blindness than before. Being made in God's image is a source of joy and the basis for asking the newly-blinded person to start using a cane to improve mobility and walk about with dignity.

Exodus 4:10-12: God entrusted Moses with a most difficult task and refused to accept the "disability excuse" for not doing what he was commanded to do. God has no problem with putting people with disabilities to work in His kingdom and among His people. Does His church?

Leviticus 19:14: Instead of a mere legalistic view of this verse, we are called to be a blessing to the deaf and to clear a path for the blind. It certainly involves proclaiming the Good News to the deaf and blind as well as to others whose lives are complicated by disabilities. It involves addressing the special needs of each one. Communication needs must be addressed in the case of the deaf and mobility concerns in the case of the blind. The family of a 75-year-old newly-blinded lady scolded her when she caused their dirty dishes to fall down the steps of their home that they were too lazy to take to the kitchen. A 16-year-old deaf girl with parents who still do not know sign language is yet another example of practical changes that need to be made for people to begin to obey this Scripture.

Job 29:15: The grace of God at work in Job's life caused him to be "eyes to the blind and feet to the lame."

Isaiah 61:1-3, Luke 4:16-21, Luke 7:18-23: Clearly Jesus understood He was the fulfilment of Isaiah's prophecy and applied the blessings mentioned to those with disabilities among others. His Church is challenged to follow in His footsteps.

Mark 7:31-37: Jesus took the deaf man away from the frightening crowd and used actions (sign language) that would communicate to him what he was doing. The man was completely healed and could hear and speak as a result of Jesus' miracle. Jesus undid all the consequences of the man's disability, ridding him of the actual disability. While we may not witness miracles, we certainly can minimize the effects of disabilities by addressing practical concerns. Teaching Braille and adaptive computer technology helps address the issue of literacy among the blind, for example. At the CEMIPRE Foundation, we seek to move people from being disabled to becoming differently enabled by addressing physical, emotional, and spiritual needs, in the spirit of the miracles of Jesus.

Luke 13:10-17: In our haste to focus on the actual healing of the woman who "was bent over and could not straighten up at all," we miss the fact that Jesus broke all kinds of rules to do what He did. Considering the seating/standing order in the synagogue, she was in back and likely outside the building (due to the large crowds that often followed Jesus). He called her forward from her "proper" place and even put His hands on her during the miracle. His willingness to include one who had been marginalized by the covenant people is instructive for Christ's church today. How many people with disabilities are in our congregations because we actually encouraged them to come in?

Luke 14:13 and 21: Judging from the overall context of these verses, it is not hard to imagine that the Pharisees were quite uncomfortable with Jesus' priorities, "the poor, the crippled, the blind, and the lame." This has everything to do with hospitality and evangelism.

Luke 14:15-24 (Matthew 22:1-14, Luke 22:30, Matthew 8:10-13, Luke 13:28-29): These passages have to do with the glorious banquet at the second coming of Christ. That great event, though in the future, sheds light upon present priorities Christ's church ought to have.

Luke 22:63-65: Jesus experienced blindness during His passion. He understands the child on the playground who is mocked by his peers because of his disability.

John 9:1-7, 35-41 (Revelation 3:17-18): Spiritual blindness and the need for repentance is compared to physical blindness. They are normal symptoms of an abnormal (fallen) world (*Same Lake, Different Boat* by Stephanie Hubach). By going and washing in the pool of Siloam, the man acknowledged his blindness and need of healing. In John 9:35-38, he sees his need of the Savior and has his spiritual blindness lifted unlike the Pharisees (39-41). Jesus drew the spiritual parallel: even the Pharisees got that much. But He didn't "spiritualize" His concern for those with disabilities. He addressed the physical need of many of them as should we.

Acts 13:6-12: Spiritual blindness was later accompanied by physical blindness.

---

1   Stephanie Hubach, *Same Lake, Different Boat* (P&R Publishing: 2006).

2   All Scripture quotes were taken from the *Holy Bible, New International Version.* Copyright 1973, 1978, 1984, International Bible Society. For maximum benefit, please look up all Scripture references.

7

The Journey to Shalom:
Peacemaking and Missions

by Natee Tanchanpongs, Ph.D.

INTRODUCTION

Thailand has a color problem! In past years, there have been waves of social and political upheavals in Thailand. Thais were wearing different color clothing based on their political stance. These colors represented viewpoints that often seem irreconcilable. The country has been so divided that at various points civil war felt imminent. It took a military coup in 2014 to bring civility back to the country.

This color problem is but one of many situations of conflict in the world. How should the church mitigate the problems of strife that we face? As the evangelical church recover from the reactive paranoia of the Social Gospel movement,[1] we are rediscovering our root in caring for society. Because of this, evangelicals are becoming more involved in ministries of reconciliation.[2] This paper seeks to support that trajectory by highlighting a robust biblical theology of peacemaking in order to better understand the church's role as agents of peacemaking. Specifically, a reading of 1 Corinthians 12 in the context of the whole Bible produces a redemptive historical understanding of peacemaking that has important implications for the mission of the church. In this way, the oneness and the many-ness of the visible church is not an end to itself, but a starting point of and a means toward the oneness and the many-ness of the redeemed humanity. By placing this passage in the canonical context we can see a fuller picture of oneness and many-ness, which in turn would shed light on our responsibilities as peacemakers.

1 CORINTHIANS 12 AND THE BIBLICAL THEOLOGY OF PEACEMAKING

1 Corinthians 12 is one of four primary passages on the unity and diversity of the church.[3] Each passage gives us reasons why a Christian should use his or her diverse set of God-given gifts.[4] This passage is often used to emphasize the need for unity in the church. The typical sermon might go something like this. There is division in the congregation. The solution is to put away our differences for the sake of harmony and to dissolve diverse many-ness for the sake of oneness. In the end, unity is appropriated by uniformity. However, 1 Corinthians 12 suggests that the unity of the church presupposes the diversity of its members. Therefore this unity cannot mean uniformity. True Christian unity is a unity of many-ness, not the unity of sameness. Even though most Christians today might agree that diversity has value, we do not always act this belief out in real life, perhaps because we fear diversity. Christians are not exempt from sin that more often than not leads diversity into disunity. Thus we are tempted to think that unity comes when diversity is dissolved.

True Christian unity is a unity of many-ness, not the unity of sameness. Even though most Christians today might agree that diversity has value, we do not always act this belief out in real life, perhaps because we fear diversity.

There is disunity in the church and thus peacemaking is necessary. However, 1 Corinthians 12 is a clear call for a unity of diverse multiplicity. In this passage, we see a twin emphasis on unity and diversity. 1 Corinthians 12 is a classic text that addresses a complex relationship between the one and the many of the church. A reflection on the ecclesial oneness and many-ness recalls the corresponding oneness and many-ness of the Godhead. Many biblical scholars and theologians have contributed to this discussion, but theologian Miroslav Volf, perhaps better than anyone else, has attempted to make sense of the actual connection between the one and the many of the Church and those of the Trinity. His desire is to examine the correspondences and limits between the Trinity and the church, seeing the former as a foundation for the latter.[5] For Volf, the key to understanding this link is not to focus on the numerical, but the relational. He argues that the *one* universal church and its *many* local churches and individuals can never correspond to the *one* divine nature and the *many* divine persons of the Trinity. The relationship between the numerical *oneness* of the universal church and the *many-ness* of her members is of a totally different kind than the relationship between the numerical *oneness* of the Godhead and *three-ness* of the divine persons of the Trinity. Humanity can never be many-in-one like God is Three-in-One numerically, but relationally this is possible. A more significant analogy lies in the relationships between the divine persons and those between the ecclesial many. Volf adds that the correspondence between Trinity and church is not purely the formal construct of relationship, but this relationship must have a material content in that "[t]he relations between the many in the church must reflect the mutual love of the divine persons." [6]

Thus the source of the Church's oneness of many-ness is the perichoretic love within the Trinity. Just as the Father, the Son, and the Holy Spirit are one in love for one another so also the many persons of the church must be one in love for one another. The mutual love within the Trinity is therefore the foundation for the oneness of many-ness in the church. And when this oneness is threatened, we need peacemaking.

Even so, the unity of the church is never an end to itself and the church is never called to fellowship just for the sake of fellowship. Our fellowship and unity must always be seen in light of the bigger purpose of God, situated in the redemptive historical context of creation, fall, redemption, and consummation.

We begin with God creating humanity to reflect His own being. Humankind was made in the divine image to reflect the Triune Godhead in various ways.[7] In one sense, humanity reflects the tri-unity of the Trinity. The Father is not the Son, the Son is not the Spirit, and the Spirit is not the Father, but all three are one in their mutual love. Humanity from within a social Trinitarian framework must include both particularity and *perichoresis* as its twin make-up, and to consider them so in a proper biblical tension. Concerning his view of the Trinity, J. Scott Horrel writes: "Rather than the either/or of the West's Boethian individuality *(persona est naturae rationalis individual substance)* or the somewhat Eastern and postmodern perspective that "person" is a mere knot of relationships with no substance or nature in itself, it seems that both ontological and relational perspectives must be held together when we think of the tripersonal God." [8]

Similarly, Volf writes: "To think consistently in Trinitarian terms means to escape this dichotomy between universalization and pluralization. If the triune God is *unum multiplex in se ipso* (John Scotus Erigena), if unity and multiplicity are equiprimal in him, then God is the ground for both unity and multiplicity .... Trinitarian thinking suggests that in a successful world drama, unity and multiplicity must enjoy a complementary relationship."[9]

We could thus say that humanity's oneness of many-ness originated from the Triune oneness of many-ness. As such, humanity's unity of diverse multiplicity is "very good" because we are made to reflect God. Our oneness of many-ness reflects God's oneness of many-ness.

Then the Fall happened. The effect of sin is extensive and total, leaving its path of destruction especially on the *imago dei*. Because of sin, the good and necessary diversity of humanity deteriorates into disputes, dissensions, and disagreements. The many became divided and are not united as one. The eye says to the hand, "I don't need you." This discord leads to alienation, strife, oppression, abuse, selfishness, and other relational problems at the personal, societal, and national levels. How do we alleviate the problem of disunity caused by the Fall? Is disunity overcome by reducing diversity, that is to say, by making the many think the same, believe the same, and do the same things, in effect, by making the whole body an eye or an ear?

Scripture does not condone making everyone the same, but offers reconciliation of the alienated many as the answer to estrangement. The solution is peacemaking. Salvation that God ushers in includes the redemption of humanity's oneness of many-ness; salvation involves the return of the true unity in diverse multiplicity. If sin disrupts the harmony of many-ness, then salvation through the Lord Jesus must at least include a return of this harmony.

This is where the oneness of many-ness in the church fits in. The church of Jesus Christ is both the beginning and an agent of this return to harmony. The trajectory of the church's oneness of many-ness must culminate in the redemption of humanity's oneness of many-ness. God has given His church the privilege and responsibilities in His plan of redemption. A task of the church is to proclaim the gospel, but the scope of the gospel is more than the spiritual task of soul-saving. Salvation must be holistic and comprehensive in the redemption of all things from the effects of sin. As such, the church is the first fruit community of the New Creation and an agent of redemption. The redemption through the Lord Jesus Christ must address all aspects of creation affected by the

Fall. Within this scope, we must conclude that reconciliation within the church cannot be an end to itself, but it is a trajectory that consummates in the reconciliation of humanity through the church as a community built for peacemaking.

THE CHURCH AS A COMMUNITY BUILT FOR PEACEMAKING

A relationship that focuses inward can easily turn away from a corporate mission to just feeling good together. The church functions better when it centers on a common goal rather than merely on being a community. Just as Jeremiah's exilic community was called to "seek the welfare of the city," churches have social responsibilities within our larger contexts. In this light, the church is a community built for peacemaking in our fallen world.

The church can appropriate this peacemaking mission in several ways. First, the church must learn to model reconciliation that advocates true unity of diverse multiplicity. For example, how do we move toward a unity of diverse theological multiplicity? Dogmatism tries to achieve oneness at the expense of many-ness. But in the end, dogmatism fosters discords and dissensions. Relativism, on the other hand, focuses on many-ness at the expense of oneness. But in the end, relativism leads to anarchy. 1 Corinthians 12 models for us a unity of diverse multiplicity. Such unity values the diverse parts and tries to understand other theological positions through the lens of discernment and charity—discernment because not all theological views are equally valid and must be tested and guided by Scripture, and charity because it is that which allows us to see the good and value others. Furthermore in the unity of diverse multiplicity, various theological parts must work together to build up one another toward one common goal. It is a unity that does not ignore our diverse multiplicity, but actively uses diversity toward the common goal *soli Deo Gloria*.

How the church addresses disunity within impacts her witness to the outside world. The founder of Peacemaker Ministries, Ken Sande, explains this impact saying:

> *"Conflict is inevitable in a fallen world; Christians and unbelievers alike struggle with disputes and broken relationships. So when unsaved people see Christians admitting their failures and forgiving and reconciling with one another even after intense disputes, they cannot help but take notice. The more our relationships reflect the amazing love and mercy*

of God, the more people would want to know about the power that is working in us to maintain peace and unity." [10]

The Lausanne paper on reconciliation reminds us that "in a deeply broken world, faithful Christian evangelism can only be envisioned and embodied in direct relationship with the vision and practice of biblical Christian peacemaking."[11] Yet the church is not only to be a model of peacemaking by working toward a unity within, we must also be agents of peacemaking to our society. The church cannot ignore the problem of strife in our world. For the work of reconciliation is an important part of seeking the welfare of the city. When we ignore and refuse to be agents of reconciliation, we are withholding love to a neighbor, and our lives are under the influence of a defective gospel.[12] Conversely, Christians are peacemakers when we forgive those who have wronged us, confront unjust situations, assist those in distress, turn the other cheek, help amidst hostilities, offer hospitality to all sides, continue seeking peace, suffer—or even die—rather than participate in destruction, host peace dialogues, stop violence, reduce persecution, cease hostilities, advocate restorative justice, heal the victims, work toward a state of tolerance and a more just societal structure and practice, etc.[13]

An understanding of oneness of many-ness in a proper redemptive historical context gives us a clearer picture of our role as the church. The unity in our churches is not itself the ultimate objective, but a trajectory that moves toward eschatological harmony. For Jesus Himself promises, "Blessed are the peacemakers, for they will be called the children of God."

THE CHURCH AS AN AGENT FOR DIVINE SHALOM-MAKING

God's Holistic Mission

Theologian Graham Cole writes, "Atonement brings shalom by defeating the enemies of peace, overcoming barriers both to reconciliation and to the restoration of creation. This is God the peacemaker's mission."[14] Yet peace is not just peace and biblical peacemaking is not just a ministry of relational reconciliation. A redemptive historical examination yields further insights to our understanding of peacemaking. Biblical shalom is richer than the notions of peace as a state of mind or peace as a relational state of being. For Nicholas Wolterstorff, shalom is the human being dwelling at peace in all his or her relationships. To live in it is to enjoy living before God, to enjoy living in one's surroundings, to enjoy living with other people, to enjoy life with oneself.[15] Biblical shalom is the wholeness that redemption brings to all areas of brokenness.

Shalom as God's peace envisions the wholeness, well-being and flourishing of all people and the rest of creation both individually and corporately in their interrelatedness with God and with each other. Shalom as God's peace encompasses all dimensions of human life, including the spiritual, physical, cognitive, emotional, social, societal, and economic. Shalom pursues mercy, truth, justice, and peacefulness through both personal conversion in Christ and social transformation.[16]

Thus God's mission is holistic and our mission is to participate in the divine shalom making and to be its living sign and an agent of hope and holistic reconciliation in our fallen world. God's mission is to create a just world that will express the divine shalom. The gospel is to provide hope for today and tomorrow, reconciliation between God and human, human and human, and human and creation. There are implications of the Gospel for our lives and our social responsibilities to the communities in which we live.

THE CHURCH INTEGRAL MISSION OF SHALOM-MAKING

A former Executive Director of the World Evangelical Alliance Theological Commission, Justin Thacker, traces the history from the 1974 Lausanne Covenant to Micah Network, outlining how evangelicals have grappled with the notion of integral mission that brings together social engagement and evangelism.[17] Micah Network was started in 2001 with an aim to promote evangelicals to do integral missions especially among the poor.[18] As such, Micah Network defines integral mission as, "the proclamation and demonstration of the gospel. It is not simply that evangelism and social involvement are to be done alongside each other. Rather, in integral mission our proclamation has social consequences as we call people to love and repentance in all areas of life. And our social involvement has evangelistic consequences as we bear witness to the transforming grace of Jesus Christ."[19]

The Micah Network Declaration states that the task of integral mission properly belongs to local churches. It elaborates, "The future of integral mission is in planting and enabling local churches to transform the communities of which they are part. Churches as caring and inclusive communities are at the heart of what it means to do integral mission."[20]

Vinoth Ramachandra clarifies and augments the Micah Network

statement. He points out that integral mission as defined in the declaration is often interpreted as "a strategy or methodology for our mission outreach." [21] However, Ramachandra suggests that integral mission has more to do with the church's integrity and less with the activities of the church. He explains:

> "Integral mission is then a way of calling the church to keep together, in her theology as well as in her practice, what the Triune God of the Biblical narrative always brings together: 'being' and 'doing,' the 'spiritual' and the 'physical,' the 'individual' and the 'social,' 'justice' and 'mercy,' 'witness' and 'unity,' 'preaching truth' and 'practising the truth,' and so on. The emphasis lies, then, not so much in the practical 'balancing' of our various activities, but rather in the firm refusal to draw unbiblical distinctions." [22]

That which Ramachandra proposes is simple but profound: Be God's people and do *everything* God's way. Doing integral mission, thus, is to stay true to who God has made us to be in every area of our lives and to do everything God's way.

The ministry of shalom-making is an integral mission that seeks to bring justice in all its aspects to this world. According to Gary Haugen, justice has to do with the exercise of power and God is a God of justice because He cares about the right exercise of power or authority in conformity with His standards. [23] God is just because He who has the supreme power and the ultimate authority uses His power and authority with mercy and compassion to care for those under His rule. Tim Keller gives a more comprehensive definition of biblical justice saying, "*Mishpat* . . . is giving people what they are due, whether punishment or protection or care." [24]

Nicholas Wolterstorff writes that,

> "An unjust society is one that lacks shalom. People in such a society exist on the margins, on the periphery, hanging on rather than being incorporated into the life and flourishing of the community. Such a society fails to mirror the wholeness of God. And when we as Christians recall that this God whose holiness we are called to reflect in our lives and societies is Himself a Trinitarian community, then it is obvious that the unjust society is an unholy society. It does not mirror God's communitarian wholeness." [25]

JUSTICE AS SHALOM-MAKING

The Church is called to demonstrate God's kingdom and extend its justice and righteousness into the world. The salvation that the church is called to proclaim transforms the whole person by the presence of shalom. The work of justice is an essential part of this shalom making. In this light, divine deliverance is a central theme of the biblical storyline, in which God is liberating His people from the bondage of sin. This storyline requires the concept of divine justice.

In Scripture, God is repeatedly characterized as just, as doing justice, and as loving justice.[26] Consequently, God wants His people to imitate Him and obey His command to do justice (Deut 16:20). Why is doing justice the response God wants? First, when we do justice, we are reflecting God as His image bearer (cf. Deut 10:18-19; 24:17-18). When we do justice we are reflecting who God is; the God who is just. We mirror God when we hear the cries of the oppressed and seek to alleviate them just as God has heard our cries and cared for our sufferings.[27] God loves justice because it is His character. He wants us to do justice to reflect who He is.

Second, we do justice as part of divine shalom-making. In expounding Micah 6, Wolterstorff writes:

> *"Micah represented God as calling for justice in response to God's saving acts . . . God saves for shalom, for life abundant. And there is no life abundant without the people's justice. The significance of the covenant is that God and the people have jointly pledged to travel together on the road to human flourishing—God's blessing, the people exhibiting wisdom, righteousness, justice, love, and mercy."*[28]

Justice is indispensable to shalom, because shalom cannot be secured in an unjust situation. As such, reconciliation and the pursuit of justice must go hand in hand. In shalom-making, reconciliation must be just and justice must be redemptive. There is no reconciliation if sin is not exposed, judged publicly, and condemned. However, how is justice redemptive?

Wolterstorff distinguishes between two kinds of justice. Retributive justice focuses on punishing the offenders. Civil criminal justice systems are based on retributive justice. Judgment is the negative notion of justice as giving what is due to wrongdoers. This includes the process of truth finding, the acknowledgement of violation, and the punishment that keeps the perpetrator accountable for the crime. Liberating justice, however, focuses on freeing the victims from injustice done to them.

This includes showing compassion, protecting, seeking restitution, and vindication on behalf of the victims. Wolterstorff points out that there are instances appropriate to retributive justice only, and at times liberating justice only. However, intrinsic to the storyline of redemption is God's liberating justice.[29] He explains the implication saying:

> *"Christian hope for liberating justice is not an optimism grounded in the potentials of creation but hope grounded in the promise that Christ will bring about His just and holy kingdom. That hope is to take the form, in part, of our participation in Christ's cause by ourselves working for liberating justice . . . . Christian hope for liberating justice takes the form of working to undo injustice in the confidence that, in ways mysterious to us, Christ will make use of what we have done, along with that which others have done, good and bad, for the coming of the rule of justice in His kingdom."*[30]

In addition, an appropriate quest for justice in the integral mission of shalom making must be restorative. Lausanne explains:

> *"In Jesus' death, God judged all sins, abuses, and atrocities. God's forgiveness in Christ "while we were yet sinners" guides our pursuit of justice toward healing. One mark of holistic reconciliation is a commitment to pursuing justice that is primarily restorative rather than retributive, keeping open the hope for future common life between enemies and alienated peoples."*[31]

Bishop Desmond Tutu defines restorative justice as "the healing of breaches, the redressing of imbalances, the restoration of broken relationships, a seeking to rehabilitate both the victims and the perpetrators, who should be given the opportunity to be reintegrated into the community he has injured by his offence."[32] Restorative justice executes justice for the sakes of reconciliation and shalom-making. It can accommodate for peace or a measure thereof in an imperfect justice system. New Testament Scholar Chrisopher D. Marshall makes a similar point when he writes:

> *"Attempts at reconciliation cannot be conditional on the prior achievement of perfect justice, else it will never happen. To use Volf's well-known metaphor, the will to embrace precedes the act of embrace, and while the act of embrace, if it is genuine, requires a commitment to equal justice,*

the choice to embrace is ultimately an expression of grace. Religious
traditions have a unique capacity to unlock the well springs of grace ...
so that peacemaking becomes an active partner in justice-building, not
just its eventual outcome."[33]

Restorative justice leaves room for humility, genuine repentance, forgiveness, reconciliation, and grace. It is a unique contribution of the church to help alleviate strife in our societies.

Justice that fits the divine mission of re-establishing shalom to the whole creation must be 1) liberating, in which the primary focus is on alleviating injustice done to the victims and only secondarily about retributive justice, and 2) restorative, in which the goal is the return of shalom.

Types of Injustice

As shalom-makers, we inevitably bump up against different forms of injustice in our society that heed our progress, including economic injustice and social injustice.

If justice is giving people what they are due, then economic justice is giving people what they are due economically. In the realm of economic injustice, the issue of poverty comes to the fore.[34] Wolterstorff makes an important assertion that the alleviation of involuntary poverty is not a case of charity as we commonly think, but that of justice.[35] He begins by linking the "natural human rights" of every human person to the intrinsic worth of being made in God's image.[36] He further explains that "...one's right to be treated a certain way by one's fellows is grounded in what respect for one's worth requires: if respect for my worth requires that I be treated in such-and-such a way by my fellows, then I have a right to such treatment."[37] Thus not giving another human person what they are due is therefore injustice.[38] If this is so, then the work to alleviate involuntary avoidable poverty does not just fall on the social welfare branch of the government or just on the mercy ministry arm of the church. Poverty is an economic injustice that is the responsibility of everyone in the society: governments, churches, businesses, and individuals. Every person has natural human rights to adequate housing, to means of sustenance, and to decent healthcare. Within these scopes, Wolterstroff makes a provocative statement saying:

"Since poverty is a violation of rights, the poor person is fully entitled to
stand up and demand what is hers by right. She does not have to beg

for it; she may demand it. That's what's implied in rights. Further, as Chrysostom emphasized, she is entitled to demand it not on the basis of her good behavior but on the basis of her personhood—this in turn grounding her imaging of God."[39]

Social injustice has much in common with and is related at many points to economic injustice. Their arguments go along the same trajectory: being made in the image of God gives inherent worth that leads to the rights to be treated as a human person. As such, not being given what is due is unjust and must be remedied. Social injustice resides in issues such as human rights, human trafficking, caste system, class warfare, human atrocities and war crimes, inequality, double-standard judicial system, religious liberty, protect the family and the sanctity of life, caring for and defending the "orphans, widows, aliens and the poor" of our days, just to name a few.[40]

Shalom-making is an extended process that requires resolve, fortitude, and patience. Shalom-making is a journey that starts with God who has taken the first step in Jesus Christ.

CONCLUSION

We began by rediscovering our identity and calling as peacemakers and explored a broader mission of shalom-making. Founded on the *missio dei* of redeeming the whole creation for shalom, the church is called to be an agent of reconciliation in a traditional peacemaking role and of justice in a more comprehensive integral mission sense.[41] God's redemptive mission has always been to recreate a just world that would best express His shalom. This gospel must be verbally proclaimed, but it must also include the battle against extreme poverty and the care for the orphans and widows of our days. The gospel must embrace proper advocacy and liberation of the oppressed. It must fight against all forms of injustice and corruption. In the end, the gospel is the chief impetus for doing justice as individuals and as churches.

Yet it should be noted that shalom-making is an extended process that requires resolve, fortitude, and patience. Shalom-making is a journey that starts with God who has taken the first step in Jesus Christ. He is spurring us on in the power of the Holy Spirit as we faithfully journey on with hope for the return of our Lord Jesus and the establishment of the New Heaven and the New Earth. Deborah Storie wisely reminds us of this journey saying:

> *"There are many paths to Shalom and many ways to travel them. God's Spirit gifts us with the ability to see the world as it is and to dream of the world made whole. Yet, we do not see perfectly, but through a glass darkly. Being committed to Integral Mission doesn't mean that we understand it all or can do it all. We are not experts who bring answers and solutions. We are disciples searching together to find and take the next step on the journey to Shalom. We are peace-makers, not the Prince of Peace."* [42]

Natee is a Teaching Elder in the Missouri Presbytery (PCA) and a missionary with Presbyterian Mission International (PMI). He served World Evangelical Alliance Theological Commission (WEA-TC) in a Study Unit on Contextualization. Natee was the academic dean of Bangkok Bible Seminary (2011-2015). Currently he is the senior pastor of Grace City Church—Bangkok. He is married to Bee.

---

1   Social Gospel was a movement led by a group of liberal Protestants in response to the social problems raised by industrialization, urbanization, and increasing immigration. It prioritized social reform over individual salvation. Believing that laissez-faire capitalism was un-Christian, social gospel advocates supported the labor movement and called for an interventionist welfare state. Their ultimate vision was a Christianized society in which cooperation, mutual respect, and compassion replaced greed, competition, and conflict among social and economic classes.

2   Lausanne Committee for World Evangelization gave some case studies of reconciliation stories around the world including Burundi, Bethlehem, Kosovo, Australia, etc. (Lausanne, *Reconciliation as The Mission of God: Faithful Christian Witness in a World of Destructive Conflicts and Divisions*, Lausanne Occasional Paper No. 51, http://www.lausanne.org/wp-content/uploads/2007/06/LOP51_IG22.pdf, 2005)

3   The others are Romans 12, Ephesians 4, and 1 Peter 4.

4   In Romans 12, Paul urges believers to use the gifts that God has uniquely bestowed upon us as a response to God's mercy. 1 Corinthians 12 tells us to use the gifts that

God has uniquely given us to serve the church. Ephesians 4 commands us to use our unique set of gifts to prepare others to serve God. Finally, 1 Peter 4 tells us to use our gifts so that in all things God alone may be glorified.

5   Miroslav Volf, *After Our Likeness: The Church in the Image of the Trinity*, Grand Rapids: Eerdmans, 1998, p. 191.

6   Volf, *After Our Likeness*, p. 195.

7   The discussions on the nature of this image have been extensive and there are various proposed views on the image. Perhaps the intensity of the debate concerning the image would be alleviated if we could accept that there is a complexity to the question of the imago dei. Perhaps it is safe to say that humanity has been created to reflect God in more than one way. For our purpose, we could view the image of God through a lens of social Trinitarianism without the need to abandon the other alternatives completely.

8   J. Scott Horrel, "Toward a Biblical Model of Social Trinity: Avoiding Equivocation of Nature and Order." *Journal of the Evangelical Theological Society 47* (2004), 403.

9   Volf, *After Our Likeness*, 193.

10 Ken Sande, *The Peacemaker: A Biblical Guide to Resolving Personal Conflict*, 3rd Edition, Grand Rapids: Baker, 2004, p. 290.

11 Lausanne, *Reconciliation*, p. 7.

12 Lausanne, *Reconciliation*, p. 13. Lausanne goes on to give possible reasons why churches ignore their role as agents of reconciliation, which include holding to dualistic theologies that detaches personal conversion from social involvement; syncretistic beliefs influenced by ethnocentrism, racialism, sexism or nationalism; a focus merely quantity as the measure of growth. (Lausanne, *Reconciliation*, p. 14)

13 Lausanne, *Reconciliation*, pp. 18-19.

14 Graham Cole, *God the Peacemaker: How atonement brings shalom?*, Downers Grove: IVP Academic, 2009, p. 229.

15 Nicholas Wolterstorff, "For Justice in Shalom," *Hearing the Call: Liturgy, Justice, Church and World*, Grand Rapids: Eerdmans, pp. 109-110.

16 Lausanne, *Reconciliation*, p. 15. For examples of the biblical understanding of shalom, see: Leviticus 26:4-6; Psalms 34:14; Isaiah 1:1617, 32, 11:6-9a, 16-17; Jeremiah 29:10-14; Ezekiel 34:25-31; Amos 5:14-15; Micah 4:2-4; Mark 4:37-29; Luke 4:1621; Ephesians 2:12-14; Revelation 7:9, 21:1-4. (*Reconciliation*, p. 15n4)

17 Justin Thacker, "A Holistic Gospel: Some Biblical, Historical and Ethical Considerations," (October 2008) http://www.eauk.org/theology/wea/upload/A-Holistic-Gospel.pdf, pp. 1-4.

18 Micah Network Declaration on Integral Mission, http://www.micahnetwork.org/sites/default/files/doc/page/mn_integral_mission_declaration_en.pdf.

19 Ibid.

20 Ibid, p. 2.

21 Vinoth Ramachandra, "What is Integral Mission?" in Micah Network Integral Mission Initiative, http://www.micahnetwork.org/sites/default/files/doc/library/whatisintegralmission_imi-the-001.pdf, p. 1.

22 Ibid., 1-2.

23 Gary Haugen, *Good News about Justice: A Witness of Courage in a Hurting World*, Downers Grove: IVP, 2009, p. 85.

24 Tim Keller, *Generous Justice: How God's Grace Makes Us Just*, New York: Penguin, 2010, p. 4. (Emphasis mine)

25 Nicholas Wolterstorff, "Liturgy, Justice and Holiness," Hearing the Call: Liturgy, Justice, Church and World, Grand Rapids: Eerdmans, 2011, p. 73.

26 Nicholas Wolterstorff, "Seeking Justice in Hope," *Hearing the Call: Liturgy, Justice, Church and World*, Grand Rapids: Eerdmans, 2011, p. 175. God loves justice (Isaiah 61:8; Psalm 37:28), God does justice (Psalm 103:6) and he does so because he loves the marginalized and victims of injustice (Psalm 146:7-9; Psalm 140:12; Psalm 68:5-6; Psalm 113:5-9). (Wolterstorff, "Why Care about Justice?," *Hearing the Call: Liturgy, Justice, Church and World*, Grand Rapids: Eerdmans, 2011, pp. 96-99)

27 Wolterstorff, "Why Care about Justice?," p. 101.

28 Nicholas Wolterstorff, "Justice as a Condition of Authentic Liturgy," *Hearing the Call: Liturgy, Justice, Church and World*, Grand Rapids: Eerdmans, 2011, p. 51.

29 Wolterstorff, "Seeking Justice in Hope," p. 176.

30 Wolterstorff, "Seeking Justice in Hope," pp. 184-185.

31 Lausanne, *Reconciliation*, p. 16.

32 Desmond Tutu, *No Future Without Forgiveness*, New York: Doubleday, 1999, p. 55.

33 Chrisopher D. Marshall, *For God's Sake! Religious Violence, Terrorism, and the Peace of Christ*, Trinity Newman Foundation, 2005, pp. 15-16.

34 There are various causes of poverty in general: oppression (double standard judicial system, excessive interest loads, unjust wages), natural disaster, personal moral failures, etc. Preventable involuntary poverty that Wolterstorff talks about has more to do with those caused by oppression.

35 Nicholas Wolterstorff, "Justice, Not Charity: Social Work through the Eyes of Faith," *Hearing the Call: Liturgy, Justice, Church and World*, Grand Rapids: Eerdmans, 2011.

36 Wolterstorff, "Justice, Not Charity: Social Work through the Eyes of Faith," pp. 402-404.

37 Wolterstorff, "Justice, Not Charity: Social Work through the Eyes of Faith," p. 403.

38 For this reason, Wolterstorff argues elsewhere that the problem of poverty has moral significance (Nicholas Wolterstorff, "The Moral Significance of Poverty," *Hearing the Call: Liturgy, Justice, Church and World*, Grand Rapids: Eerdmans, 2011, p. 296.)

39 Wolterstorff, "The Moral Significance of Poverty," p. 296.

40 Space does not permit the discussions of Marketplace Ministry and Business as Mission movement, but these ventures are considered parts of integral mission of shalom making. Cf. Lausanne Occasional Papers #40 (Marketplace Ministry: http://www.lausanne.org/wp-content/uploads/2007/06/LOP40_IG11.pdf) and #59 (Business and Mission: http://www.lausanne.org/wp-content/uploads/2007/06/LOP59_IG30.pdf).

41 We should note here that traditional role of peacemaking is not detach from its broader counterpart. Violent conflicts are costly in various ways. Concerning the human costs, Ramachandra writes, "In protracted conflicts, whole generations of children and youth are brutalized by the effects of war. Families and communities pass on the trauma of rape, looting and violent deaths to posterity. Natural habitats are devastated, food production and local markets are disrupted, leading to widespread malnutrition and undermining gains made in health and education .... Violent conflict gives rise to chain reactions that extend the suffering of ordinary people." (Vinoth Ramachandra, *Globalisation of Conflict: A Case Study*, Micah Network Global Consultation, Thailand 2006, http://www.micahnetwork.org/sites/default/files/doc/library/global_conflict.pdf, pp. 5-6) Therefore, in dealing with peacemaking, one must also be concerned about shalom making.

42 Deborah Storie, *Integral Mission and Violent Conflict: Journeying toward Shalom*, Micah Network Global Consultation, Thailand 2006, http://www.micahnetwork.org/sites/default/files/doc/library/integral_mission_and_conflict_-_journeying_toward_shalom.pdf, p. 16.

8

God's Covenant Commitment to Local and Global Interdependency

by William Yarbrough

The Bible describes the interdependency of God's people using various living images and metaphors. Accordingly, each unique member of the community of faith has been united to God and to a global family that is called "one new man" (Ephesians 2:15) and each of us comprising this multi-member new person are variously described as "fellow heirs, members of the same body, and partakers of the promise" (Ephesians 3:6). Rooted in the realities of the covenantal Israel, today's Israel of God is called a "spiritual house ... a holy priesthood" (1 Peter 2:5), a "chosen race, a royal priesthood, a holy nation, and a people of his own possession" (1 Peter 2:9). It is from this new humanity, priesthood, race, house, body, and nation that Christ promises, "I will build my church" (Matthew 16:18) and promises to do so with believers who share varying degrees of association on a local and global scale. From smaller groupings in homes (Romans 16:5), to larger and more numerous associations of Christians in a city (1 Corinthians 1:2 and 1 Thessalonians 1:1), and then to congregations connected regionally and internationally, God graciously weaves His people together (Acts 9:31).

As evident throughout the pages of Scripture, in God's economy no one was ever to be overlooked, excluded, or displaced as members of this global, multicultural, multinational, and interdependent movement. According to the Apostle Paul's inspired understanding of interdependency, "in one Spirit we were all baptized into one body—Jews or Greeks, slaves or free" (1 Corinthians 12:13), and God has uniquely arranged the members of His body, "each of them, as he chose" (1 Corinthians 12:18). Paul assures this diverse Christian community that each member, regardless of social or economic tags, is significant and contributive and that no member could ever say to another member of the community that "I have no need of you" (1 Corinthians 12:21).

As Paul has it, the collective need of the people of God is related not only to the administrative, teaching, preaching, and mercy gifts evident within a specific demographic or culture, but is a multicultural, multiethnic, and multi-socioeconomic dynamic made possible only through a deep and powerful work of the Holy Spirit. Of this dynamic reality David Prior, biblical commentator who has pastored churches in South Africa and Oxford, England, notes, "It is important not so to identify Christ with his church that we lose sight of his pre-eminence and transcendence. Nevertheless, Paul is clearly referring here to the way Christ today manifests himself by the Spirit to the world through his church."[1]

The collective need of the people of God is related not only to the administrative, teaching, preaching, and mercy gifts evident within a specific demographic or culture, but is a multicultural, multiethnic, and multi-socioeconomic dynamic made possible only through a deep and powerful work of the Holy Spirit.

With respect to working and walking together, especially across socioeconomic and geopolitical divides, and uniquely among the poorer members of Christ's church, Jayakumar Christian, associate director of World Vision India-North Zone, professor at the Asian Institute of Christian Communication, and adjunct professor at the School of World Mission, comments that:

> *"Jesus rebuilt community by challenging the very lines that divided people. He further made those lines a religious issue about which God was deeply concerned. While issue-based community organization techniques exploit numbers and mobilize people around issues, covenantal communities deal with issues without reducing the poor to mere numbers. Personhood is*

valued; diversity is celebrated and not exploited. Rebuilding relationships demands investing in relationships." [2]

He goes on to say with respect to the poorest members of the covenant community, "If poverty is about broken relationships—exclusion from society's mainstream and the fragmentation of community—then our transformational initiatives must result in rebuilding community. We must move beyond community organizing to something more radical and fundamental." [3] In the Apostle Paul's mind, our interdependency included and was and is dependent on each and every member of Christ's body being a participative member. Paul insisted that every member of the church is essential to its well-being and "the parts of the body that seem to be weaker are indispensable, on those parts of the body that we think less honorable we bestow the greater honor, and our unpresentable parts should be treated with greater modesty" (1 Corinthians 12:22-23). The interdependent weaving together of the body, socially, ethnically, and culturally is God's doing. Prior goes on to note that God has so composed the body " ... mixing different parts together with a specific purpose in mind, i.e. to produce mutual support and interdependence." [4] According to Paul, our need is for the input and perspective of colleagues and friends from other nations whether they are the poorest of the earth, literate or illiterate, a displaced immigrant or refugee community, or the international élite.

How then to become an interdependent people with the seemingly weaker, less honorable, and unpresentable parts of the global community has proved to be a challenge to the "World Christian Movement," with the practical sharing and distribution of resources, economic and otherwise. Such interdependence, on a global scale, is especially challenging in the areas of acute global disparity and/or health concerns such as HIV/AIDS which, according to Steven Fouch, are "inextricably linked to poverty." [5]

THE IMPORTANCE OF "PRAGMATIC SOLIDARITY"

Dr. Paul Farmer, Presley Professor of Medical Anthropology at Harvard Medical School, founding director of Partners in Health, and chief of the Division of Social Medicine and Health Inequalities at Boston's Brigham and Women's Hospital, discusses interdependency in terms of "pragmatic solidarity" with the world's neediest: "Pragmatic solidarity is different from but nourished by solidarity per se, the desire to make common cause with those in need. Solidarity is a precious thing: people enduring great hardship often remark that they are grateful for the prayers and good wishes of fellow human beings. But when sentiment is accompanied by the goods and services that might diminish unjust hardship, surely it is enriched. To those in great need, solidarity without the pragmatic component can seem like so much abstract piety."[6]

From Scripture, the Apostle John speaks of the "pragmatic component" simply and succinctly: "But if anyone has the world's goods and sees his brother in need, yet closes his heart against him, how does God's love abide in him? Little children, let us not love in word or talk but in deed and in truth."[7] For the believing community, such freedom, focus, and generosity is rooted in the power of the gospel of grace: "By this we know love, that he laid down his life for us, and we ought to lay down our lives for the brothers."[8] At the end of the day, it is the power and freedom of the gospel that leads God's people to build relational bridges, by moving into each other's neighborhoods to share each other's lives and stories and so to begin to learn how to build those heartfelt, relational ties with the world's neediest. Christian writes, "Poverty by its very nature demands a spiritual response. We need to respond at a level that goes deeper than our traditional level of engagement. We need to expand our scope from addressing dignity issues to clarifying the very identity of the poor."[9]

From the pages of Scripture, we see that the interdependence discussed by Farmer—"pragmatic solidarity"—gripped the early church on a number of levels. Luke tells us that as a direct result of a deep work of conversion to Christ, those who "received [the] word and were baptized" not only dedicated themselves to the study of the apostles' teaching, to fellowship, to the breaking of bread, and to prayer, but "were selling their possessions and belongings and distributing the proceeds to all, as any had need" (Acts 2:41 and 2:45).[10] The palpable, practical interdependency of God's people worked itself out in the pervasive worship of God, the believing community having favor with all the people, and a daily increase of the number of disciples (Acts 2:46-47). This description of the common life of the early church continues to paint a compelling picture of local and regional interdependence for societies and churches growing increasingly materialistic and individualistic. Beyond the local dynamics of practical sharing, Scripture gives examples of trans-local economic interdependence during times of famine and distress that is described as a work of "the grace of God" (2 Corinthians 8:1). In 2 Corinthians, Paul writes of the churches of Macedonia, "in a severe test of affliction, their abundance of joy and their extreme poverty . . . overflowed in a wealth of generosity" for the neediest among God's people in distant Jerusalem (2 Corinthians 8:2). Christopher Wright, an ordained Anglican priest and international director of Langham Partnership International, in discussing this merciful sharing between geographically separated communities, notes: "It is very probable that Paul saw in the collection he organized among his Gentile churches to take to the poverty-stricken believers in Jerusalem . . . a token or symbol of the tribute of the nations as prophesied in the Old Testament. He invested a lot of energy, both theologically and logistically, in this act, which doubtless had straightforward charitable objectives as its primary motivation."[11]

It is the power and freedom of the gospel that leads God's people to build relational bridges, by moving into each other's neighborhoods to share each other's lives and stories and so to begin to learn how to build those heartfelt, relational ties with the world's neediest.

THE GENEROSITY OF GOD

Paul, in commending the generosity of the Macedonians to the believers in Corinth, affirms that generous sharing of resources on a global scale has its genesis not simply in humanitarian concerns, but in the generosity of God in Christ. The apostle writes, "For you know the grace of our Lord Jesus Christ, that though he was rich, yet for your sake he became poor, so that you by his poverty might become rich" (2 Corinthians 8:2).

Our contemporary understanding of global independency, as it was for the New Testament church, is founded on the guidance of God's loving instruction to His people expressed in Genesis through Deuteronomy. Those earlier texts bear testimony to the generosity of God and of His intentionality about the care of the poor, the oppressed, the needy, the widow, the orphan, and the alien. These documents give foundational guidance about how to care for the most vulnerable in the midst of our covenant community and how resources can and should be shared. These precious books demonstrate how God and His grace are the source of kindness, generosity, justice, and truth. Scottish theologian John Drane writes:

"When the Old Testament demands justice, mercy and truth in human relationships, it does not appeal to some abstract notion of morality. Instead, it goes back to the roots of the covenant faith, in the justice, mercy and truth of God himself .... And it is no surprise that one of the most eloquent statements of God's will—the Ten Commandments— begins not with a command, but with a statement: 'I am the Lord your God who brought you out of Egypt, where you were slaves.' Right behavior should stem naturally from the response of a grateful people to what God has done for them. Morality and theology are inextricably interwoven with each other—for it is within the context of a personal relationship between God and his people that the ethical principles of the Old Testament can most fully be understood." [12]

ADDRESSING DISPARITY

As contemporary, covenantal people, we listen as Exodus 16:18 instructs the community of faith about the just and equitable distribution of manna, thus assuring that the basic nutritional needs of the community of God's people were met (2 Corinthians 8:13-21). The Apostle Paul, citing the distribution of manna in the Exodus account, tells the Corinthian church, in relationship to his appeal for the distribution of resources to the Jerusalem church in times of famine, "I do not mean that you should be burdened, but that as a matter of fairness your abundance at the present time should supply their need, so that their abundance may supply your need, that there may be fairness. As it is written, 'Whoever gathered much had nothing left over, and whoever gathered little had no lack'" (2 Corinthians 8:13-15). The distribution of manna was, according to Paul, a guiding light on the path toward economic interdependence between members of the covenant community who found themselves in dire straits. Such guidance about the basic needs of food and sustenance should move us toward practical generosity locally and globally through our relational and organizational networks.

Throughout the Pentateuch, God speaks of practical, positive ways to address disparity among His people. Exodus 22:25 states that "if you lend money to any of my people with you who is poor, you shall not be like a moneylender to him and you shall not exact interest from him," addressing the possibility of interest-free loans and, on a local and global scale, could have practical application in the areas of micro-enterprise and financing opportunities. Exodus 23:12 guaranteed a day of rest for the slave and sojourner throughout the year, instructing contemporary business owners and organizational managers to make rest core to our life together with the most needy and marginalized. Leviticus 19:10 instructs the covenant community to assure that there is a continual provision for the community's neediest during the time of harvest: "And you shall not strip your vineyard bare, neither shall you gather the fallen grapes of your vineyard. You shall leave them for the poor and for the sojourner: I am the Lord your God." God instructs us to simply give away, no questions asked, a portion of the harvest. Leviticus 19:13 instructs those who hire workers to pay wages immediately ("the wages of a hired servant shall not remain with you all night"); laborers were never to be left unpaid. Deuteronomy 14, in discussing the tithe, addresses the requirement for the community of faith to meet basic alimentary needs for the most defenseless members of the covenant family: "At the end of every three years you shall bring out all the tithe of your produce in the same year and lay it up within your town. And the Levite, because he has no portion or inheritance with you, and the sojourner, the fatherless, and the widow, who are within your towns, shall come and eat and be filled, that the Lord your God may bless you in all the work of your hands that you do" (Deuteronomy 14:28-29).

Deuteronomy 15 instructs God's people how to deal with members of the community whose needs are such that they are unable to provide for the basic domestic requirements of their everyday lives. God addresses the release of credit debt and seeks to insure that, while there will "never cease to be poor in the land," among His people "there will be no poor" (Deuteronomy 15:2-3, 15:11, and 15:4). Centuries later, Jesus referenced these very words in Deuteronomy in a discussion in the house of Simon the leper. About that encounter John Stott comments that "when Jesus said, 'the poor you will always have with you' . . . he was not acquiescing in the permanence of poverty. He was echoing the Old Testament statement 'there will always be poor people in the land' (Deuteronomy 15:11). Yet this was not intended to excuse complacency but as an incentive to generosity . . . ."[13]

LOVINGLY RELIANT, COMPASSIONATELY INTERDEPENDENT

In practical terms, the first eleven verses of Deuteronomy 15 address the duty to lend to the poor but put "specific limits on the power of those who do so."[14] After discussing directives for forgivable loans, Moses discusses possibilities for helping former slaves by furnishing them "liberally out of your flock, out of your threshing floor, and out of your winepress" (Deuteronomy 15:14). Such a provision does not simply provide for the initial sustenance of the individual or family, but opens up the possibility of an initial resource for local business and the possibility that all peoples might flourish in the land.

As Gustavo Gutierrez, a Dominican priest, who spent many years of his life living and working among the poorest of Lima, Peru, and who is known as the founder of liberation theology, notes, "Poverty contradicts the very meaning of *the Mosaic Religion*. Moses led his people out of the slavery, exploitation, and alienation of Egypt so that they might inhabit a land where they could live with human dignity." [15] Gutierrez goes on to say, in a working paper prepared for Peruvian bishops, "The privilege of the poor . . . has its theological basis in God. The poor are 'blessed' not because of the mere fact that they are poor, but because the kingdom of God is expressed in the manifestation of his justice and love in their favor." [16] The heartbeat of God, from Genesis to Revelation, through the incarnational labor of love of our dear Lord Jesus and in and through His Spirit-filled community of faith, is that we "open wide [our] hand to [our] brother, to the needy and to the poor, in [our] land" (Deuteronomy 15:11). That is what is means to be lovingly reliant and compassionately interdependent, one with another.

William (Bill) Yarbrough served as a church planter/pastor in Alaska from 1972 until 1980 when he moved to Mexico to lead a multicultural church planting team until his return to the USA in 1996. Stateside, from 1996 until 2003, Bill served as both a church planter and pastor with an emphasis on mission and the immigrant and refugee population in St. Louis. From 2003 until the present Bill has been serving as the International Director for Sub-Saharan Africa and Latin America with Mission to the World.

---

1   David Prior, *The Message of 1 Corinthians*, eds., John R. W. Stott and J. A. Motyer, *The Bible Speaks Today* (Downers Grove, Illinois: InterVarsity Press, 1985), 210.

2   Bryant L. Myers, ed., *Working with the Poor: New Insights and Learnings from Development Practitioners* (Monrovia, California: World Vision, 1999), 8.

3   Myers, *Working with the Poor: New Insights and Learnings from Development Practitioners*, 7.

4   Prior, *The Message of 1 Corinthians*, 215.

5   Richard Tiplady, ed., *One World or Many? The Impact of Globalisation on Mission* (Pasadena, California: William Carey Library, 2003), 135.

6   Paul Farmer, P*athologies of Power: Health, Human Rights, and the New War on the Poor: With a New Preface by the Author* [2005 ed.], California Series in Public Anthropology 4 (Berkeley: University of California Press, 2005), 146.

7   1 John 3:17-18.

8   1 John 3:16.

9   Myers, *Working with the Poor: New Insights and Learnings from Development Practitioners*, 22.

10 Acts 2:45.

11 Christopher J. H. Wright, *Understanding the Bible Commentary Series: Deuteronomy* (Grand Rapids, Michigan: Baker Book House, 1996), 524.

12 John Drane, *Introducing the Old Testament* (Oxford: Lion Publishing, 1987), 286.

13 John Stott, *Issues Facing Christians Today*, 239.

14 Wright, *Understanding the Bible Commentary Series: Deuteronomy*, 289.

15 Gustavo Gutiérrez, *A Theology of Liberation: History, Politics, and Salvation* (Maryknoll, New York: Orbis Books, 1988), 167. Author's emphasis.

16 Robert Benne, Richard John Neuhaus, and Center on Religion & Society (New York, New York), *The Preferential Option for the Poor: Essays*, ed. Richard John Neuhaus, Encounter Series (Grand Rapids, Michigan: W.B. Eerdmans, 1988), 37.

9

Ministry to Women in India

by Colleen Bales, with Sue Harris

In 2012, an Indian female medical student, Jyoti Singh, was brutally and repeatedly raped and then murdered on a public bus while it circled India's capital city. This incident, as horrifying as the details were, wasn't as shocking as the reason for it: this rape and murder was characterized by many as men teaching a woman a lesson.[1] The public outcry from this attack brought India's view of women to the forefront of world news. There was a shocking exposé unearthing a dark secret: women are not just marginalized in India, they are often hated simply because they are women.

One of Jyoti's six rapists claimed that female victims of rape are more responsible than the men who attack them. "A girl is far more responsible for rape than a boy. Boy and girl are not equal. Housework and housekeeping is for girls, not roaming in discos and bars at night doing wrong things, wearing wrong clothes. About 20 percent of girls are good."[2]

In India, as throughout much of South Asia, a girl child is thought to be a burden or even a curse from birth on.

What is a believer in Christ, a child of God, to do with this incident? Beyond that, what are we intended to do with this pervasive attitude in India and other countries about women? How do we respond? And, even more personally, how can a female American missionary pour out the grace of the Lord Jesus in this context when it seems like a steep, never-ending, uphill battle? How can I minister with perseverance when such an overwhelming need for justice hovers over every moment of every day?

WIDESPREAD INJUSTICE FOR WOMEN IN INDIA

The more I look, the more I learn that Jyoti's story is not an isolated one. A 2012 poll of 370 gender specialists around the world voted India the worst place to be a woman out of all the G20 countries. "In India, women and girls continue to be sold as chattels, married off as young as 10, burned alive as a result of dowry-related disputes, and young girls exploited and abused as domestic slave labor," said Gulshun Rehman, health program development adviser at Save the Children UK, who was included in this poll.[3] In addition, 53 percent of adolescent girls (and 57 percent of adolescent boys) think it is justifiable for a man to beat his wife.[4]

In India, as throughout much of South Asia, a girl child is thought to be a burden or even a curse from birth on. In this male-dominated culture, men are considered a necessary asset to their family. The male will carry on the family line and name, stature, and standing in their community. A male child is necessary to perform many of the Hindu rituals and will be responsible to provide for his parents as they age. Men are thought to be stronger and more dominant in all areas of life while "bringing up a daughter is like watering a neighbor's plant."[5]

In contrast, when a girl child is born, parents must begin to put aside money for the dowry that will be necessary to obtain a match for her marriage. Otherwise, if unwed, she will be a lifelong financial burden and embarrassment. In the meantime, as the girl child grows up, she is under scrutiny by her family and entire community. She must remain spotless in the eyes of the community for the sake of the family's reputation. A girl child brings no benefit, only financial burden and liability. A preference for sons and fear of having to pay a dowry has resulted in 12 million girls being aborted over the past three decades, according to a 2011 study by UK medical journal The Lancet.[6] Even in the womb, girls are cast aside. It is not uncommon at the birth of a girl child, to receive the condolences of a neighbor: "I'm sorry. Maybe the next one will be a boy."

If and when girls do marry, they are frequently expected to move into the home of their husband's family. There, the mother-in-law rules and calls all of the shots for the new bride's life. If the husband's family believes that enough dowry was not received for the bride, her life becomes one of constant harassment by the groom's family, often sadly ending with a fatal "kitchen accident," freeing the groom to remarry. In India, more than 15,000 women are killed every year from a kitchen accident or dowry death.[7] In fact, in the southern state of Karnataka, a dentist was arrested after his wife accused him of forcing her to drink his urine because she refused to meet dowry demands.[8] Indeed, females in India are, in my mind, one of the "least of these" (Matthew 25:31-40).

A preference for sons and fear of having to pay a dowry has resulted in 12 million girls being aborted over the past three decades, according to a 2011 study by UK medical journal The Lancet.

Although laws in India may affirm women's rights, the societal norms often trump the law. In the wake of his daughter's death, Jyoti's father posed a question to his countrymen: "What is the meaning of 'a woman'? How is she looked upon by society today? And I wish that whatever darkness there is in this world should be dispelled by this light."[9]

As believers, we understand that Jesus is, and we have become, light in the darkness. We also know that the darkness has not overcome the light. Yet, what real kingdom impact can we make in the spiritual lives of women in India?

PROVIDING DIGNITY TO WOMEN THROUGH THE GOSPEL

So frequently in India a woman sees herself as a daughter, a wife, and a daughter-in-law—unloved, insecure, vulnerable, defenseless, unintelligent, fearful, and insignificant. Often these women have never heard of a God who protects them, a Heavenly Father who cares for them, or a Bridegroom who gives His very life for the one He loves (Psalm 84:11, Ruth 2:11-16, Ephesians 5:25-33). The God of the Bible who created man in His image, both male and female, is unknown and even when He is known, He is often misunderstood in this country (Genesis 1:27).

In this context, opportunities that provide dignity to women create a bridge for the gospel. Undoing this worldview is nothing short of a miracle. Some might question the purpose of establishing a business that teaches a skill to women. But I will testify to how the Lord has used such ministries for His glory through sharing the gospel with the marginalized women in India.

Often these women have never heard of a God who protects them, a Heavenly Father who cares for them, or a Bridegroom who gives His very life for the one He loves.

The ministry of Women's Livelihood Projects is designed to begin by opening up a relationship between a Christian woman who has a desire to share God's love and mercy to the defenseless, the harassed women of India. Started in 2010, the Women's Livelihood Projects began raising money for sewing machines, accessories and fabric in three different churches. Then, the project would provide basic training and individual sewing kits so that women could begin to offer sewing services on their own. The rural-living families of India struggle daily with providing the most basic needs for the family, so when an opportunity for skills training is made available to women in these poor communities, they are eager to learn anything that might help their home situations.

The skills training that we provide, through the gracious donations of supporters, teaches women basic stitching and sewing. In India, the cheapest way to purchase clothing for men, women, and children is to purchase fabric and pay a tailor to sew the items. Ready-made clothing is far more costly. So when a woman learns to sew for herself and her family, it is a financial benefit to her family. Not only does this give a woman a sense of pride and viability, but in most cases, it also brings admiration and appreciation from her husband, family, and community. In one of our national partner churches where we were able to place sewing machines and a trained sewing instructor (the pastor's wife), the pastor shared with me that when one of the woman students made her own saree blouse, her husband was so pleased and proud of her that he took that blouse around to his neighbors to show what she had done. The pastor also shared that that same husband normally treated her with disdain, which affected how the community had viewed her.

Skills training is good, but the key to this ministry is the environment in which the training takes place. Relationships in India take time to build, but they go very deep into the heart and life of the individuals. This is where the opportunity arises for the teacher to begin to speak to the women students about God's love for them and to disciple these women. In time, transformation takes place in the lives of the women, in their family relations, and in the communities. It is a wonderful chance to invite women and families into the churches out of which the ministry work is being held. It is a joy to introduce these women and their families to our good and gracious Heavenly Father.

OASIS: A CASE STUDY

For about six months, I attended a stitching class that was held in a poor community by an organization called "Oasis." I knew sewing, but wanted to learn more about the types of stitching done here in India. And I also wanted to learn from Oasis—what they've learned over the years of this type of ministry. Oasis not only provided stitching classes, but basic computer instruction, English lessons, a once-a-month medical clinic, and topical teaching for teenage girls and women who live in the community (topics such as basic as proper hygiene and the truths about STDs).

The majority of students at this stitching center were young women: some married, some singles. I only attended this class once a week while the community women attended almost every day. It was obvious to me that this became a safe place for these girls and women. Hema, the woman who managed this particular center, shared with me some of the women's stories—how each one came into class on one or many occasions burdened with pressures in their life. When Hema interacts with them, they easily and quickly pour out their stories and situations which allows Hema, who happens to be a strong believer, to begin to speak into their lives with the gospel.

I try hard to understand the cultural demands and expectations for young women in India to be given in marriage as soon as possible. There is unbelievable pressure for both the women and their families. For most Indian women, marriage is the last chance for human dignity. Women who are unmarried often have no place in this society, and marriage seems to be the only context for a woman to be valued. And as we've learned, even in this context, the marriage relationship doesn't typically provide the intended and hoped for love, care, and security. Jyoti's story was rare. She was living outside of normal Indian custom. She was 23 and unmarried. She was finishing medical school. And, according to at least one of her rapists, she was guilty and so were her parents.[10]

I remember one young woman in my class who was somewhat awkward, but also a little feisty. It didn't take long in conversation to realize she was at the age where marriage needed to happen or else shame would come to her family. Still, for her, it didn't look promising. For months I was traveling and when I returned to India, I found that the center had been closed due to lack of funds. It broke my heart, but so much of what I see in India breaks my heart. Maybe a year later I visited "Jacob's Well," a small company that grew out of the Oasis Stitching Center. Jacob's Well is a for-profit center that sews clothing and bags and other items for international clients. When I stepped in, I saw my friend. She had gotten a job stitching at Jacob's Well. This was life changing! I was so proud of her, and I knew that she now had this skill which gave her some dignity. It started with her responding to an invitation to a stitching center that opened up in her very poor community. And it changed the course of her life.

OVERCOMING OBSTACLES

Of course there are problems. Funding and leadership are the biggest challenges I see. This type of ministry requires a leader who is devoted to these women, someone who understands the pressures of their lives, someone who knows how to sew and wants to disciple and mentor with the gospel message. Sometimes you can find the leader, but they need funding, or funding is there without someone to lead.

Neetu is a young, smart, extremely talented and creative Indian woman and mother. Neetu connects amazingly well with women on the streets of India. She has some biblical knowledge, and may not be as orthodox as we'd like, but she has a passion to share Christ with women while teaching them skills they can use to keep them from begging on the streets. These women live in "beggar" communities, mostly made up of women with children, without husbands and fathers. Their only option to feed themselves and their children is begging. But Neetu pursues these women and talks to them, asks them about their situation, their lives. She offers them stitching lessons, and then she's invited into the beggar community where more women and children live. Today, Neetu is teaching stitching to women in two different beggar communities, and also leads home schooling classes for the women's children who are too poor to attend school. She has even organized medical teams to come in to serve these women and children. Neetu needs more funds to support the growth of this ministry.

Opportunities that provide dignity to women create a bridge for the gospel.

Sadly, I never approached Neetu about working with us because her husband is already affiliated with another mission agency. Consequently, I could not figure out how to partner more closely with Neetu. It is difficult to have a heart to minister and partner with others only to find out that, although we have the same Heavenly Father and worship the same King, we may not officially partner together. These ministry challenges exist everywhere on earth, including the mission field.

Currently we have funds available, but no leadership in place with the same gifts and talents that Neetu has. Funds have been raised that have allowed us to open three stitching centers within our partnership churches, but there is no one leader in place to oversee them. Each center is in a different region and language area of India, which is a big challenge.

I don't have all of the answers. Frankly, I don't even feel like I have some of the answers. But, I do know that my Heavenly Father does. He has a purpose for these women and a purpose for me. I also know He's given me a heart for these women. He has a heart to love them. He wants to care for, protect, and feed the least of these, and so do I.

Colleen Bales was born and raised in Southern California. Colleen and her husband, Cartee, received Christ in 1982. Colleen worked in business for 20 years while active in her local church missions and mercy ministries. She and her husband joined MTW in 2009 and moved to India where they lived almost seven years. In the process of learning about the culture of South Asia, Colleen was struck by the marginalization of women, and was led to begin a program for national women's training in theology and life-skills. Colleen and her husband have been married for 36 years and have two adult sons and two grandchildren.

Sue Harris served at Mission to the World from 2007-2016 aiding churches by equipping them to extend a passion for missions in their congregations and challenging the next generation in missions. She also filled a unique role at MTW of caring for single missionaries and leading short-term women's teaching teams to multiple countries including Mexico, India and Kenya. Sue currently serves as the Women's Ministries Director at Oak Mountain Presbyterian Church in Birmingham.

---

1   Ryan Barrell, "India Gang Rape Convict Blames Victim Jyoti Singh for Her Own Rape and Death," *Huffington Post UK*, (March 3, 2015).

2   Barrell, "India Gang Rape Convict Blames Victim Jyoti Singh for Her Own Rape and Death."

3   Helen Pidd, "Why is India so Bad for Women?" *The Guardian*, (July 23, 2012).

4   Kounteya Sinha, "57% of Boys, 53% of Girls Think Wife Beating Is Justified," *The Times of India, Indiatimes*, (April 25, 2012).

5   Gethin Chamberlain, "Where a Baby Girl Is a Mother's Awful Shame," *The Guardian*, (November 22, 2008).

6   Helen Pidd, "Why Is India so Bad for Women?"

7   Darrow Miller, *Nurturing the Nations: Reclaiming the Dignity of Women in Building Healthy Culture* (Downers Grove, Illinois: Biblica Books, InterVaristy Press, 2007), 31.

8   Pidd, "Why Is India so Bad for Women?"

9   Barrell, "Indian Gang Rape Convict Blames Victim Jyoti Singh for Her Own Rape and Death."

10 Colin Freeman, "Delhi Bus Rapist Blames His Victim in Prison Interview," *The Telegraph*, Telegraph Media Group Limited (March 1, 2015).

SECTION 2

Collaboration and Partnership

10

A West African Pastor's Perspective on Partnerships

by Mamadou Diop

Collaborative partnership, the relationship of partners, is the framework in which those engaged together can exchange information, as well as experience, in order to develop and accomplish their objectives.

This type of collaboration is without a doubt built on mutual objectives defined by common strategies. To even consider such a partnership structure, it is necessary to determine the overarching priorities for each step envisioned. The different discussions, meetings, and visits to the ministry field must contribute to reinforcing the relationships that allow each partner to clearly define their roles. The most successful partnerships bring together each partner's varying experience as they plan and accomplish various objectives. Out of this, shared values surface which allow the group to envision and initiate new ways of relating between the Global North and the Global South based on our mutual faith in Jesus Christ and in the pure Truth. This unity brings together our initiatives, organizing ourselves in networks and raising and pooling resources, knowhow, and expertise.

In such a partnership, each partner must keep his own identity. The fact that I keep my identity permits the other partner to view me in a positive sense so that we can better collaborate and communicate. It isn't necessary to change their surname and family name to a local one to be integrated into the local community. A name does not make us fit into our place, but it is the way in which we fulfill the responsibilities of our social role toward the group or community that will decide if we are accepted or rejected.

HOW MISSIONARIES ARE PERCEIVED BY LOCALS

If our contextualization stops at having a local name without adapting to the other aspects of culture, we will be moving forward on the wrong foot and will be considered by the local community to be duplicitous. This duplicity does not help other people really know who we are. They will see us, they will well know the local name we have given ourselves. But this attempt to adopt a surface identity creates problems where we could be seen to be lying, lack seriousness, or be hiding our real identity.

In reality, the local people often don't even know who the missionary really is. For some, you might be a spy from the United States, simply a long-term tourist, perhaps an opportunist who is trying to co-opt some local resources, or perhaps a photographer seeking interesting subjects that he might sell. Who are you? Depending on the identity you try to adopt, you may even seem to be a person who has no religious affiliation at all. Evidence that seems to support this includes your lack of a fixed separate physical location for worship and the fact that you are always in your own home with your wife, your children, your dog, and your car. Often you may be seen only out around the city of Dakar or perhaps out at one of the tourist beaches.

Love as it is presented in the Bible is an end and not a means to an end. It is because we love a people that we want their conversion and not because we want their conversion that we set ourselves to love them.

What sort of impression does this create in the local workers that you interact with? You are the boss and they are the poorly paid workers. In the eyes of the local community, your national partners are seen as traitors who have been bought by the white man. The local worker is also often abandoned by his family. And in his relationship with you he isn't connected with any level of life in community. Sadly, often this issue isn't even on the table to be discussed.

Your partnership functions such that the local is informed but not consulted. The local worker often feels left to himself to face the hardships of life without the benefit of real community. The result is the local partner often can barely even accomplish his ministry. Reinforcing this lack of community, the local worker sees the families of the missionaries themselves often living in isolation. This is contrary to local culture, but is also off the table for discussion.

A FLAWED FOUNDATION

The mission comes with its vison, plans, and objectives to accomplish its vision in a predetermined timeframe. The mission recruits one or several locals in order to accomplish this vision. Sadly the result is little fruit because the local workers are not competent for many reasons.

- Often the overall vision and supporting plans aren't communicated to the local workers.
- Local workers are not given adequate training to do the necessary work.
- The means of community life are completely absent.
- The means for doing ministry are not provided either.
- Real life in community as a working group—including missionaries and nationals—was not the basis for starting their program at the outset.

In this manner of partnering, the national is at times used as bait to catch others. Treating your national partner like the bait that one puts on the hook to catch a fish isn't a good way to reach shared objectives. In this way of partnership, we don't demonstrate any love for the bait or the fish. What we show is a desire to eat the fish and the necessity of finding bait. In a strategy where the national is only a means, the love and respect you owe him is absent. At this stage, the national is left in complete isolation, having no connection with his community of origin nor being integrated into missionary community and taken into account in their plans and strategies.

PROPOSITION FOR A NEW PARTNERSHIP

1. Restore true love

Often we use love simply as a strategy. And this strategy is simply a means to accomplish an end. If we don't accomplish our goals after some period of time we are tempted to change our strategy. That means if we love a people because we want to bring them to Christ, we risk hating this same people if they refuse to convert. Is this really love?

Love as it is presented in the Bible is an end and not a means to an end. It is because we love a people that we want their conversion and not because we want their conversion that we set ourselves to love them. The Great Commission does not replace the great commandment of love for God and neighbor. The Bible says that the greatest love is to give one's life (John 15:13). Have we truly laid down our lives for other people or simply laid down what we think might be important to them?

2. Invest in people

When the people of a neighborhood or village need some type of assistance, whether material or financial, who will they approach first for help? When they have a problem in their lives, their families, their neighborhood, who will they ask? When they need help with a local public service such as police, mayor, water company, or electric company, who do they turn to? If in the group of people you have gathered to plant churches, you have no people like this turning to you, know that you have had no influence on the community in which you are members. If this is the case, the ideas that you want to impart to the community will be accepted only with great difficulty. Only the marginal people—those with no influence who themselves are not listened to, who themselves are only surviving and not really living fully—will espouse the ideas you are trying to share. The result will be years of time invested but no changes.

If you want to work with a national partner, make him first of all a friend and not a servant. Jesus said, "No longer do I call you servants, for the servant does not know what his master is doing; but I have called you friends, for all that I have heard from my Father I have made known to you."(John 15:15) Make known to your friend everything—your vision, your plans, the goals you want to reach. Help your friend to benefit from all the training needed for your work together. Seek always that there is understanding, acceptance, and mutual devotion to your vision, plans, and goals. Invest in all aspects of his life so that his life changes radically. Make available to your friend all that is needed to allow him to work and to live out a good life in community. Make your friend someone the local community can't do without. Model the kind of power Jesus gave His disciples in Matthew 28:19, 20.

PCPC PARTNERSHIP: A CASE STUDY

Today as I write these lines, the Presbyterian Church of Senegal (EPS) is in a position of wonderful influence in several areas:

- Influence in its relationships with other groups: government authorities, traditional authorities, majority religious organizations, and other Christian denominations.
- Influence in the promotion of our own holistic strategy for evangelization and planting churches, which is reaching different people groups in Senegal and is expanding to other neighboring countries.
- Influence in the management of our own training plan to select, train, and examine new young church leaders. After their successful examination, they are established according to the call of God as elders in the churches. Cases of discipline are also dealt with according to the Word of God and exercised with both the complete rigor and love befitting.
- The last area of influence is for us to completely realize our plans in the area of self-financing. We can say that now the main plans are already underway in this area and we hope by the grace of God to fully realize our plans.

So how did we arrive at this stage?

We can certainly say that the partnership that we began with Park Cities Presbyterian Church of Dallas, Texas, through the work of Curt Dobbs and others, has played a big role. Through many of its leaders PCPC took the risk to follow a different track in innovating a different kind of missions partnership. Normally missions partnerships are "owned" by the Western organizations with Western norms and standards. Typically, this sort of partnership is between Western churches and the Western missionaries living overseas. In this type of partnership there isn't a place for relationship and communication directly with nationals. The relationship of the Western and non-Western church is almost completely absent. PCPC's innovation was to bypass the normal strategy of Western missions, which consists of sending their own missionaries and putting everything under them. I still remember a phrase Curt used during our first meeting in Senegal: "We are here to work with the nationals directly and to do this without the intermediary of foreign missionaries." I looked at my colleague Frank, a foreign missionary, who was translating and he was very much at ease with this new direction which he later called "even more right." During this meeting, I thought to myself, "I am seeing the world remade anew and missionary strategy is taking a new form!"

PUTTING LOVE IN ITS TRUE PLACE

Since that first meeting, PCPC has not reversed course. The first step was to work with the EPS to begin to restore the true form of love. They did not make love a strategy for working with us, but an end in itself. They loved us as we were and tried to do with us what no other Western church had tried to do. They gave us responsibility without constraint and they did not miss any effort to help us accomplish our own vision. Their collaboration restored to us a sentiment of dignity. This is because their collaboration was not just a desire to give us what they thought we needed, but a desire to give us themselves.

In a culture that places emphasis on relationships above all else the partnership with PCPC and EPS and the fruit that has come from it is a testimony that resembles more a city built on a hill than a collection of small individual lights which shine here and there.

PCPC invested in our people and did not use them as bait. The financial and training support PCPC gave us allowed us to become indispensable in the communities to which we belonged. They helped us attain the ability needed to fully live out the appropriate social roles in our communities so we became leaders of influence among the leaders of these communities.

This new position that we have in these communities has made the preaching of the gospel much less difficult, even communities where recently it had been impossible to preach the gospel. They made us their friends and not their servants. They gave us access to all sorts of training that has equipped us for the work God has called us to. In a word, they invested in all aspects of our lives to the young, children, families, couples, etc., such that we are radically different. Above all, they have helped the EPS and its leaders to be an entity that our communities cannot do without. In a culture that places emphasis on relationships above all else, the partnership with PCPC and EPS and the fruit that has come from it is a testimony that resembles more a city built on a hill than a collection of small individual lights which shine here and there. In a world that is more and more a global village and in the face of the ethnic rivalries that tear the world apart, the church has to show the bonds of love in Christ, which unites ancient enemies to become forever friends and sisters in the Lord. Jesus said you will love one another and by this the world will know you are My disciples.

Mamadou grew up as a Muslim in West Africa. Around the age of 20 he came to faith in Jesus Christ as the result of seeking out answers to questions about his relationship with God. Today, Mamadou is a pastor in a West African Presbyterian denomination, the president of the denomination, the director of training and church planting, and recently was elected as the president of a new association of Presbyterian churches that includes churches in five countries. The national church in his country now has about forty churches and possesses a strong vision for planting sustainable churches and seeing the gospel holistically transform communities. He is married with five children and he and His wife lead an orphanage which is home to 40 girls.

ADDENDUM

African Culture: A Primer

From an African perspective, success is defined according to relationships, shame, and good done for the community. This is contrary to how a Westerner understands success. In the West, success is summarized by money, power, and standard achievement.

1. Investing in relationships. This aspect of success depends on an individual's ability to cultivate close relationships with family, in the African sense, and with the community to which the family belongs. In order to cultivate close relationships with people and to maintain them long-term, the necessary investment can be measured in terms of how much time, counsel, and support people have invested in or for the individual. The second important factor is our concept of generosity, that is, our ability to share with others the little that we have. It's in this sense that the community becomes the individual's bank. Whether the person can afford it or not, the little that he or she has is invested in the family and the community. And when the days of want come knocking at his or her door, in turn, the person looks to the family or the community. The members of this community are pleased to participate in resolving the problem of one of their members.

2. Shame brings dishonor, humiliation. This aspect of success means not becoming a source of shame for the family and the community. To be successful, a person is expected to do everything—in being, acts, and possessions—to not be the person through which shame comes upon the family or the community. In this sense, a person can spend a lot of money not on a business that will bring a return, but rather on roadblocks that will prevent shame from reaching the family or close friend.

3. Good done for the community. The individual exists solely because of his or her membership in a community, in a family. It is this membership which provides his or her identity, reason for being, and sure safety net in old age. Therefore rejection by the community means that the person loses all of that, and going on living becomes a terror. The person sees his or her life as devoid of value, and his or her birth as a waste; for the individual no longer has an identity and therefore no longer has a reason for being. At this point the person no longer sees purpose in living and starts walking down a path leading to suicide, the depreciation of his or her body, or a fierce fight against the community through criminal acts. For this reason, the identity and purpose which a person receives by way of membership in a community or family is priceless. That's why the individual will do everything in his or her power to secure membership in the community.

In Western thought, these principles, which are fundamental to the daily lives of Africans, are divided into three points. But in actuality, they go hand in hand and create a harmonious and fluid system in which the individual evolves. The harmonious overlap of these principles becomes a training ground in which the individual crafts his or her soul, thoughts, behavior, acts, and gestures, and especially his or her wisdom. This training gives the individual the ability to develop and maintain relationships; to avoid being a cause of shame, or the entry by which it reaches the family or community; and lastly, to be useful to the community which gave him or her everything.

11

Building Trust between National Partners and the Church

by Curt Dobbs

How does the local church go about building trust between its national partners and the church? Quick answer: personal relationship and long-term commitment. I hope this article helps the reader see the importance of personal relationship and commitment and how vital both are to the issue of trust.

First, some background. In 1997 the session (board of elders) of Park Cities Presbyterian Church (PCPC) approved a long-term vision for church planting in the Southwest U.S. and overseas. The 2020 Vision was to plant 100 churches by the year 2020. As of the end of 2015, more than 125 churches had been planted through U.S. and international partnerships. God has truly blessed PCPC by allowing us to be a part of this kingdom growth.

In this article I will focus on overseas church planting and give examples from PCPC's experience over the last 20 years. PCPC strongly believes in the importance of U.S. churches partnering with indigenous leaders to plant evangelical churches and therefore to follow the Great Commission given by Christ to His church.

We have found that building trust with national partners takes time and considerable effort. But, it is worth it! The two most important foundations are developing a true relationship and being willing to commit long-term. Both of these take planning and dedicated work on the part of the local church.

Planning for this work includes developing a strategy for church planting based on location, commitment to national leaders, accountability of all partners, involvement of a mission agency, identifying local church participants, and funding. Don't overlook planning. "Seat of the pants" approaches do not work in hard places. Your church's dedication to overseas church-planting partnerships can emerge from the planning process. Be sure to get key church leaders involved in developing the plan. Get them "over there" even for short visits, and they will begin to develop a feel for the people and needs. Ultimately, church leadership buy-in and approval (not "rubber stamped") is necessary.

Long-term commitment is just that—a commitment to plant churches with indigenous leadership, realizing that it will take years of hard work and years of funding. There will inevitably be major bumps along the way. It really can't be done in one year or one budget cycle. It will take years. We must understand and accept that years of effort and prayer must be planned for and anticipated.

Building trust with national partners takes time and considerable effort. But, it is worth it! The two most important foundations are developing a true relationship and being willing to commit long-term.

THE GREAT COMMISSION

Jesus commanded us in Matthew 28:18-20: "And Jesus came and said to them, 'All authority in heaven and on earth has been given to me. Go therefore and make disciples of all nations, baptizing them in the name of the Father and of the Son and of the Holy Spirit, teaching them to observe all that I have commanded you. And behold, I am with you always, to the end of the age.'"

PCPC set out to follow the Great Commission as His command, but we realized that we certainly did not have all the gifts, knowledge, and experience to pull it off. Our indigenous brothers on the ground have knowledge, language, and experience that we did not have. Mission agencies had experience and manpower to provide on-the-ground oversight and accountability. But, we had some gifts and experience that our brothers did not have. It seemed like we should work together, and we determined to do just that. It meant building trust and relationships and making sure that national leaders were full partners.

Here is how the PCPC World 50, the international part of the 2020 Vision, was inspired. This is a true story, but with some names changed.

A Mighty God: Initial Emphasis for the PCPC World 50

Communists came to power in Laos in 1975. By 1978, they had established an oppressive socialist society and had confiscated all the land in the country. Ninety percent of all Laotians were farmers—but now their land belonged to the state. Anyone who resisted was killed and anyone who was suspected of being traitorous was killed. Thousands were murdered, and consequently many Laotians tried to flee the country. The best way to do that was to cross the Mekong River, a very wide, fast-moving, dangerous river, to Thailand. The Communist government dispatched gunboats to patrol the river with orders to shoot Laotians trying to cross it.

Boun was a young man living in Laos. He feared for his life and that of his new bride, Nang. He had a plan of escape, but it was dangerous. Nang's sister feared for her children's lives, as well, and she asked Nang to take her son and two daughters with her. Nang agreed.

Boun made a deal with a man to build a raft out of bamboo and leave it hidden at a designated spot on the Laos side of the Mekong River. At midnight Boun took his bride, her two-year old nephew, and her two nieces (four and six years old) to the designated spot. The bamboo raft was there. The frightened little band climbed aboard. As Boun paddled away from shore, he prayed "to the Mighty God whose name I do not know: 'Please keep us safe and get us to the other side of the river.'" A strange prayer indeed since Boun and Nang were Buddhists, along with most of the Lao population.

An hour or two later, still in the deep darkness of night, Boun had managed to paddle the raft to the middle of the river. They heard a motor boat approaching. It was a Lao gunboat. As the spotlight was shined on them, Boun immediately stood up and started shouting, "Shoot me, shoot me, spare my family!" Nang grabbed Boun by his clothes and jerked him down to the raft. The gunboat slowed, but no shots were fired! The gunboat went on down the river.

Finally, in the early morning, Boun had managed to paddle all the way across the Mekong to the Thailand side. They hoped they were safe! They climbed up the embankment to a dirt road, and a man approached them. Boun thought he was there to rob them and they were all afraid. But the man spoke kindly to them and asked them where they were headed. Boun said, "To the refugee camp. We have just crossed the Mekong River." The man asked, "Do you have any money?" Scared again, Boun shook his head "no." The man reached into his pocket and gave them what he had! Then he directed them to the camp.

At the refugee camp Boun and his little family were welcomed and housed in a tent, where they eventually stayed for two years. During that time, there was a young 18-year-old Christian Thai man, Sumran, who came every day and rode his bicycle up and down the rows and rows of tents. He would get off his bike and talk to the refugees. He also held large group meetings with the refugees. He spoke about a "Mighty God" who loves people and takes care of them and protects them. Boun blurted out, "I know this Mighty God! I met Him on the Mekong River! He saved me and my family!" Boun wanted to know more, and the young Thai evangelist was eager to share about God and Jesus Christ, His Son. Boun believed with all his heart and was soon baptized.

In 1981, Boun and Nang, with the three children they now claimed as their own, were granted refugee status by the United States and they were eventually flown to Dallas, Texas, for resettlement. The U.S. government supplied them with a small apartment, a chicken, and a pot. Upon arrival, the little family discovered that one of their neighbors was Laotian. O happy day! This man had previously traveled to a Presbyterian church in Dallas to ask for help. The church had assigned an elder to help the growing group of needy people, and church members gathered furniture, cooking utensils, clothes, and food for Boun and his family. Word spread and even more Laotian people were helped. Soon they wanted to know more about this Mighty God who is so loving and kind. Boun already knew Him. He had met Him on the Mekong River!

The church's elders made a commitment to have a relationship with Lao people in need of mercy and love. It was messy and not convenient, but it grew as more Lao families came to church and many became believers. Even though they did not speak English, it was decided that those who became Christians would be members of the church, just like the *farang* (a generic Thai word, also used in Laos, for specifying a white person or white foreigner).

This is how PCPC's Lao Presbyterian Fellowship (LPF) began in the late 1980's. It is now more than 30 years old. Hopefully, the story helps you see more personally what the gospel and relationships with real people can mean.

Boun became PCPC's Lao leader for many years. The Thai evangelist,

Sumran, who shared the gospel with Boun, became a pastor and eventually became PCPC's national project director in Thailand. He has taught PCPC much about partnerships and being brothers in Christ.

PCPC decided to get personal with Lao refugees through Word and deed ministry. It was an active decision and one that would feature personal one-on-one connection. It would be messy.

It took years to learn about Lao culture. It took time. It took prayer. It took personal effort. It took hurt feelings. There are heroes at PCPC who pioneered this effort with strong long-term commitments to Lao families. And, there were kingdom results! Seeds were planted in PCPC leaders that would take root a few years later as the church embarked on the 2020 Vision.

Relational partnership uniquely combines the strengths, gifts, and experiences necessary to do His work with strong results.

THE THAO PROJECT

Let's look more deeply at how relationship and long-term commitment are developed and also look at kingdom results.

Familiar verses from Ephesians 4:11, 12, 16 helped us focus. "And he gave the apostles, the prophets, the evangelists, the shepherds and teachers, to equip the saints for the work of ministry, for building up the body of Christ, from whom the whole body, joined and held together by every joint with which it is equipped, when each part is working properly, makes the body grow so that it builds itself up in love."

And from Romans 12:4-6a: "For as in one body we have many members, and the members do not all have the same function, so we, though many, are one body in Christ, and individually members one of another. Having gifts that differ according to the grace given to us, let us use them . . . "

We recognized we had to be unified to accomplish our part of extending His kingdom. We needed to bring all parts of His body together: PCPC was not enough. Our unity developed through our relationships and long-term commitments with leaders on the ground. PCPC has long felt that this type of relational partnership uniquely combines the strengths, gifts, and experiences necessary to do His work with strong results.

When PCPC first determined to plant churches internationally in 1998, we targeted Southeast Asia, particularly Laos and Thailand. Why there? It was because of our relationship, commitment and love for Lao refugees and their home country. Thailand became important since Communist Laos is quite difficult to use as a base. We chose Nong Khai in northeast Thailand as a base because it is immediately across the Mekong River from Vientiane, the capital of Laos. Nong Khai was also the location of the refugee camps in Boun's story. You see, we had a deep relationship with Lao and Thai people already. This relationship was built over many years and had become a part of PCPC's DNA. Relationship would become the foundation of most of our church-planting efforts all over the world.

We started looking for local partners in northeast Thailand and Laos, but we also had to develop a strategy for reaching a strongly Buddhist culture. How could we get people's attention? Why should they care? Over several visits we talked with many Thai and Lao believers and even government officials (very carefully). In both Laos and Thailand there was a huge need for medical attention. So, after more meetings with local folks and much prayer, we decided that the initial ministry would be a medical clinic. It would become a model for PCPC's World Missions' Word and deed ministries.

So, how about relationships? As already noted, the pastor who had shared the Gospel with Boun became our consultant and advisor. *Achan* (Thai word for pastor, leader, teacher) Sumran by then had a 350-member church in another city in northeast Thailand. We spent many days and visits traveling with him and his wife, meeting people in Laos and northeast Thailand. He came to the U.S. to see refugees from the Nong Khai camps in which he worked. He found that many had moved into various forms of Christian ministry. And he visited PCPC to meet with leadership, both pastoral and lay. At first Achan Sumran was our consultant, but eventually he joined us as our lead national partner for what we called the Thao Project (a combination of Thai and Lao). This was a huge move for a pastor with a national reputation and a large church, but one that was based on the relationship and commitment we developed over several years. We learned much from him that we could not have learned without his committed relationship with us and to God's purposes.

Soon, the medical clinic spawned a small church. PCPC continued to send finances, leadership and special teams to work with our brothers and sisters in Nong Khai, Thailand. The church was called Gennesaret and would become the cornerstone for the work which continues today.

This has been PCPC's most ambitious and complex project. God has blessed His children in Northeast Thailand and Laos in many ways, and we have learned much over the years. Here are some highlights of the ministry so far:

- Thousands of professions of faith.
- Four churches planted in Thailand, including the cornerstone church, Gennesaret, with 150-200 members. (Three of the four churches are daughter churches of Gennesaret.)
- Eight churches started in Laos in villages with no or few believers.
- A medical clinic serving thousands of patients (at one time seeing more than 600 patients/week).
- Thousands from Laos and Thailand hearing the gospel at the main church, at the medical clinic in Nong Khai, and through children's and school ministries.
- A Christian school, with all Lao staff, established in Vientiane, the capital city of Communist Laos.
- Many thousands hearing the gospel in both countries through an indigenous radio Ministry.
- Hundreds taught at seminars at Gennesaret Church, including pastors and potential leaders from Laos.
- Churches from Thailand and Laos, plus other countries (e.g., Singapore, Malaysia, Philippines) visiting Gennesaret to see and learn about the work.
- More than 200 from PCPC visiting through short-term trips and oversight visits—lay people, pastors, elders, deacons, doctors, and nurses.
- The Thao ministry consistently led by indigenous, national leaders.

What was the key to all this? Building trust in a purposeful and determinedly personal way based on long-lasting, true relationships. We had already developed a good relationship with Achan Sumran as our consultant. But after carefully and prayerfully partnering with him as the on-site national leader, we purposed to grow and deepen in connection and fellowship with him.

Over time, indigenous leaders came to trust PCPC. Yes, there has been significant funding from PCPC, but this has now been a 18-year *relationship* based on much more than funding. Admittedly, the partnership has been quite long and unique. But many of the components are evident in other relationships even with shorter duration, such as on-site visits, phone calls, prayer times, members working on site, preaching, teaching, helping with Word and deed ministry, and long-term commitment. All of these are components of PCPC's church-planting projects in varying ways.

CHOOSING TO COMMIT LONG-TERM

In the late 1990s, our session approved the World Missions Team making long-term commitments with PCPC's church-planting efforts. The terms were five years and sometimes up to 10 years. That commitment was based on a well-conceived and planned project, with accountability. An annual review was always built in, but the intent was only to end a project if something truly dire happened on the field or within PCPC. By God's grace, we have never had to end a project for such a reason. (One project ended when agreed upon planned preliminary goals could not be met.)

So, how did these long-term commitments build trust? To the indigenous leader, many of whom are accustomed to short-term and somewhat trendy commitments, confidence grew from PCPC's decision to partner long-term. The local leadership did not have to worry about losing its U.S. partner every 12 months. This meant there could be concentration on long-term goals. Churches cannot be planted by indigenous pastors in difficult countries in just 12 months. It often takes years. With this arrangement, national partners could trust PCPC to stick with it even in difficult times. And, there are always such times.

It also was a relief to mission agencies for the same reasons, as they did not have to look for new partners and funding every year. PCPC has heard many times from national partners and agencies that this long-term commitment was vital (and often unique) to ongoing and successful ministry. It does, indeed, build trust.

PCPC WORLD MISSIONS AND
WORLD 50 DISTINCTIVES

Over the years, PCPC has learned much ... sometimes painfully. Not every indigenous pastor has stayed with the project, but a large percentage have. Not every church plant has continued, but amazingly almost 95 percent of them have. That is God at work!

140

We tend to plan and strategize a lot. And, yes, we review and make changes. Flexibility is vital. We set goals based on prayerful vision and strategy. And we try to stick with our plans while still being flexible.

Several distinctives have emerged as we work in countries in Asia, Europe, South America, and Africa through prayer, on-the-field experience, and input from missionaries, mission agencies, national leaders, and PCPC leadership teams.

- Church planting has been our major world missions focus (and our eventual end goal of overseas ministry activities).
- We target hard, strategic places (e.g., unreached peoples, less than one percent evangelical, 10/40 window).
- We partner with indigenous pastors and leaders.
- Word and deed ministry (not "mercy" only) is a key component.
- Personal relationships (missionaries, national partners) are developed in key field and country locations.
- Continuity is planned for long-term partnerships and commitments.
- We build around field-driven efforts (not plans made in Dallas).
- We focus on theological education whenever possible.
- Short-term team impact increases by focusing on church-planting efforts and areas where PCPC home church missionaries minister.

WORD AND DEED MINISTRY

Here's another ministry story with some changed names. It illustrates the importance of Word and deed ministry in church-planting efforts.

In a rural village in Thailand, a lady named Kosum was very sick. She was Buddhist. Kosum had talked with monks and others and prayed to spirits. But she couldn't get well. After many months, she was getting sicker and sicker. She was at the point of giving up.

A friend in the village mentioned a medical clinic in a town almost two hours away. The neighbor said the people at the clinic seemed to really care about patients and treated them with love. She got someone to take her.

The clinic was in Nong Khai. It operated as a part of a church called Gennesaret. There, Kosum was greeted by a clerk at the clinic who kindly greeted her and asked what was bothering her. She saw people in the clinic who seemed to care about all of the 100+ other patients who were there. Then, a Thai Christian pastor (yes, Achan Sumran again) started talking with the patients. He explained who God is and talked about how the world began and even talked about sin and the problems in the world. Finally, he talked about someone called Jesus.

He even prayed for the patients. There was a video about Jesus also. The *Jesus Film* in Thai.

Kosum was moved, but she did not know why. The pastor said the patients could be healed if they became believers in Jesus. He was talking about being spiritually healed, but she wondered about her body. Could that be healed also?

Finally, Kosum saw the Thai doctor who caringly asked about her problems. The doctor said something about what might be wrong and prayed for her. The doctor also shared what she called "good news" about Jesus. It was the same message Kosum had heard from the pastor. The doctor gave her some medicine (at a small cost) and instructions and prayed for her again. Kosum wondered why the doctor cared. Why did everyone seem to care?

Before Kosum left, she saw the pastor again. He told her about God's love and asked if she knew of things she might have done wrong in her life. Kosum didn't want to admit it, but she knew that she had done some bad things, some very bad, and she had thought many bad thoughts. The pastor asked her if she would like to confess those sins and if she would like to be free of those sins. By this time, something was happening in Kosum's heart. Something she did not fully understand. She felt sad and guilty and confused and hopeless—all at once. But the pastor's words had a soothing effect on her. Kosum decided to pray to this "Mighty God," asking His forgiveness and accepting Jesus as her Lord. Kosum didn't fully understand this, but she felt strangely relieved. Like a heavy burden had been lifted. Then, Kosum felt something else. Her body did not hurt! She did not feel sick! Could it be that she was healed? All the way back to her village, Kosum wondered about what had happened and wondered if she would start feeling bad again. She didn't.

Back in the village, Kosum talked to her husband about what happened. He didn't fully understand, but she was excited and told him, "I know you are not sick, but you need to go to the clinic also!" He did and he became a believer too.

Six years later, that village has 40 to 50 believers and is meeting in its own church building. It is a daughter church of Gennesaret. All because of Word and deed ministry. All because of a loving God. All because Thai believers love Thai people who are "sick" and need to hear the gospel. So, what can be learned?

• PCPC sent short-term teams (lay and medical), funding, and prayer.

- PCPC and its national partners stayed with the plan and worked together more than 15 years in the clinic. A strong, long-term relationship developed through God's love.
- This relationship became apparent in the way the clinic was operated as some patients came from hundreds of kilometers away.
- Patients saw a love they had not seen before.
- The kingdom grew!

WRAPPING UP

The basics of the ministry is built on personal relationships and long-term commitment. But, other keys became important as we worked in many countries:

- The basic foundation became a "three-legged stool:" the local U.S. church (PCPC), indigenous partners, and a mission agency.
- Goals, objectives, and timetables must be in writing, with regular review and flexibility.
- Accountability must be established—clarity on who is responsible for what, and how it will be monitored.
- Funding amounts, conditions, and reductions must be made clear from the beginning, including the process of weaning off support (the latter must be clear and made known from the start and must be regularly reviewed).
- Reporting and communications must be established and maintained.
- The local church must regularly visit the field—not just short-term teams, but pastors and/or missions leaders.
- Short-term trips (unless not possible as in some countries), should be targeted to support the work and designed to meet on-the-ground efforts as the first objective.
- Follow-through on all commitments or written responsibilities.
- Be honest and admit mistakes.
- Be flexible.
- Organize prayer—local church, indigenous church, leaders, and agency.

Some things *not to do* also became apparent:

- Do not assume that you are the expert. You are not!
- Do not think that new churches must look like your church.
- Do not forget to recognize that it is the national partner who knows the people and culture.

- Do not make a partnership in which the national partner is not an equal partner.
- Do not neglect to follow through on all commitments.
- Do not forget to communicate regularly.

There is one more set of verses that has driven PCPC, from John 17:20-24: "I do not ask for these only, but also for those who will believe in me through their word, that they may all be one, just as you, Father, are in me, and I in you, that they also may be in us, so that the world may believe that you have sent me. The glory that you have given me I have given to them, that they may be one even as we are one, I in them and you in me, that they may become perfectly one, so that the world may know that you sent me and loved them even as you loved me. Father, I desire that they also, whom you have given me, may be with me where I am, to see my glory that you have given me because you loved me before the foundation of the world."

This unity, these partnerships and relationships, are a prime way people all over the world can know of God's love. When Buddhists, Hindus, Muslims, and other non-believers see Christians working together, it makes a difference.

Here we see the divine importance of unity, of being one in Christ. Why? Well, because God's Son prayed that for us. Why else? "... so that the world may know." Get that? This unity, these partnerships and relationships, are a prime way people all over the world can know of God's love. When Buddhists, Hindus, Muslims, and other non-believers see Christians working together, it makes a difference. They see indigenous people working with foreigners. They see white people and brown people working side by side. They may even see people from different kinds of churches working together. Typically, that is not what people experience in their own cultures. They take notice because it is different, and it is different in positive ways. It opens the door to sharing more about a Father who loves them and wants a relationship with them.

In my view, partnering with national leaders to plant churches, especially in difficult places, is the best approach. There are cultural differences as well as theological hurdles that are huge. This makes the development of solid relationships and long-term commitments a must. That requires the local church's time, money, and considerable effort. That means getting "up close and personal;" it means being vulnerable; it means caring on a personal basis; it means committing a lot of time; it means getting buy-in from church leadership; it means spending time on communications; and it means travel.

Hmm . . . sounds like work, doesn't it? You bet it is. But the kingdom results are worth it.

Curtis was Senior Director of Mission & Church Planting for 17 years at Park Cities Presbyterian Church (PCPC) Dallas, Texas and was active in missions since 1980. He has worked with indigenous leaders and missionaries in over 25 countries and directed 10 indigenous-centered church planting projects. At PCPC Curt had staff responsibility for PCPC's "2020 Vision," a plan to plant 100 churches in the U.S. and overseas. As of 2015, approximately 125 churches had been started overseas and the U.S. He retired in 2014.

12

Multi-Ethnic Teams

by Jonathan Eide

In our first years of church planting in Ukraine, we had many long meetings with our multi-ethnic team, dissecting and disagreeing about everything from potential leaders to the length of the worship service. We couldn't reach a consensus on issues from tithing (box in back or plate handed around?), Bible distribution (old or new translation?), or church outreach events (does it smell of bait and switch?). Our different backgrounds and perspectives pushed us in different directions, produced conflict, and necessitated compromise; and that was just among the multi-ethnic Americans. Our team and emerging church session of this fledgling church consisted of an Afrikaner, a Kazakstanian, a Minnesotan, a Pennsylvanian, a Texan, and later a number of Ukrainians with their own ethnic nuances. When we think hard about our ethnicity informing our work together in church planting, it quickly goes beyond us and them, and often the fine nuances are harder to work through than the big obvious differences, so unless a missions team all happens to share the same last name, all mission teams are multi-ethnic.

The longer one lives in any area, the more one sees the finer points of culture that inform the actions and reactions of the people who share that culture. Ukraine is now in the deep throes of searching for its ethnicity after part of the country was annexed and another is being fought over for this very question. It is the question that is now (sometimes forcibly) put in front of each person—what is your ethnicity? Who are you? This is a stark example, but every country has its own *shibboleths* which subtly and not so subtly divide the country into little parts. What you would see at a wedding or funeral differs drastically from Jackson to Los Angeles to Portland to Dayton. What's considered rude in the South is polite in New York, and what is polite in Kyrgszstan may be rude in Switzerland. Ethnicity is complicated.

When people from different places and different cultures form a team for the purpose of planting a church or being involved in a mission of the church, these big differences (language, leadership, and lifestyle) have to be overcome, as do the smaller ones (sensibilities, sports, and soul food). Both big and small cultural and ethnic differences are subservient to the commitment to the kingdom, but working that out gets tricky. It may be too easy to use the cliché "what unites us is stronger than what separates us." But in this case it's true, and in this short treatment we'll look into the biblical, historical, and practical elements of that unity.

A BIBLICAL EXAMPLE

Genesis 1, of course, lays the foundation of the dignity that is given us as image bearers of God. We understand that, despite the qualities of any given culture which annoy us most (including our own), we are all created in His image, and Psalm 8 tells us we have been crowned with glory and honor (while reminding us "what is man that you are mindful of him"), but we recognize that faint glory in each other, both those we work for and those we work with. Lewis reminds us to "remember that the dullest, most uninteresting person you can talk to may one day be a creature which, if you saw it now, you would be strongly tempted to worship . . . ." [1]

The one who has made us in His image as spiritual beings, Himself exists in a unity of three persons that points to our unity in His church. If He has made us in this unity as members of His church, this unity is certainly strong enough to plant His church together.

Cross-cultural missions is often defined as "incarnational missions," a missions that takes the form of the people we have set out to love, in the same way that Christ took human form. But this, too, is related to the image of God:

> *"We see an important relationship between the image of God and the incarnation ... it was only because man had been created in the image of God that the Second Person of the Trinity could assume human nature. That the Second Person, it would seem, could not have assumed a nature that had no resemblance whatsoever to God. In other words, the Incarnation confirms the doctrine of the image of God."* [2]

147

It was because of the Incarnation that we also seek to assume a foreign nature, and in this way show the love of Christ through us. All ethnicities and cultures reflect this image, and, in fact, embody this image. There is no monopoly on who, or what group, portrays or conveys this image to others.

Paul, in his church planting and his letters to the churches, reminds the churches of the unity in Christ they have in common. Ephesians 3:6 reminds us that Jews and Gentiles are "members of the same body."

These few words, *as it is now revealed*, throw additional light on the admission of the Gentiles to be the people of God. It is on the condition that they shall be placed on a level with the Jews, and form one body. That the novelty might give no offense, he states that this must be accomplished *by the gospel.*[3]

If Jew and Gentile, through the gospel, form one distinct body which is now the church, it should follow that the church, being this one body with different ethnic groups, should be able to send out people who would represent that diversity and form new bodies of Christ. We can and should be involved in planting and growing together.

Paul also thanks God often for the "partnership in the gospel" that is present in the churches, and, tellingly, the harshest words Paul has are not for those who are different ethnically or culturally, but those who have cut at the root of what unites in the first place. Take Paul's rebuke in Galatians 2. The division on ethnic lines "when they came he drew back and separated himself" is met with Paul's judgment: "Their conduct was not in step with the truth of the gospel." The truth of the gospel for Cephas in Antioch, as well as for me in Kyiv, unites me with my fellow whom God has called to His Church, and in those who join at my side to further His church.

AN HISTORICAL EXAMPLE

"It is unlikely that there would be any disagreement with the idea that the Jerusalem church in the first century was an indigenous church. The Jerusalem Christians were so strongly Jewish in their attitudes that they resented the conversion of Gentiles unless they joined the Jewish ritualistic performance of the law. That church, however, in its time of need received gifts from abroad ... Paul himself carried some of those gifts to Jerusalem."[4]

We would see, even from the early church in its apparent desire to care for and reach out to only its own, an organic interconnectedness that the Church is built on and for.

We look no further than the muti-ethnic teams that Paul formed in Acts for church planting:

4:36—*Joseph, a Levite from Cyprus, whom the apostles called Barnabas (which means "son of encouragement").*

16:1—*Paul came to Derbe and then to Lystra, where a disciple named Timothy lived, whose mother was Jewish and a believer, but whose father was a Greek.*

18:1-4—*After this, Paul left Athens and went to Corinth. There he met a Jew named Aquila, a native of Pontus, who had recently come from Italy with his wife Priscilla, because Claudius had ordered all Jews to leave Rome. Paul went to see them, and because he was a tentmaker as they were, he stayed and worked with them. Every Sabbath he reasoned in the synagogue, trying to persuade Jews and Greeks.*

Both in the team who was sent, and in the people sent to, we see the nuances of ethnicity and the promise of the gospel.

This desire for unity in the church and in church planting, while not always carried out well, at least has been a goal. The five solas of the Reformation all centered around the church—only in the body of Christ can one have Scripture, faith, grace, Christ, and the glory of God alone—and only in the church is our unity in these things larger than the cultures or languages that come together in it.

This invisible church represented and visible church presented is the church that the Nicene creed "one, holy, Catholic, apostolic people" describes. The history of missions after the Reformation, and especially in the last 100 years, has been a struggle to make that unity into a cohesive missiology that would, in its presentation and formation of new churches, show the unity that it is built around.

In Christian missions, be it the partnership between nations to reach a people, or the partnerships that exist between those sent and local believers, there have been many difficulties and co-opted efforts to work together because of the task to build His church.

MISSIONS PRAXIS IN KYIV

Here in our short history of missions in post-Soviet Ukraine, we have been engaged in just this idea of incarnational church planting. The "multi" in multi-ethnic has referred both to American Ukrainian as well as "intra-ethnic" Ukrainian and American relationships, which have been as hard, if not harder, to manage.

One such team I was privileged to work with brought together a Ukrainian church planter along with a team of Ukrainian "volunteers" as well as myself, an American church planter, and a team of American missionaries. We were all aligned, by God's grace, theologically and missiologically, but not culturally or ethnically. We agreed that it was our goal to plant a church, agreed on what kind of church that would be, but came at it from different angles and with different metrics. The hesitancy and difference we felt in strategy would have to be constantly mediated—meeting after meeting, prayer after prayer, study of Scripture after study of Scripture. The unity of the church we were setting out to plant had to be matched by the unity of the multi-ethnic team who was planting it. Many conflicts later, I can say that the ultimate goal remained in front of us and ethnic differences were, sometimes painfully, overcome.

As I think through the task before us, a few practical steps come to mind.

First, when coming from different perspectives or ethnicities, we remind ourselves of the God we worship, the Savior we receive, and the Spirit who empowers us. In that light, worship and prayer are essential. Worshipping and praying together as a norm are ways we can both remind ourselves of the goal and of the one who set that goal. When we are worshipping with our brothers and sisters, we are more likely to engage in the kind of kingdom unity we are trying to produce.

Second, the parameters for our cooperation must align in the end. I write as an American missionary of the Presbyterian Church, working in a different culture yet among those who agree theologically. There is a sense that if we cannot agree on the task that is set before us, we will not be able to have unity in what we do. I have been privileged to be involved in a denomination in Ukraine and in America, both of which have made the goal of our work clear—to plant healthy, Reformed churches. But without some form of alignment, a group can be cross-culturally adept and organizationally pointless. The former is healthy, the latter less so.

Third, the task before us exists both in the short term and in the long term. It can be exciting and fun to gather a group of diverse people for a task like this in the short term, but how the group handles the inevitable conflict and heartache that church planting brings in the long term is where the gospel is shown, and the team is unified under it. While it may be easier to set aside cultural and ethnic differences for a week or month or year, it's decidedly harder for decades when children go off to different educations, when the pull of the ethnicity comes for children and grandchildren, and when differences which seemed trivial grow significant. The power of the gospel is real, and it is possible by the power of the Holy Spirit in us to realize our goal as servants of His kingdom, no matter our stage or status or ethnicity.

Timothy C. Tennent wrote, "In contrast, we discover in the New Testament that suffering is one of the ways in which we embody the gospel and reflect Christ's work in the world . . . Jesus envisions persecution as one of the ways in which the Spirit of God proclaims the gospel, through His church, to the rulers of this present age." [5]

The relationship we are to have with each other should be a mirror of the relationship that exists in the Trinity. God as the sender toward this mission we seek to engage in, Christ as the incarnational model that we follow as we become less and He and others become more, and the Holy Spirit who convicts and empowers toward these ends.

The suffering that comes in any form of incarnational missions points us to Christ, and it is Christ's church that points us toward incarnational missions. We see a picture from Genesis through the New Testament of His church bridging ethnic lines, and we would expect to see that the way the church is established should bridge those lines as well.

Jon Eide with his wife Tracy have served in the Slavic world for fifteen years, twelve of them being in Ukraine in two different cities. They have been a part of four different church plants, all of which are now pastored by nationals and are independent churches. Jon currently serves as the Country Director for Mission To the World Ukraine, and helps with a current church plant in the Kyiv. He serves to develop Ukrainian pastors, and be involved in the evangelism and discipleship that God is using to establish and grow His church.

---

1   C.S. Lewis, *The Weight of Glory* (Grand Rapids: Eerdmans, 1949).

2   Anthony A. Hoekma, *Created in God's Image* (Grand Rapids: Eerdmans, 1986), 22.

3   Andrew T. Lincoln, *Ephesians: Word Biblical Commentary* (Nashville: Thomas Nelson, 1990), 42.

4   Ralph Winter and Steven Hawthorne ed., *Perspectives on the World Christian Movement* (Pasadena: William Carey Library: 1981), 494.

5   Timothy C. Tennent, *World Missions* (Grand Rapids: Kregel Publications) 97.

13

A New Way of Partnership: Directional Koinonia

by Tim M. (full name withheld for security reasons)

When my family and I arrived in China years ago, I never could have imagined the things that were in store for us. We were not strangers to the challenges of cross-cultural living and ministry. To begin with my wife is Chinese, born in Taiwan. I was born and raised in the U.S but had several years of living abroad in China as a single man. As a couple, we had assisted in two Chinese church plants in the United States and had years of ministry experience with Chinese students and visiting scholars at a major university campus in the Washington, D.C. area. Both of us were fluent in Mandarin and when we arrived we wanted to dive right into ministry.

On July 7, 2010, when our family of five landed at the airport, we were greeted by two local house church pastors and an Australian-born Chinese brother, all of whom became trusted and crucial ministry partners. The years of ministry that followed would teach me lessons about partnering with national leaders that I am certain I will never forget. In this piece, I want to focus on the two house church pastors who met us at the airport that day and what I have learned from collaborating with them since we began working together.

CHURCH PLANTING AS TREKKING

In 2012, I went to Nepal for leadership meetings with my sending agency and had the opportunity to do some trekking in the Himalayas with some of my fellow Asia Pacific missionaries. While my respect and admiration for mountain climbers grew as we spent several days trekking, there were some profound ministry lessons that I learned from that experience as well. I learned that sometimes progress is slow and acclimatization to altitude (metaphorically speaking) is difficult. Sometimes trekkers cannot continue and must turn back due to the challenges that are brought about by the trekking. There were so many parallels between that trekking experience and my experience of doing long-term ministry in China.

Inevitably, along the journey you run into those who are fit for the task, acclimatize well, and seem to be making good progress but you also run into those who are not prepared, are not handling the conditions well, and who are having a very rough go of it.

After that trip, I did a lot of research on mountain climbers and in particular those who climb Mount Everest. I found it helpful to draw certain parallels between cross-cultural ministry in China and the climbing of Mount Everest. I have never climbed Everest and do not plan on ever doing so, but I have done enough research to understand the difficulties and dangers of climbing Everest to know how similar it is to my experience of ministry with Chinese. I believe this to be true not only for ministry in my context in China, but for many other cultural contexts that missionaries face.

Both missionaries and mountain climbers go through much preparation before they embark on their long journey. After nearly 30 years of ministry experience with Chinese both in the U.S. and China, I have seen many people and organizations do well. I have also seen some horrible disasters. Inevitably, along the journey you run into those who are fit for the task, acclimatize well, and seem to be making good progress but you also run into those who are not prepared, are not handling the conditions well, and who are having a very rough go of it.

In addition, both missionaries and mountain climbers face tremendous risks. One out of every five climbers on Everest dies. In a similar vein, missionaries sacrifice a lot to go on the field and can face dangerous living conditions, not only for themselves, but for their families. At some point, the decision to turn someone back could save their life and the lives of others but that decision often comes with a lot of pain and difficulty.

Both the experienced and the inexperienced must face the challenges of being on the journey and in some cases both the experts and the novices are not able to finish the task. In some cases the inexperienced ones can drain precious resources from the more experienced ones and in the end there is a disastrous toll on both.

The journey is long and grueling and at many points the participants (missionaries and climbers alike) ask themselves if it is really worth it. "Is it worth it to put my family through this?" "Am I depriving my children of important opportunities?" "Is it worth it to give up all the comforts of home?" "Is it worth it to face the risks and dangers of living in a developing country?"

In the end, those of us who answer "yes" all know that we are working toward an eternal goal. Here is where the similarity between the mountaineer and the missionary ends. Unlike the fleeting glory of reaching the top of a mountain, which is the goal of the climber, the missionary works toward the eternal purpose of seeing God's kingdom expand. It is truly a high calling (pun intended) and the cost cannot be compared with the ultimate reward of seeing lost souls won for the kingdom.

There is one final similarity, however, between the missionary and the mountain climber. Trying to accomplish the goal without the cooperation of locals, whether it is reaching the top of the mountain or planting a church, is an unwise choice. In climbing Everest, every expert climber knows that the Sherpas, the indigenous people who live in the Everest region, know the lay of the land better than any non-native, can acclimatize faster, and can assist the climbers in ways the non-locals are incapable of doing.

This was one of the greatest lessons I have learned working alongside the two house church pastors who picked me up from the airport that day. They have been my Sherpas, my guides, my partners, and my friends. They have taught me many valuable lessons and I, in turn, have been able to help them in areas where my experience was needed. Working alongside them has not only made this journey more fruitful and enjoyable, it has provided me with critical ministry lessons that I hope I can pass along to others.

The results of our partnership with local leaders are evident. Two years after arriving on the field, we started a seminary that has grown from 40 students to more than 160 in just three years. Several years after arriving, we were able to start a local presbytery, which now includes more than 1,000 church members from over half a dozen churches and is still growing. From this network, we have seen other ministries such as campus ministry, ministry to the elderly, pro-life/adoption ministry, ministry to unwed, single mothers and many others, not to mention the countless individuals whose lives have been touched by one-on-one encounters with church members.

In addition, this church network has influenced churches in six other cities around China that want to use this model and we are actively coaching them in this process. Within the coming five years, we hope to see these six other cities fully developed and influencing their surrounding areas. This represents the lives of literally thousands of Christians.

Alongside God's sovereign hand in all of this, none of these things would have been possible without the Sherpas who guided and navigated the journey. The terrain where I live is too difficult spiritually and culturally for us as missionaries to have been able to pull any of this off on our own. The Sherpas have been essential.

SHARED MINISTRY: A HEALTHY PERSPECTIVE

The first two men to accomplish climbing Mount Everest were partners Edmund Hillary and Tenzin Norgay, a Sherpa. There were many elements outside of their control that made their climb successful. Many natural variable are all part of what can make or break a mountaineer's success in reaching the goal. All such variables were completely outside of the control of the climbers. Hillary and Norgay were successful in large part because these variables played out in their favor.

In a similar fashion, it needs to be understood that success or failure in ministry is ultimately not in our hands. We must to do the hard work of learning language, studying the culture, and sacrificing the comforts of home, but we also know that "unless the Lord builds the house we labor in vain." Every successful ministry owes more to those variables outside of human control and planning than it does to the ones we inevitably accredit to the "bright minds" of men. Often the truth is that ministry success meant they were fortunate to be at the right place at the right time.

For those of us now who are fortunate enough to see ministry growth in China, and in many other countries, we must remember it was the missionaries who served 100 years ago who paved the way for today's ministries successes. They themselves often saw little fruit in their own lifetime. While this is certainly a reminder to us to be humble, the ultimate thrust toward humility rests in the fact that every single variable that contributes to ministry success is ultimately not in our hands. God reserves the right to claim those ministry successes and our joy is in being a participant in that success.

We have been fortunate to experience a level of ministry success since we arrived in China in 2010 and have partnered with national leaders to promote church growth and theological education. This partnership between foreign missionaries and local leaders has been a sweet taste of kingdom fellowship as well as a thrilling experience of watching the Spirit work in powerful ways. Many lives have been changed as a result including our own, but in the end we all must humbly admit that the Lord has orchestrated it all.

PARTNERSHIP MUST BE CONTEXTUALIZED

It would be an enormous mistake for me to take what I have experienced and try to duplicate the same experience in another city in China or another country in some other part of the world. There have been so many variables at work that we had no control over. The timing of how I met the other local leaders, the economy, the political climate, the needs of the church at this time, the resources available, the church's particular stage of growth, and many other variables were factors that we did not control. All of these factors affected the outcome of our ministry efforts and all of them were orchestrated by God.

Both secular and Christian bookstores are littered with "how to" books written by people who experienced success and then wrote a book to explain to others how they too can experience the same success. Whether it's church planting, running a business, or some other form of ministry, the mistake is to try to focus on the experience and ignore the variables.

As I set out to write this, I am painfully aware that I am treading dangerously close to the same territory of focusing on the experience and ignoring the variables. My aim, however, is to bring out one particular element that I think cannot be absent from a fruitful cross-cultural ministry. That element is the partnership between the foreign missionary and the local church leader. The way I suggest going about this partnership is to understand the context you serve in and choose a partnership style that is fitting. Generally speaking, partnership styles range between a more hands-off, facilitative approach and one where the missionary needs to play a larger role in leading.

No matter which partnership style suits our context best, it is also crucial to carefully consider what that partnership will look like in great detail before launching into it. What I would like to focus on within this topic are three factors. First, I would like to propose it is essential to have a robust theology of contextualization. How one approaches the culture into which they have been called and how they present the gospel is crucial. Second, a healthy philosophy of partnership. In working with a multi-cultural team of both nationals and foreign missionaries, it is critical to avoid patronizing the local culture, and unintentionally promoting the missionary's culture as synonymous with gospel living. Finally, there is a profound need for wisdom in choosing national partners. Not everyone who is willing to work with you, the missionary, is a good fit and spending time getting to know your local leaders is absolutely essential.

My aim, however, is to bring out one particular element that I think cannot be absent from a fruitful cross-cultural ministry. That element is the partnership between the foreign missionary and the local church leader.

A THEOLOGY OF CONTEXTUALIZATION

When it comes to cross-cultural missions and church planting, we need the help of local leaders to help us navigate the cultural landscape. In gospel terms this equates to contextualization. More than twenty years ago, when I was a young teacher in China teaching at a university in the foreign language department I would frequently visit our foreign affairs office to take care of certain essential matters. I would practice my Chinese with the non-English speaking staff sometimes and one of the men who knew Russian but not English would often speak with me. He brought me back a Muslim skull cap from a business trip to Central Asia, the kind that are worn by many Muslim men. He handed me the hat as a gift one day. I wondered, "Why would he give me such a nice hat?"

Years later after I got married, I showed the hat to my wife, who, as I mentioned previously, is Chinese. After I put the hat on she said to me, "Never wear that outside while we are together." Why was she so adamant? Was it because the hat was a Muslim hat and we are Christians?

No. The hat was a green hat and in Chinese culture the one who "wears the green hat" is a husband whose wife is cheating on him.

Lesson number one in contextualization is that things are not often what they seem. Stepping into a cross-cultural context does not always mean we have left our native culture. It is essential that we spend time studying the culture we are called to serve. In the case of being a cross-cultural missionary, the Sherpa (local church leader) is going to help a great deal in navigating the missionary through the cultural landscape.

In discussing contextualization, it is crucial that the foundational ground work of presenting what things are transcultural (universal truths that apply to all cultures at all times) and which are subject to change be clearly stated. It can be simply stated by saying that these universal truths are the fundamental aspects of the gospel that Christians have agreed upon for centuries including the existence of God, the fallen nature of man and sin, God's image within mankind, and the need for redemption. There are many others, of course, but without a clear understanding of what these universal truths are, we run the risk of departing from the life-giving message that makes the gospel what it is.

In addition, there must be a robust theology of how we contextualize. There are multiple thorny issues currently being debated on the mission field. The current debate over the Insider Movement related to ministry toward Muslims is one such example. I have had a decent amount of interaction with those who do ministry to Muslim minority groups in China, and some of the issues being discussed are issues that touch upon what is universal and what is cultural. On the other hand, there are many big issues that fall under the broader heading of how to contextualize the gospel in the worldview and community of a Muslim. Some are suggesting ways that over-contextualize the gospel and some under-contextualize. How much is too much and how much is too little? The specific details are thorny and there is much disagreement in the missionary community on this issue.

To be sure, the discussion of universal truths and how to contextualize are intimately related. It would be wrong to draw too sharp a distinction between these two topics, but for the sake of discussion it is helpful to categorize.

The answers to difficult questions about contextualization require a proper amount of research. To approach this issue it helps immensely if we have a robust theology of contextualization to help us avoid the obstacles and pitfalls that have plagued previous generations when similar types of issues have been addressed.

To begin we must ask, why contextualize? To answer the question directly, we need only look at the Bible. The Bible gives us many clear examples of how its own message is contextualized. Perhaps the most explicit example, we can look at Paul's message to the Greek intellectuals in Acts 17. Paul is making the point that God is the sovereign Lord they are looking for in their searching for ultimate truth by putting it in a language and context that the Greek audience would understand. There were risks of communicating the message in a way that could be misunderstood by the local listeners but my point is simply that contextualization is a given. How we contextualize, however, is where we really must roll up our sleeves and get busy.

We must approach the culture by understanding the areas where the gospel both affirms and challenges the values held dear by the culture we are seeking to reach.

How do we do contextualization? This topic is much broader than we can cover in an article of this scope but I find it immensely helpful to draw from the work of Dr. Timothy Keller in his book *Center Church* where he addresses the issue of contextualization. Keller gives us a helpful paradigm of contextualization. His paradigm operates off the idea that there is no such thing as a Christian culture outside of the culture of any particular people group. In other words, Christianity always functions within a particular culture of a nation or people group; therefore, when we take the gospel into a culture we are not working off a blueprint marked "Christian culture." We must approach the culture by understanding the areas where the gospel both affirms and challenges the values held dear by the culture we are seeking to reach. "This is why it is so important to enter a culture before challenging it. Our criticism of the culture will have no power to persuade unless it is based on something that we can affirm in the beliefs and values of that culture. We can challenge some of the wrong things they believe from the foundation of those right things they believe. As we have said, each culture includes some rough areas of overlap between its own beliefs and Christian beliefs." [1]

PHILOSOPHY OF PARTNERSHIP

Partnership is not a term foreign to the Bible. Paul and Barnabas were partners in their missionary endeavors. Even cross-cultural partnership is not something strange to the pages of Scripture. Based on our understanding of Philippians 1:4-5 Christians share a common understanding that true partnership (κοινονια, Greek = communion or fellowship) among Christians is based on our partnership with God through Christ. Our union with Christ corporately and individually must be the key factor in informing our unity with one another.

Using this as our foundation, we see that "partnership" is something that is written into the DNA of our faith; therefore, we ought to naturally gravitate toward partnering with other believers. However, we see that even in the early church problems arose with partnering. Paul and Barnabas split up over a difference of opinions and 2,000 years of church history shows us much disunity. My point is simply this: partnership is not always something that happens easily and we should not be naïve about how Christians partner.

Partnership, therefore, is a given, but how *koinonia* practically works itself out is not simple. What does it look like for a Western mission agency to partner with a Chinese house church to send out a Chinese missionary to Thailand? How does a team in Cambodia function with second generation Korean-Americans, Filipinos, a second generation Chinese-American, and Caucasian Americans? Questions of communication in a common language, financial provision, cultural expectations, and many others are complicated. In addition, there are issues of theological and ministry style differences. One can get so burdened by the complexity of these issues to the point that we throw our hands in the air and give up. Is it possible to come up with practical, biblical principles and guidelines that would help us to better understand how to work toward that koinonia?

A NEW WAY OF PARTNERSHIP: DIRECTIONAL KOINONIA

I believe there is and therefore the purpose of my writing this is to point us toward that end in something I would like to call directional koinonia. The "directional" refers to a starting point and a goal. The starting point takes seriously the different identities that define much of who we are, but that often leads to separation and fracturing (denominations, theology, methods, and even culture and language, to name just a few) of koinonia. I call these identities "subordinate identities." The goal of biblical koinonia must be pursued with a biblical, spirit-filled wisdom, recognizing that we will never fully realize the consummate unity with one another in Christ until the new heavens and new earth, but always striving toward that goal. Koinonia refers to what we already possess as part of our identity in Christ, a common identity, a "primary identity."

The primary identity and subordinate identity are God-given blessings. Acts 17:26-28 makes it clear how we should view that subordinate identity as part of God's sovereign plan:

> *"From one man he made every nation of men, that they should inhabit the whole earth; and he determined the times set for them and the exact places where they should live. God did this so that men would seek him and perhaps reach out for him and find him, though he is not far from each one of us. 'For in him we live and move and have our being.' As some of your own poets have said, 'We are his offspring.'"*

In determining the time and location of both of our community (nation, culture, language) and our individual lives, God shapes our subordinate identity and calls us to seek Him. This biblical text is crucial for us understanding the role of our subordinate identity in directional koinonia. As Christians we cannot afford to think of either our primary or subordinate identities in fundamentally negative terms since God is the one who preordained them.

Since it is often in the realm of our secondary identity that we experience the greatest level of breakdown in Christian koinonia (e.g. racism, factionalism, sexism), it is crucial to address the subordinate identity with wisdom and spirit-filled guidance. What we are called to do is reflect upon what aspects of our subordinate identity unnecessarily prevent koinonia while not abandoning our own subordinate identity altogether. Abandoning our subordinate identity would be perilous and even unbiblical.

I have reflected on my experience in my calling to be a missionary. In my pursuit of understanding the context and culture to which I sought to minister, I made some crucial errors related to my subordinate identity. God called me to minister in China in 1986. I set about studying the language, learning the culture, and ministering among the Chinese in mainland China. In 1993, after seven years of ministry to the Chinese, two and a half of which were spent in China, I met a young Chinese woman from Taiwan who is now my wife. We shared the same passion for reaching China and over time we grew in our love for one another.

In 1996 we were married and the real adventure of cross-cultural understanding began. Of course we experienced conflict but I often felt a profound inability to understand the nature of that conflict. After two years of marriage, I realized something about myself that was causing a tremendous amount of tension and confusion in me. I had been expecting myself to essentially become Chinese in order to win my wife's love and approval. This unwittingly prevented us from understanding the true source of our marital conflict. When I felt the freedom to be who I was (a white American who grew up in the suburbs of Washington D.C., who loved God, loved China, and loved my wife) our marriage and communication began to experience a level of profound richness and understanding that we did not have before. As long as my understanding of her love for me was based on how 'Chinese' I could become, it prevented us from experiencing a true intimacy that comes when we accept one another's secondary identities. It prevented our koinonia. This example has implications for us as we seek to partner together. To share a common task is not enough. We must learn how to grow in our understanding of one another.

CHOOSING PARTNERS

Who should we partner with when we engage in the ministry of church planting? The brother in Christ who discipled me as a young Christian was a wise man. Early on in our discipleship relationship he gave me some sage advice. "Before you partner together with another Christian you should 'date' them." The idea was that it is often unwise to jump into partnerships, even with fellow Christians, before we get to know and understand them. Their personality, gifts, theological stance, situation in life, and many other factors will be relevant when we consider how to partner with another individual.

I realized the wisdom in this brother's advice after I had invited a member in our church to work with our ministry only to find out later he was not suitable for the responsibilities I gave him. I asked him to lead our weekly bible study with Chinese graduate students. After the first study, I realized I had made a big mistake. He often would focus the discussion on controversial political issues during the Bible study that were a distraction for the non-Christian Chinese students. We were trying to help them understand the gospel but this brother kept putting up obstacles. Despite my continued warnings, this brother could not resist the temptation to discuss these issues. The decision I made to place him in this position was too hasty. I "married" him to the ministry role before "dating."

Could I have koinonia with this brother? Absolutely yes. Should I ask him to lead a small group in our investigative Bible study? Probably not. At least not until I trained him for the role. Koinonia, therefore, must necessarily be understood in a broader sense than the specific area of whether or not I include this brother in leading our Bible study. Directionally, I could seek to understand and even look for new ways to partner with this brother but it must be based on understanding those elements of his subordinate identity (namely personality, gifting, theology, political views, and many others).

With respect to choosing national ministry partners, there are two potential groups. In many cases with Group A, the selection pool might be quite small or even non-existent. In those cases the problem you face is whether you should start with those you already have among the small Christian community or wait until God raises up new leaders that may hold greater long-term partnership potential. For Group B, there is a larger pool of potential local ministry partners to choose from in which case the missionary may find it more prudent to be more selective with whom he or she chooses to partner based on the principle stated above. I would like to focus my comments mostly on Group B, although some of the principles I address would also be applicable for Group A.

Three principles can help us choose national ministry partners. These are not the only things to consider but these are the things I have seen most often neglected among the missionary community I have interacted with over the past years. The three principles are:

1. *Balancing your primary and secondary identity*
2. *Finding a common vision*
3. *Considering the uniting potential of creeds and confessions*

1. Balancing your primary and secondary identity

As a young seminary student, I was invited by Chinese church leaders in the U.S. to join with them in planting a church. I was excited and eager to share what I had learned in seminary but it quickly became obvious that many of the Chinese who wanted to work with me did not like my theology. They assumed we were all on the same page because we are all Christians and I probably assumed they would like what I had to say. Those assumptions were based on a naïve view that differences such as theology and ministry philosophy are not important. While it is true that these should not separate us, time must be spent understanding each other's positions before working on some ministry endeavor. We must be realistic about those issues that can divide us and diligent about searching for ways we can cultivate real directional koinonia despite those issues.

The first principle means we do not underestimate secondary identity. To truly engage in koinonia we must merge an intensely realistic perspective with a faith-filled passion to see God do what man cannot, namely unite in directional koinonia. We cannot afford to ignore our subordinate identity as Baptists or Presbyterians or non-denominational any more than we can ignore our national. We must understand and live out the truth that those identities are subordinate to our primary identity in Christ. Our union with Christ is fundamental and must form the foundation of any true koinonia. Sometimes in our efforts to move toward greater koinonia, we downplay those differences only to find out later, when conflict arises, that those differences played an important role in the conflict that occurred.

2. Finding a common vision

The second principle has to do with finding common ground. Something that has been immensely helpful to our church-planting ministry in China has been the presence of a common ground through which people from different theological backgrounds (different secondary identities) can work together. This common ground rests between the two common areas of conflict—doctrinal beliefs and ministry methods. This is what Dr. Keller calls a "theological vision." He writes, "between one's doctrinal beliefs and ministry practices should be a well-conceived vision for how to bring the gospel to bear on the particular cultural setting and historical moment. This is something more practical than just doctrinal beliefs but much more theological than 'how-to steps' for carrying out a particular ministry." [2]

18 house church leaders gathered together in Manhattan, New York to start church-planting training in 2010. Most of the 18 did not follow through and there was no pressure for them to do so. Four of the 18 did

want to continue. Four years later that group had grown from four churches to more than 500. Some of these were new church plants but most were existing churches. Those four pastors that underwent the training were in China. They partnered with three North American Chinese church leaders and spent the following three years canvassing different cities in China, doing the basic training that constituted the theological vision. The focus was on one simple question, "What is the gospel and what are the implications of it in my life and the life of my church?" Churches, pastors, and lay leaders were hungry for the training and the community that came out of this group. There were Presbyterians, Baptists, and non-denominational churches that flocked to these trainings and the work continues to expand as of the writing of this article.

There are opportunities to partner with all kinds of people on the mission field but we must approach this with a sense of both godly conviction and Spirit-led discernment.

This common theological vision has helped us to foster a directional koinonia that has enabled churches from all over the country representing many varying theological stances and ministry philosophies to work together in real partnership for the sake of the gospel. It serves as a common final goal that all team participants agree to work toward.

But having a common vision must be coupled with an agreement among the team of how to reach that goal. There must be short-term goals, a mission statement of how to reach that final vision and what strategies the team plans to use to reach that vision. In their book *Leading Multicultural Teams*, Evelyn and Richard Hibbert give some valuable tools to help develop these aspects of the team. Chapter five highlights how a multicultural team should go about developing these areas.

There was a defining moment in our church-planting movement in China when we gathered 20 leaders together in December 2012 to hash out the mission, core values, and strategy of the movement. The churches represented had a common theological vision, but the mission statement, strategy, and core values were not clear. During the meeting the group split up into several groups representing churches from the four regions of China

165

(north, south, east and west). After the work groups convened, they were astonished to see that what they had written had nearly identical content. This was a defining moment for the group. Not only did it highlight the presence of the Holy Spirit working to unify these churches (they were all existing churches coming from differing theological stances), it also showed the strength of having a common theological vision as a starting point.

At the end of the following year, a board was elected and in mid-2014 an official statement of faith was adopted. Through this, we have seen and continue to see a growing church-planting movement that involves both expats and nationals in a self-sustaining, organically-grown community with a common vision.

3. Consider the uniting potential of creeds and confessions

The use of creeds and confessions can help cultivate this sense of directional koinonia. We recently formed a coalition of 10 seminaries in China to work together around our common theology and belief in the classic Reformed confessions. In our group we have Baptists and Presbyterians working side by side. Although we are only three years old, I have been surprised at how quickly the group gelled and then got down to business.

Creeds and confession can be historical or modern. Consider, however, the Apostle's Creed and how many Christians subscribe to this simple statement of the Christian faith. Some other examples would be the Cape Town Commitment, a document written by a working group led by Christopher Wright and the Lausanne Covenant, which was written under John Stott's leadership. Consider the positive elements of how a commonly agreed-upon creed can foster unity and partnership.

Avoiding the historical traps of creeds and confessions is important. These documents are fashioned to unite and divide. When they instruct to avoid certain errors we ought not to look at this as dividing, but rather preserving the orthodox faith of our forerunners in the faith.

SUMMARY

Whether you are serving in a field where locals are mature in their Christian faith or one where the work is just getting going, the need to partner is necessary. In some cases that partnership may only be a plan for the future, on others it is a living reality. No matter what the situation, it is my hope that we follow the wisdom and instruction of the Holy Spirit as we approach this indispensable aspect of ministry.

There are opportunities to partner with all kinds of people on the mission field, but we must approach this with a sense of both godly conviction and Spirit-led discernment. I trust that the principles outlined in this chapter will provide a needed bit of helpful counsel for the missionary, regardless of what his or her field looks like. May the Lord bless the work of His church and may His kingdom come and His will be done, on earth as it is in heaven.

Tim, and his wife, Huilan, a native of Taiwan, ministered with Asian graduate students in the U.S. for 15 years, and were part of a Chinese church plant in Florida. They now minister in East Asia in the areas of Church Planting and Church Maturity. They work with pastors and church leaders who are in need of theological and pastoral ministry training. In 2012 they helped start a seminary in East Asia and in 2013 were part of helping local pastors start a presbytery.

---

1   Timothy J. Keller, *Center Church: Doing Balanced, Gospel-Centered Ministry in Your City* (Zondervan: Kindle Edition, 2012), 124.

2   Keller, ibid., 17.

14

Breaking Bread while Building Bonds

by Neal W. (last name withheld for security reasons)

In March of 2011, a local family invited my family to join them for the spring equinox celebration in Central Asia. We had gotten to know this family through our handicraft project. In a country where most souvenir shops are filled with imported trinkets, our project had earned the reputation of helping local handicraft producers no matter what they made.

Life, for their family, unfolded as a difficult story. They had three children. Their only son, the eldest, was deaf and mute. Their two girls were shy but friendly. The house they lived in 30 kilometers outside of the capital was located in the center of the village but lacked even basic repair. Although the wife's handmade souvenir work was unique and expensive to buy in the city center, the family received very little on the large markup of their product. They were struggling to make ends meet.

What is it about bread that is so sacred?
Although viewed as a staple of life and substance,
it is more than that—a symbol of life itself.

So here we were, their family of five and my family of five, all sitting together preparing to break bread and to celebrate the coming of spring. How did an American family find their way halfway around the globe into the rural house of a Central Asian family? And why were we here? The simple reason was to break bread. In Central Asia, bread is central to life. They eat it with every meal, they kiss it, they do not throw it away, and they even swear by it. What is it about bread that is so sacred? Although viewed as a staple of life and substance, it is more than that. I believe they really understand it to be a symbol of life itself. In the local language, the word for bread also means food. To ask someone if they have eaten, one simply asks, "Have you had bread?" It is that central to life.

THE IMPORTANCE OF BREAKING BREAD

As our families sat around the table and chatted, our hosts explained the importance of breaking bread together. It is a ceremony of sorts that recognizes, seals, and celebrates friendship. Later, I would come to understand that it is unthinkable to betray someone with whom you have actually broken bread. If you show that you doubt your friend's words, they may remind you: "But we have broken bread." This is supposed to reassure you that it is impossible that their trust could be broken. I did not realize it at the time, but this would be one of many meals with this family. Over the course of several years, we would break bread together many times, each time giving testimony to our relationship.

Many times I have wondered how we Americans can actually build genuine relationships with people whose culture is so different from ours. The languages and cultures we encounter are very different from our own. There is certainly a novelty in such relationships and, in some instances, they also convey status and/or economic benefits. Over our family's 16 years of living and working in Central Asia, I have found a number of close friendships with a great deal of intimacy and trust. As I have reflected on my life, my techniques, and my values, there is one passage of Scripture which stands out to me and which, I believe, serves as a guide to building cross-cultural relationships.

LEARNING TO LOVE LIKE JESUS

The night our Savior was betrayed, denied, and deserted by His closest friends, He broke bread with them. Though the meal that He celebrated with His disciples happened very close to the spring equinox, it was not the same meal I celebrated with my Central Asian friends, although the intent and meaning may have a number of parallels.

In John 15:12-15, Jesus talks to His disciples the night before giving His life for them on the cross. He teaches them what He has done for them and what He would have them do. Several times in these last chapters of John we see Jesus modeling for His disciples and trying to help them understand the task that He has given to them. Even though they would desert Him, He knew they would not depart from Him forever but would return to be His instruments of the gospel of the kingdom to the ends of the earth.

The night He was betrayed, Jesus spoke these words to the 12 men He had invested in for three years of His life: "My command is this: Love each other as I have loved you. Greater love has no one than this: to lay down one's life for one's friends. You are my friends if you do what I command. I no longer call you servants, because a servant does not know his master's business. Instead, I have called you friends, for everything that I learned from my Father I have made known to you."

God the Father sent God the Son into the world to love. This is Christianity 101: God is love. We all know, "For God so loved the world that He gave His only begotten Son." But here Jesus explains that this love has now overflowed from the Father through Him to His disciples. In these three chapters from 13 to 15 of John, love is mentioned 29 times. It is a major theme of Jesus' last night with His disciples. We know that the entire law is summed up in loving God and loving our neighbor, so is it odd that Jesus would command His disciples to love?

The difference is that Jesus came and demonstrated the kind of love He requires. In verse 9 He explains that He loved His disciples as the Father loved Him. It is an all-encompassing love. The love of family. A love without conditions, beautiful and complete. This love that Jesus received from the Father He passed on to His disciples and now instructs them to pass on to others. This love had never been seen or experienced before.

This is one simple principle that has guided my interactions with those I minister to cross-culturally: love them as I have been loved. Rocket science? Nope. Yes, it is quite simple, but how often we forget the simplest things when engaged in the complex. It is also encouraging that it is to be a family love. It isn't really dependent upon anything other than the fact that we are related. That is the type of love Jesus bestowed on us, the love the Father had for the Son. Should we not also have that same love for our brothers and sisters in Christ? It is disheartening how often I hear cross-cultural workers struggling to love those with whom they work. The focus primarily falls upon the differences or the faults, but that is not what we are challenged with when Jesus commands us to love. He tells us to love others as family, despite how different we may be.

I am not sure what kind of family you grew up in, but my family was a mess. There was alcoholism, divorce, adultery, bitterness, selfishness, lack of forgiveness, and deception, just to name a few of the precious moments I enjoyed growing up. So is this the kind of family love that Jesus is talking about? It sure is. How? Our family was still family and despite all of these things, we still loved each other; no matter what happened and no matter how we hurt each other, we were still family. Oh, how poorly we love our brothers and sisters from different lands and languages! But this has to be a foundational principle for us as we cross the seas. We must be committed to loving others as Jesus has loved us.

But like most things Jesus asks of us or commands us to do, it is impossible without Him. Is that not what He teaches us in this very chapter? Our first challenge is to believe we are loved. John 15 repeats again and again the word "abide." This is simply the idea that we are to remain, stay, dwell in the love of Jesus through His word and commands. We often neglect this spiritual discipline, but it is only by abiding in His love that we will ever be able to love others. Perhaps when we struggle to love our national partners we are really struggling to understand how Jesus has loved us. Instead of trying harder to love better, maybe we should take time to grow in our understanding of how we are loved by Jesus.

LIFE-GIVING FRIENDSHIP

Jesus follows this by showing just how sacrificial this type of love is: it is a love which enables one to actually lay one's life down for a friend. This is the second value that guides me in my interactions with my brothers and sisters of a different tongue—be their friend. Once again, this is not rocket science, but coming from cultures where relationships are often utilitarian, we can have a misguided perspective when it comes to our national partners.

In the country where we presently work, it did not take long before we heard the effects of workers who had gone before us. At a church-wide celebration, cameras came out to snap group photos. Our language had progressed to a level that we could understand much of the muttering, and apparently, our national partners were used to the drill. Smile for the camera held by the foreign workers who would take pictures, send them abroad, raise money, and the national partners would never see a dime of it or even get a copy of the photo. All they really wanted was a picture. They were in it, and at the time, very few of them owned cameras. The practice had come to communicate that the cross-cultural worker needed to document what God was doing through them so that support would keep coming for them personally.

It is only by abiding in His love that we will ever be able to love others. Perhaps when we struggle to love our national partners we are really struggling to understand how Jesus has loved us. Instead of trying harder to love better, maybe we should take time to grow in our understanding of how we are loved by Jesus.

The relationship was not one of friendship or family; rather, it was one of economics. The unreached heathen provided a means for the cross-cultural worker to live "high on the hog" with the support of foreign dollars while the national partners really did all of the work.

In the passage in the gospel of John, Jesus explains that He is giving His life for His friends. The relationship Jesus describes is not employer/ worker or master/slave, it is not even father/child, but it is friend/ friend. This is a relationship of mutual respect. It is a life of giving, not taking. So much has been written on the dangers of paternalism, yet we still commit the same errors time and time again. These errors can only be avoided when we embrace our national partners as friends instead of projects. There are so many ways to skew this relationship, and the result will not be healthy. The only way I have found to engage with nationals in a way that really builds trust is to embrace one another as friends.

This certainly means different things in different contexts. For our family, it has often meant our entire family hanging out with other families. We have gone on holiday, spent the night watching the World Cup, and played Wii all afternoon with national partners. What is it that you do with friends? We pray together. We mourn together. We have fun together. A local proverb teaches, "If you want to know someone, travel with them." Do you travel with your national partners? As foreign workers, we can be quick to isolate our national partners because they don't know our language or customs. How can we break down these walls? Just as Jesus did.

MODELING CHRIST'S LOVE

We lay our lives down for our friends. Again, only as we understand how Jesus loved us can we love others. Only as we understand what it meant for Jesus to give up His life for us will we be able to give up our lives for others. Do you want to build trust and relationship with your national partners? It will take laying your life down, figuratively, if not literally.

Jesus modeled this for us by washing the disciples' feet. What a shock it was for them as the Master took on the role of a servant. In our Western culture, this is not so unusual for us. We often talk about "servant leadership." But as we cross cultures this plays out differently, and wisdom and relationship are needed as we find the best ways to lay our lives down. What friendship looks like is a very cultural thing, and we need to strive to be friends in the way our national partners understand friendship.

Another aspect of friendship Jesus showed His disciples involved transparency. Jesus said to His disciples, "I have called you friends, for everything that I learned from my Father I have made known to you."

TRANSPARENCY BUILDS TRUST

As if sacrificial love—laying one's life down for another—was not enough, Jesus now shows us that our love should be transparent. For some people transparency in relationship is easy and for others it is extremely difficult, but it lies at the heart of building trust in relationships. As before, Jesus modeled this transparency for us: He made known to His disciples His Father's plan just as He received it. Information is power. We live in an age of information. Most information is now quickly and easily available—all we need to do is Google it. That was not the case in the days of Jesus. But He explained everything the Father had given to Him. Is this how we relate to one another? Are we consistently transparent with our information and plans?

One foreign team in our local context had written their team strategy and plans before arriving on the field. It took about three years before they realized they did not really know the context, much less had they dialogued with any local believers before coming up with their strategy.

They revised their strategy, but once again, it was accomplished without much advice or input from local experts. This is not an uncommon story, and I have been guilty of it myself. We should make plans, but perhaps our first plan should be to engage the local believers and befriend them so they can help us know what we should do with the gifts God has given us. Perhaps we could develop plans together. Of course, Jesus did not run the Father's plans by the disciples and ask if they thought it was a good idea for Galilee or not. However, the principle remains that Jesus was transparent with His disciples as to what He was doing and who He was.

As if sacrificial love—laying one's life down for another—was not enough, Jesus now shows us that our love should be transparent. For some people transparency in relationship is easy and for others it is extremely difficult, but it lies at the heart of building trust in relationships.

Living in a context where you must be careful in how to communicate who you are and what you are doing, many workers are super secretive. I believe this has greatly contributed to mistrust between local believers and workers in our context. Most foreign workers do not even know each other's last names, what church they are from, what organization has sent them, or what they actually have been called to accomplish. If this is not known among the foreign workers, how much more unlikely it is to be known among the local believers! It is not infrequently that I hear a local believer say, "I don't even know why they are here or what they are doing."

This is very different from the greeting that Paul gives at the beginning of most of his letters, "Paul, an apostle of Christ Jesus by the will of God, To the saints who are in Ephesus, and are faithful in Christ Jesus." Paul knew who he was and with whom he was engaging, and he made known to them who he was. In longer passages, he openly shared much about his life, education, experience, and ministry. Do your national partners know you that well? Do they know who you are and why you have come to their country? This transparency in sharing information goes a long way toward building trust.

Love your national partners. Love them with a love that is found in families. Love them with the kind of sacrificial love found among friends. Love them with a transparent love. No, it is not earth-shattering new information. But it is impossible without the Holy Spirit's power to love others with the love that Jesus showed us. It is when we love like this that we build the foundation for genuine relationships of trust.

What does Jesus call us to, but to trust Him? Why would He love us this way? It is because He wants us to trust Him. He has proven Himself to be trustworthy through the way He has loved. In my experience, only as we love our national partners in this way will we really be able to experience genuine relationships of trust.

When we do not love this way, the result will be a relationship based on economics or work or projects and will not result in the type of multiplication Jesus instilled in His disciples. Love as Jesus has loved us, for that is how He was loved by the Father. This is reproducible love.

It is also a love that Jesus built around the table. John 13:2 sets the scene as "during supper." All of the four following chapters take place while Jesus broke bread with His disciples. He demonstrated to them how to build trust while around the table. The verses we reviewed in chapter 15 are in the midst of this whole dialogue and are lived out in the other chapters. Cultures vary around the world, but where I make my home among Central Asians, this type of trust is most easily built while breaking bread. Even as Jesus demonstrated the Father's love to the disciples and called them to love while breaking bread, may we too demonstrate Jesus' love to the world as we break bread with others. May breaking bread result in building bonds of trust.

Neal and Debbie, along with their three children, have served with MTW in Central Asia since 2000. Neal became the International Director for all of our teams serving among Muslim communities in July 2014. Their ministry endeavors have included ESOL, Theological Training, Business as Missions, and Evangelism.

15

I Can't. You Can't. God Can. We Can.

by Paul Taylor

Most of us face some pretty daunting tasks in our lives. Getting someone to love us enough to be willing to leave mom and dad and marry us. Saving up enough money to be able to buy a house. Raising kids. Establishing a church. Raising support to become a missionary. Reaching an unreached people group. Learning another language. You have your own list of difficult tasks that you have faced. Some people shrink away from these daunting challenges and simply say, "I can't." So they don't.

But we're missionaries. Each one of us is called to face and to overcome many challenging tasks. We are not expected to say, "I can't," or at least we are not expected to say, "I won't." So we start by saying, "I'll try."

However, as some particularly difficult task stares us in the face, we know that we can't—we really can't. We don't have the experience. We don't have the track record. We don't have the wisdom or the strength or the time or the.... Therefore we can't do it. In spite of our desire to be strong, in spite of other people's expectations, we know that this thing is too big for us.

WHEN "I CAN'T" BECOMES "WE CAN"

As my wife and I arrived in our field of service 23 years ago, we didn't know the language, we didn't know the culture, we didn't know anyone, we didn't have a team that arrived at the same time as we did. And we had the challenge given to us by our mission to develop a church-planting ministry in that country. We had never lived overseas before. And no one was going to follow us closely and tell us how to proceed each step along the way. We were expected to lead many to Christ. We knew that we couldn't do that, because theologically we knew that no evangelist, pastor, or missionary ever really leads people to Christ. That is always the work of God's Spirit. We were expected to build the church. And we knew also that we couldn't do that. If we can't lead one person to Christ, how could we hope to lead enough people to Christ so that a church could be developed. We couldn't. Again, we knew theologically that it is always Christ who builds His own church.

We cannot do ministry well without dependency. The same principle applies in doing ministry together. How great it is when I freely depend on others, reveling in who they are, and honoring them for what they bring into the ministry and our relationship.

But in time, the "I can't" began to go away. It went away as we found partners to teach us the language. It diminished as teammates began to arrive on the field. It began to go away as some key Filipino leaders agreed to be an advisory board for us over the first couple of years. Our "I can't" receded as Filipino pastors agreed to work with us to develop a number of churches. And it went away big time as the Spirit of God enabled some people to respond to the Good News as we shared it. People were coming to Christ, and we could begin to envision not only one church, but many. Then we knew, if not before, that "God Can," and therefore the team (with Him) could.

In time, we came to have a small team of a half a dozen American missionaries working with us. That was great. We helped one another. But the help that we gave one another paled by comparison with the great help that came from our national partners and from the Lord. Over the next four or five years, the number of those national partners steadily grew—10, then 20, then 40, then 60. Much of this article will center on our relationships with these people. But, true to the original sense of calling that God gave us, the ministry in that country soon turned into ministry to many other countries in that region of the world.

In every country the story was the same. As we contemplated entering a new country, the same old cry rose up in our hearts, "I can't." And sure enough we could not. There were just too many obstacles. Government opposition. Religious opposition. Enormous populations. Financial challenges. No personnel. Hundreds and literally thousands of languages. But the same old story repeated itself. National partners were found. And God's power was seen again. And slowly but surely in place after place, with the great help of national partners, and particularly with the strong presence of our God, the "I can't" became "We can."

That's when we learned to say to ourselves, "What a wonderful thing dependency is!" We know that we can't live well or do ministry well without it. We are totally, utterly, continually, and thankfully dependent.

THE BLESSINGS OF DEPENDENCY

We can't live well without dependency. Life is made rich by our interaction with others. Interaction with others is greatly enhanced as we live in humility with them, seeing their strengths, honoring them for those strengths, and bringing their strengths into our lives. And then we bring our own strengths to bear in helpful ways so others will benefit from our strengths. We need the other person. We are dependent on him or her to do certain things or help us in certain ways. But the flip side is equally true—the other person needs us just as much as we need them. They are dependent on us to bring good things into our relationship. That's why the well-known verse in Ecclesiastes is so true: "two are better than one, and a cord of three strands cannot be easily broken" (Ecclesiastes 4:10-12).

We cannot do ministry well without dependency. The same principle applies in doing ministry together. How great it is when I freely depend on others, reveling in who they are, and honoring them for what they bring into the ministry and our relationship. Suspicion, doubt, and distrust are not part of these ministry relationships. The ministry goes from strength to strength as we work together. One level of success breeds new thinking, new faith that the future will also bring new success. And all rejoice in how God is using us.

We need the other person—we are dependent on the other person. And we don't mind the other person needing us and depending on us for certain things. Our weaknesses are largely removed as others provide where we are weak, and their weaknesses disappear as we provide strengths in their areas of weakness. And the whole enterprise becomes strong as we are dependent on each other. Actually the right word might be interdependent.

This sort of healthy, interdependent relationship cannot occur where one person believes that he needs to be in control. It is very difficult to have this healthy dependency where one person sees himself as the dominant leader to whom others ought to always yield. When one person feels that he or she has all the answers or is smarter or stronger than the rest, the healthy, mutually-dependent ministry has a hard time developing. In fact, it is this sort of strong man leadership that creates unhealthy dependency that we hear so much about. As we set ourselves up as the strong man who carefully guards all things, seeking to keep others in line and keep others from "dependency," we can easily create the very thing that we're seeking to avoid. Leaders are not allowed to emerge. Team members are not given freedom to think for themselves. All must depend on the strong leader—or so he tells them. The partners in ministry realize that the strong leader doesn't fully trust them to lead, so they constantly yield to him to provide the needed strength in many ways—leadership, strategy, and even finances. They become dependent. The ministry stays weaker than it should. The ministry would be so much better, so much stronger if the strong leader would develop the leaders and trust them to lead.

A WELL-GUARDED HEART

Let's consider the characteristics that create the trust that enables a healthy, interdependent ministry to be developed. I love these words of wisdom from Proverbs 4:20-23:

> *My son, pay attention to what I say;*
>   *listen closely to my words.*
> *Do not let them out of your sight,*
>   *Keep them within your heart;*
> *For they are life to those who find them*
>   *And health to a man's whole body.*

What on earth is the writer going to tell us? We wait with bated breath for the next words. And here they are:

> *Above all else, guard your heart*
>   *For it is the wellspring of life.*

Guard your heart. Do that and you have health for your whole body, according to Proverbs. Do that and you have the wellspring of life flowing out from you to bless the lives of others. Do that and you bring something magnificent into the ministry team enabling others to depend on you. You bring a healthy heart. One that is full of the power and wisdom of God since you "live humbly with your God." You are one who cares more for others than for yourself. One who loves yourself since you are happy with what God has done with your heart. And therefore a heart that does not need others to constantly prop it up with their words of praise and adulation. It's a heart that can be devoted to others since your own needs are supplied from God's refreshing well of blessing.

When others see in you the integrity, the humility, the love, joy, peace, long-suffering, and all of the fruits of the Spirit, they know they can trust you. They can relax in their relationship with you. They can listen to you, and know that you will listen to them.

So the first characteristic that creates or enables healthy trust is a well-guarded heart. When others see in you the integrity, the humility, the love, joy, peace, long-suffering, and all of the fruits of the Spirit, they know they can trust you. They can relax in their relationship with you. They can listen to you, and know that you will listen to them. The well-guarded heart clears away so many of the issues that get in the way of good working relationships. And trust prevails on all sides.

Just this morning I was blessed as I received an email from a wonderful national partner in Asia. I have not visited this brother or worked with him in five years. He spent most of his email talking about the relationship that we have had together for 15 years now. He talked about many shared experiences as we saw the Lord build an amazing work using this brother and MTW working in a fruitful partnership. My wife asked me some time ago, "Who are the 10 or 15 people in the world whom you love most deeply, and whom you believe love you equally in return?" I stopped to create that list as much for my own curiosity as to answer her question. This brother was on that short list. How rich my life is because of this man and others like him! I would quickly entrust my life and all that I have to this man if I needed to do so. I trust him explicitly, and I believe he would do the same with me. And that is possible because I know that he guards his heart well.

HONOR AND RESPECT

A second characteristic that creates trust and enables strong, interdependent relationships to occur is honor or respect. When people believe that we honor or respect them, barriers go down. Openness and ease of conversation become the norm. People let their guard down and become transparent as they know that we will continue to honor and respect them regardless of what they say or do. There is no fear that the other party will take advantage of us. There is no concern that the other party will seek to become dominant over us. We trust each other as peers. We both know that we need each other. We know that the other party will give of themselves to help us. We don't fear that if we give to the other party, that the other party will become unduly dependent on us. There is no hesitation to talk about difficult things. This comfort flows out of the honor and respect that we each hold for one another. We are free to give (and withhold) wisely, and we are free to receive from the other because we trust the other to have a similar open spirit of giving and receiving. Neither of us is fearing that he will always have to give, or that he will always be considered the recipient. One may give more ideas, more money, more wisdom, more physical effort than the other. But no one is counting. We don't worry about those matters because we honor and respect the other as our peer. We know that we need the other person, and the other person needs and benefits from us. We are peers in the work. As we honor and respect in this way, we are freed to listen well to others and do as they suggest unless we see some significant reason not to do so. We don't have to win the day in every conversation about strategy or personnel. We don't have to impart our wisdom to them first and make them copies of ourselves before we will honor and trust them.

I read an interesting article this morning about the concepts of "apprenticeship" versus "facilitation." The writer was strongly advocating apprenticeship over facilitation. It was a thought-provoking piece. While there are many, many strong points in favor of apprenticeship, there is at least one rather glaring landmine. In an apprentice relationship, one party is the primary teacher/mentor while the other party is the primary learner. To suggest that most work relationships need to be modeled after the apprenticeship/learner relationship suggests that one or both of the parties do not see themselves as peers. The honor or respect for the other party is lacking. There is still the sense that until I share with you the great things that I know, you still need me to teach you. In this case, the writer admittedly had less than five years of field experience while some of the nationals he was desiring to place in an apprenticeship relationship had much more experience, and were doing quite successful ministry.

That same spirit sometimes is seen when a young man just out of seminary states that his calling is to go overseas "to train national pastors." It seems the assumption is that the young, inexperienced person has something that the national pastor doesn't have. While that may be true, it is almost always equally true that the national pastor has something that the young, inexperienced pastor does not. How much better it would be if the mentality was, "I feel called to go overseas to work alongside the national pastors to learn, and to help as I can." The latter shows honor and respect, whereas the former shows an arrogance that could and probably will militate against developing that healthy, truly interdependent relationship.

EFFECTIVE WORK

Let's think about a third characteristic that builds trust and enables strong, interdependent relationships to form. This one is about effective work—the product, if you will, of our working relationships. What happens? What ministry is developed? Mission work is very much about advancing the gospel around the world. It's about advancing the kingdom of Christ. Something is supposed to happen. Of course it is God who "makes things grow" (1 Corinthians 3:6). The Lord "has assigned to each his task" to work in partnership with Himself. It is then through that great interdependent partnership with God and others that things happen on the mission field. I can't. You can't (meaning our national partners). But God can—through us. Therefore "we can."

When that three-part team is working smoothly, then we often see the "wow" factor kick in. God does great things which are sometimes unbelievable. But He does those things through us and/or through our national partners. Therefore, as you and I bring our faith into the working relationship, good things happen. As our national partners bring their faith into the working relationship, good things happen. As we both put our whole-hearted energy into the work, God makes good things happen through that energy and commitment.

This all sounds familiar. We have read about it in Matthew 25 as

Jesus told the parable of the man who entrusted his property to his workers. To each was given some amount of money to manage—some more, some less. As the owner was far away, the workers invested his funds. The first two in an entrepreneurial way earned double. The third invested using the "hide it under the mattress" principle, which kept the initial holding intact but made no profit. The master on his return praises those who had accomplished the most and strongly rebuked the one who had only maintained the status quo. God expects us to work hard.

We, His servants, can and should bring into all our partner relationships a sanctified, ecclesiastical entrepreneurship that assumes good results will happen.

To create healthy, interdependent partnerships each party needs to bring his faith, his expertise, his education, and his gifts into the work. And those assets must create some "added value" to the ministry. The missionary must do that. And the national partner must do that. When each of us sees the other's value to the ministry, we are blessed and encouraged. And our faith is stimulated to trust the Lord to bring even more results in the next adventure of our partnership together. Yes, a healthy, interdependent partnership is greatly enhanced as the results of our work become clear. Otherwise why bother to enter into the relationship to begin with? We are on a mission. His mission. Missio Dei (the mission of God). Our Master expects us to show the return on investment when He returns. As we and our national partners see those results as God blesses our work together, our love for one another grows and we move on to higher ground in our next undertaking.

WORKING HEARTILY

There are other words or phrases that lead us to that same conclusion. There is much talk in the Scripture about stewardship. That is the same concept as discussed above. It is managing the ministry that the Lord has put in our hand so that the greatest good can be accomplished. And our national partner must do the same.

Another word is "heartily" or "with your whole heart" as found in Colossians 3:23: "Whatever you do, work at it with all your heart, as working for the Lord, not for men, since you know that you will receive an inheritance from the Lord as a reward."

The Lord honors the work of those who expect things to happen. We could call that faith. It is not faith in ourselves—it is faith in Him. It is knowing that He is one of our partners, and therefore strong things can and will happen because of His Power. We often sing:

> *Let your Kingdom come;*
> *let your will be done;*
> *on earth as it is in Heaven.*

We sing that knowing that Jesus Himself taught us to say or sing those words. And as we make that prayer through song or with our eyes closed in prayer, He answers. And sure enough wonderful things happen. Therefore, we His servants can and should bring into all our partner relationships a sanctified, ecclesiastical entrepreneurship that assumes good results will happen.

Let us end where we started and rejoice together in the reality in these words: "I Can't. You Can't. God Can. Therefore We Can."

Paul and his wife, Sarah, have spent 47 years in church planting ministry. For twenty-three of those years they lived and worked in the US and Canada. Paul served nine years as Director of Church Planting for two denominations. In 1990, they felt called to foreign missions and spent the next twenty-four years serving in Asia. From 2001 until 2014 Paul served as the International Director of Mission to the World's ministry in the Asia/Pacific region.

SECTION 3

Leadership Development

16

Theological Education and the Church in Africa

by Victor Nakah

Since 1999 when I began working with the Theological College of Zimbabwe, I've attended countless consultations, most of them organized by Overseas Council International (OCI) and the All Africa Council of Churches (AACC). I was in Nairobi in February 2000 for a consultation between leaders of churches and leaders of theological institutions. Then and now, what seems to be a consensus among church leaders in Africa, is that the product coming out of our seminaries is not sufficient for the task of ministry. Churches send students who have a heart for ministry, an eagerness for mission, and a zeal for evangelism to be prepared and equipped, and three years later these students graduate from seminary theologically confused, having lost their commitment, and often totally unprepared for the task which they had hoped to accomplish and for which they had come to seminary to be trained.

Tim Dearborn, commenting on the relationship between the church and the seminary, once said, "There is no other professional organization in the world which allows its primary professional training institutions to produce graduates who are generally as functionally incompetent as the church permits her seminaries." [1]

Dearborn's assumption in making this comment is that the seminary is the church's premier leadership enterprise and it therefore exists to serve the church by training her leaders. If this is no longer the case, then something has gone terribly wrong. The Church is important in this equation because she serves two primary purposes. First, she is God's primary means of bringing His people to spiritual maturity and equipping them for the work of ministry, and second, she is God's primary means of bringing salvation to the world.

John Vawter, speaking at a meeting of pastors and Christian leaders, said this about theological education: "Seminary education in general has only four things wrong with it: it is taught by the wrong people in the wrong place with the wrong curriculum and has the wrong oversight."[2]

My experience serving with both the church and seminary has been that the church does not always prioritize the seminary as its premier training enterprise. This is often demonstrated in the lack of resource support from the church to the seminary and the caliber of leaders the church entrusts with the responsibility to train future leaders. More often than not, seminary professors thrive academically but are poor ministry practitioners. And so, you end up with professors who can't in any reasonable way practice what they teach or provide thought leadership to the church as the seminary response to issues the church is grappling with. Essentially, John Vawter is saying that there is something very wrong with seminary education in terms of its leadership, those who teach, what they teach, and how and when they teach.

CHURCH AND SEMINARY: PARTNERS IN MINISTRY

This honest evaluation of seminary education and its graduates by church leaders is driven by a deep desire for kingdom partnership between the church and the seminary. The two institutions were never designed to be separate entities, one training men and women for ministry and the other employing them to do ministry. They are designed to be partners in calling, preparing, and sending men and women into all the world to preach the Good News to all creation (Mark 16:15). Leadership development is a lifelong process that begins in the church, continues in the seminary only for a brief moment of specialized training, and then returns to the church as part of ongoing leadership development. Three years in seminary is significant but it is nothing compared to the rest of the training that happens through life and ministry experience. After all, experience is the best teacher.

One of the great partnership passages in the Bible is 1 Corinthians 12. In this chapter, the Apostle Paul reminds us that we are each uniquely gifted and as such, need one another to accomplish the mission Christ has entrusted to us. To illustrate the necessity of partnership in the body of Christ, Paul points out the foolishness of independent thinking. Paul writes, "The eye cannot say to the hand, I don't need you. And the head cannot say to the feet, I don't need you" (1 Corinthians 12:21). John Maxwell uses one of Mother Teresa's quotes to describe partnership, "You can do what I cannot do. I can do what you cannot do. Together, we can do great things."[3] Interestingly, it wasn't Mother Teresa who single-handedly blessed the slums of Calcutta, but her whole community of nuns, community members, and supporters around the world. Together, they accomplished great things.

Leadership development is a lifelong process that begins in the church, continues in the seminary only for a brief moment of specialized training, and then returns to the church as part of ongoing leadership development.

This eternal principle of partnership can and must be applied to the church and seminary relationship. God has uniquely gifted both the church and the seminary and we need one another to accomplish the mission that Christ has entrusted to us. Professor Gabriel Fackre sums it up well in an essay entitled "Educating for the Church": "Evangelical seminaries are born and raised in the bosom of the Christian community, exist to prepare its leaders, rely on its resources, and thus are schools of the church. At the same time, they aspire to academic excellence, calling the church to love God with the mind. They are schools of the church, willing to challenge the church when threatened by anti-intellectual frenzies or cultural captivities."[4]

In an essay entitled, "Thinking of the Future," R. Albert Mohler writes, "Evangelical theological education was born in the churches who understood their responsibility to train and educate ministers of the gospel."[5]

The Lausanne Movement's 2010 Cape Town Commitment articulates this in terms of the mission of God and the church and theological education: "The mission of the church on earth is to serve the mission of God, and the mission of theological education is to strengthen and accompany the mission of the Church. How does theological education do this? First, by training those who lead the Church as pastor-teachers, equipping them to teach the truth of God's Word with faithfulness, relevance, and clarity. Second, by equipping all God's people for the missional task of understanding and relevantly communicating God's truth in every cultural context."

The church lies at the center of the eternal purpose of God as His primary means of carrying out His mission, and the seminary exists purely to serve this purpose. In a very practical sense, theological schools determine the direction of the church of the future. Dr. Manfred Kohl explains it like this: "The professor's lectures, seminars, and textbooks are the foundation on which the leadership of our churches and Christian organizations is built. Pastors, missionaries, and evangelists put into practice what they are taught and pass on their knowledge and experience to people in their churches, mission work, or outreach ministries. It follows, then, that the lives of church members and the ministries in which they are involved will reflect what is taught in theological schools."[6]

What Manfred is saying here is that the ministry of the church becomes the true measurement of the effectiveness of the training that happens in seminaries. The seminary responds to the needs of the church and community by offering its faculty, graduates, and programs. This assumes that the graduate has been trained and equipped to respond to the needs of the church and community, the programs are designed to address the same, and the faculty are not just academics, but men and women of God who can demonstrate what they teach in the classroom on the field as well as provide the church with leadership. This perhaps is the ideal that we should all strive for, and the starting point is to acknowledge that seminaries exist to serve the church. We should, however, remind ourselves of the church-seminary partnership and that the seminary's work is simply part of a long process of training.

WHAT IS THE GREATEST NEED?

What is the greatest need of the church or the people of God which seminaries must meet? No one doubts the fact that Christian theological education is first and foremost about God and His glory and the need for us to know Him intimately above all else and to serve Him passionately with all that we are. We know this and we believe it, but seminaries do not make it obvious enough. Seminary professors tend to focus heavily on developing students' intellect and they forget the heart, hands, and feet in the process. This is the reason why seminaries have been called cemeteries. If theological education is God-centered and knowing Him intimately is more important than everything else, then we must make this clear in what we teach and how we teach, so that we do not lose sight of what is most important. Seminaries are not about diplomas and degrees and certificates—more important than all else is that our students come out having met with God significantly, have been changed by Him, and then are recruited into His army of effective soldiers for the church and society. My academic dean when I was a seminary president would demonstrate what seminary education was not about to first-year students on their first day by burning a sample degree certificate in front of the class. He would go on to say that the church does not care whether you have a degree or not. Instead, it is interested in your character and whether you can do the work of ministry or not.

Seminaries are not about diplomas and degrees and certificates—more important than all else is that our students come out having met with God significantly, have been changed by Him, and then are recruited into His army of effective soldiers for the church and society.

Therefore, John Piper says, "the supreme challenge of every scholar and teacher who would prepare these pastors and missionaries is: How shall I study and teach and write and live, so as to help my students know God better than they know anything, and delight in Him more than they delight in anything? That is the supreme challenge of your life."[7]

THE BATTLE FOR THE CHURCH: CONTEXTUALIZATION

The central thrust of theological education is communicating the gospel in light of a particular context (time and place). Gehman argues that, in any culture, Christ must be presented in a manner that is both true to Scripture and meaningful to the people. Just as God, the eternal Spirit, became incarnate as a human being in a particular culture, so Jesus Christ must belong to each society in a unique way.[8]

Simply defined, contextualization is the capacity to respond meaningfully to the gospel within the framework of one's own situation.[9] The gospel is always experienced in context and becomes meaningful as it addresses contextual realities (answers the problems, needs and questions). Context here refers to the whole environment in which the people of God live, including the social, economic, educational, religious, philosophical and political: in brief, man's culture.[10]

The church in Africa desperately needs African answers to these realities. For theology to be relevant, it must speak to issues of poverty, either in the material sense or in forms of marginalization and related realities. The area of ecclesiology and ministry needs serious attention if we're to address the criticism that the church in Africa is still too Western and is therefore less attractive to ordinary Africans. Everyday realities that Africans grapple with include witchcraft, corruption, polygamy and child marriages, cultural and religious syncretism, and the rampant problem of the prosperity gospel. To address these issues, the church needs lectures and textbooks that focus more on these issues and not just the global context. But it all begins with contextual leadership development, and seminaries play a critical role in this. In one sense, it is true that this battle for the contextualization of evangelical faith is won or lost at both the seminary and church leadership level.

THE IMPORTANCE OF WHOLE-LIFE DISCIPLESHIP
The Cape Town Commitment brings to our attention the missional priorities and ministry issues that should help shape theological education and keep it serving the church creatively and relevantly: "As disciples of Christ, we are called to be people of truth. We must live the truth and proclaim the truth. We urge church leaders, pastors, and evangelists to preach and teach the fullness of the biblical gospel as Paul did, in all its cosmic scope and truth. We must present the gospel not merely as offering individual salvation, or better solutions to needs than other gods can provide, but as God's plan for the whole universe in Christ. People sometimes come to Christ to meet a personal need, but they stay with Christ when they find Him to be the truth."[11]

If this is the mission of the church, then seminaries must equip church leaders, pastors, and evangelists to live and preach the fullness of the biblical gospel: "We need intensive efforts to train all God's people in whole-life discipleship, which means to live, think, work, and speak from a biblical worldview and with missional effectiveness in every place or circumstance of daily life and work. Christians in many skills, trades, businesses, and professions can often go to places where traditional church planters and evangelists may not. What these 'tentmakers' and businesspeople do in the workplace must be valued as an aspect of the ministry of local churches." [12]

The rapid growth of the church in so many places remains shallow and vulnerable, partly because of the lack of discipled leaders. The solution is "leadership training." Leadership training programs of all kinds have multiplied but the problem remains, for two reasons.

We strongly encourage seminaries, and all those who deliver leadership training programs, to focus more on spiritual and character formation, not only on imparting knowledge or grading performance, and we heartily rejoice in those who already do so as part of comprehensive "whole person" leadership development.

First, training leaders to be godly and Christlike is the wrong way around. Biblically, only those whose lives already display basic qualities of mature discipleship should be appointed to leadership. The answer to leadership failure is not just more leadership training but better discipleship training. Leaders must first be disciples of Christ before they can be leaders.

Second, some leadership training programs focus on packaged knowledge, techniques, and skills to the neglect of godly character. Yet Bible teaching is the paramount means of disciple-making and the most serious deficiency in contemporary church leaders.

We therefore long to see greatly intensified efforts in disciple-making through the long-term work of teaching and nurturing new believers, so that those whom God calls and gives to the church as leaders are qualified according to biblical criteria of maturity and servanthood.

We strongly encourage seminaries, and all those who deliver leadership training programs, to focus more on spiritual and character formation, not only on imparting knowledge or grading performance, and we heartily rejoice in those who already do so as part of comprehensive "whole person" leadership development. Ours is a theological system so heavily slanted toward lecturing, book reading, writing, and testing. It's nearly all about the grasping and repeating of concepts. The result is a form of Christianity that lives as though it's possible to really believe something without embodying it. The Bible knows nothing of disembodied belief, but this is the very thing that our current system of theological education perpetuates.[13]

CHURCH AND SEMINARY: HOLDING THE TENSION

There is no doubt that the tension between church and seminary is caused by the triangulation of many kinds of issues. However, the question is how can we hold the tension without losing relationship? The two institutions need one other, and continuous dialogue around issues that matter to both should be encouraged. But honest dialogue requires courage and perseverance if differences are to be ironed out and common vision found. Such dialogue should be driven by the knowledge that seminaries exist to serve the church. And in order for seminaries to do this well, the church must equally serve the seminary by identifying the right students for training, sending godly, gifted faculty, and providing resources that contribute toward sustainability. For the seminary to serve the church, seminary leaders and teachers must listen carefully to what the church needs and have the courage to think outside the box to find relevant, sustainable solutions. Traditional models of theological education are no longer sufficient in Africa??, and if seminaries don't find suitable models for the African context they will continue to be irrelevant to the needs of the church.

Victor Nakah is an ordained Presbyterian minister and is the current Senior Vice President for Spiritual Ministry with CURE International. He was the seminary president for ten years in Zimbabwe. Before joining CURE, he served for three years as the Africa Regional Director for Overseas Council International.

1   Tim Dearborn, *Preparing New Leaders for the Church of the Future: Transforming Theological Education Through Multi-Institutional Partnerships* (Transformation: December 1996).

2   John Vawter, *Seminaries: Surviving or Thriving?* (Faculty Dialogue 23: 1995), 41.

3   John Maxwell, *The 17 Indisputable Ways of Teamwork: Embrace Them and Empower Your Team* (Thomas Nelson: 2013), 188.

4   Gabriel Fackre, "Educating for the Future" eds. D.G. Hart and R.A. Mohler, Jr., *Theological Education in the Evangelical Tradition* (Grand Rapids: Baker, 1996), 217.

5   R. Albert Mohler, Jr., "Thinking of the Future: Evangelical Theological Education in a New Age," eds. D.G. Hart and R.A. Mohler, Jr., *Theological Education in the Evangelical Tradition* (Grand Rapids: Baker, 1996), 280.

6   Manfred W. Kohl and A.N. Lal Senanayake, editors, "Theological Education: What Needs to Be Changed" in *Educating for Tomorrow—Theological Leadership for the Asian Context* (Bangalore: 2002) , 30.

7   John Piper, "Training the Next Generation of Evangelical Pastors and Missionaries," The Evangelical Theological Society (ETS) Annual Meeting, (Orlando: November 20, 1998).

8   Richard German, *Doing African Christian Theology: An Evangelical Perspective* p.1-4

9   Shoki Coe and Aharon Sapsezian, *Ministry in Context*, 20.

10 Richard J. Gehman, *Guidelines in Contextualization*, 29.

11 Cape Town Commitment, Part II, 26.

12 Cape Town Commitment, Part II, 28.

13 Cape Town Commitment, Part II, 43.

17

Investing in the Next Generation of Leaders

by Richard Wolfe

The Apostle Paul instructed Timothy to make developing leaders a high priority in his ministry. "You then, my son, be strong in the grace that is in Christ Jesus. And the things you have heard me say in the presence of many witnesses entrust to reliable people who will also be qualified to teach others" (2 Timothy 2:1-2). And in my opinion, this same priority must be at the forefront of missionaries and mission agencies. This paper briefly looks at elements of investing in future and emerging leaders in the organization.

WHAT IS OUR PRIORITY?

Within MTW (Mission to the World, PCA) exists opportunities for new leaders to serve. Some of these include the following: the opportunity to open a new field, an opening due to a current leader providentially moving into a different ministry, the present leadership is ineffective and needs to be replaced, or it is just time to pass on the torch to another. However, on several occasions when opportunities arose, there was a vacuum of leadership, and we were hard pressed to find the person we needed. Why is there a shortage of leadership? We have not been as intentional about mentoring those we lead as we need to be.

One of our highest priorities as leaders should be to mentor emerging leaders. And one of the highest priorities of an organization should be to mentor future leaders. Theologian Hans Finzel states, "Producing leaders for the next generation should be on everyone's agenda."[1] "The future of the ministry or organization will live or die on the basis of new leadership."[2] John

196

Maxwell wrote, "Every effective leadership mentor makes the development of leaders one of his highest priorities in life. He knows the potential of the organization depends on the growth of its leadership." [3]

In practice, every effective leader should have an ongoing list of emerging, young leaders whom he is intentionally mentoring for the purpose of equipping men and women for future leadership.

WHY DON'T ALL LEADERS DEVELOP LEADERS?

Over the years, I have observed several reasons why many leaders do not develop others. First, leaders do not see the tremendous value of developing others and only have a short-term perspective. Some express that they are "too busy"—it would take time away from their hands-on ministry. Some see it as the role of the home office. And others think it will happen organically. Finally, I see an overall lack of urgency and intentionality in our organization and on the fields in developing future leaders. According to theologian Leighton Ford, "Jesus had a strategy to develop leaders—he aimed to reproduce himself in them." [4] Therefore, if MTW is going to make developing future leaders a priority, we too need a strategy. Such a strategy is an investment worth our efforts.

THE TEAM PAUL BUILT

The Apostle Paul's practice was to develop others through ministry work.

Paul was a master mentor. His practice was to take people along with him. He empowered others in his ministry and gave them opportunities for growing in their gifts. In *Called to Lead*, John MacArthur makes many insightful remarks concerning Paul's leadership.

> *"In the closing section of 2 Timothy, as Paul finished the last chapter of his final epistle—as he wrote what would literally stand as the concluding paragraph of his life—what filled the heart and mind of this great leader were the people he ministered to and worked alongside. They were the most visible and immediate legacy of his leadership . . . In fact, the true character of Paul's leadership is seen in this brief list of people he had poured his life into. They personified the team he built. This catalog of individuals is therefore instructive in assessing why Paul's leadership was not a failure."* [5]

Paul's final words to Timothy, his son in the faith, follows:

"Do your best to come to me soon. For Demas, in love with this present world, has deserted me and gone to Thessalonica. Crescens has gone to Galatia, Titus to Dalmatia. Luke alone is with me. Get Mark and bring him with you, for he is very useful to me for ministry. Tychicus I have sent to Ephesus. When you come, bring the cloak that I left with Carpus at Troas, also the books, and above all the parchments. Alexander the coppersmith did me great harm; the Lord will repay him according to his deeds. Beware of him yourself, for he strongly opposed our message. At my first defense no one came to stand by me, but all deserted me. May it not be charged against them! But the Lord stood by me and strengthened me, so that through me the message might be fully proclaimed and all the Gentiles might hear it. So I was rescued from the lion's mouth. The Lord will rescue me from every evil deed and bring me safely into his heavenly kingdom. To him be the glory forever and ever. Amen."

"Greet Priscilla and Aquila, and the household of Onesiphorus. Erastus remained at Corinth, and I left Trophimus, who was ill, at Miletus. Do your best to come before winter. Eubulus sends greetings to you, as do Pudens and Linus and Claudia and all the brothers."
(2 Timothy 4:9-21)

This passage illustrates that Paul built a network of people around him. He had a large, effective team—people on whom he depended and delegated ministry responsibility—people whom he trusted.[6] Therefore, Paul's influence was widespread. First, we must remember that Paul was serving out of his calling as an Apostle, which he received from Christ (Romans 1:1-6). Secondly, it is helpful to recall that Barnabas was first among the leaders to believe in Paul, stand with him (Acts 9:27) and give him an opportunity to serve as an Apostle (Acts 11:25). So Barnabas significantly influenced Paul who then mentored or developed many others *(see "A Biblical Mentoring Example" chart next page).*

INVESTING IN THE FUTURE

It is understandable that definitions of an effective leader from Christian authors would have a spiritual focus. Henry and Richard Blackaby center their attention on spiritual leadership. "Spiritual leadership is moving people on to God's agenda."[7] Robert Clinton defines a biblical leader as a person with a God-given capacity and a God-given responsibility to influence a specific group of God's people toward His purpose for the group.[8] In addition, "Christian leaders are servants with the credibility and capabilities to influence people in a particular context to pursue their God-given direction."[9] In order to influence God's people toward His purpose, effective leaders must invest in others. The idea of investing encourages a long-term approach to leadership. There are "get rich quick" schemes that promise returns on your investment that surpass anything else that is happening in the market. Beware! If it sounds too good to be true, it probably is. A basic investment principle is called the "Rule 72"—the percentage of return divided into 72 determines the length of time it will take to double your money (i.e. investing $1000 at 6%, will yield a total of $2000 in 12 years). In other words, it takes time. This is true with investing in others as well.

A Biblical Mentoring Example

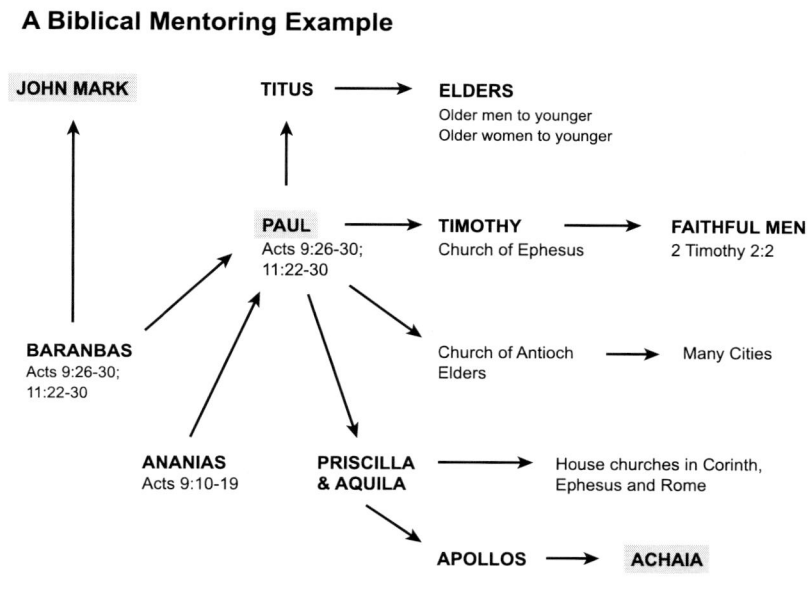

INVESTING THROUGH RELATIONSHIPS

The following verses reflect the importance of ministry being relational. Leading others involves sharing your life with those who follow. John Maxwell states, "Effective leaders know that you first have to touch people's hearts before you ask them for a hand. That is the 'Law of Connection.'"[10]

The greatest leaders are able to connect with people individually and as a group. We see this with both Jesus and Paul. While they effectively addressed crowds, they also touched the hearts of individuals.

Mark 3:14: *"He appointed twelve—designating them apostles—that they might be with him and that he might send them out to preach."*

1 Thessalonians 2:7-8: *"But we were gentle among you, like a mother caring for her little children. We loved you so much that we were delighted to share with you not only the gospel of God but our lives as well, because you had become so dear to us."*

1 Thessalonians 2:11-12: *"For you know that we dealt with each of you as a father deals with his own children, encouraging, comforting and urging you to live lives worthy of God, who calls you into his kingdom and glory."*

Leighton Anderson states, "The effective leader understands how people connect with one another. The effective leader cares about people and enables them to find satisfying relationships within the church. The effective leader never ignores the importance of relationships for the sake of accomplishing a task. "[11]

When serving in the Philippines (which is a highly relational culture), one important lesson I learned was that people are more important than tasks (even though I am very task-oriented). For example, whenever someone would enter the office, I learned to stop whatever I was doing to greet and visit with him or her. If we attended a gathering, we were expected to greet the hosts when we arrived and see them before we left. At the end of the day, task-oriented people ask, "Did I get everything done?" Filipinos would ask, "Are all my relationships in order?" I had to learn to put people over paperwork.

Hans Finzel includes "putting paperwork over peoplework" as one of the top ten mistakes leaders make. "There is a simple test," suggests Finzel, "to determine whether you are a task oriented-people or people-oriented. When someone enters his office without an appointment and interrupts the task at hand, how does he react? Does the leader view the person as an interruption or an opportunity?"[12]

In order to be an effective relational leader, Maxwell addresses the question, What can a person do to manage and cultivate good relationships as a leader? First, have a leader's head and understand people. A leader must understand how people feel and think. Second, have a leader's heart and love people. You cannot be an effective leader unless you love people. Third, extend a leader's hand and help people. If you focus on what you can put into those you lead more than what you can get from them, they'll love and respect you because they know you love and respect them.[13]

To summarize, we can say that effective leadership cannot occur in a relational vacuum. In order to influence God's people toward His purpose, effective leaders must invest in others. Carson Pue aptly states, "The conventional definition of effective ministry leadership is getting work done through people, but *real leadership is developing people through ministry work*" (italics mine).[14]

Mentoring is a relational experience in which one person empowers another by sharing God-given resources. It is a relational exchange between two people with varying levels of involvement and degrees of intensity.

INVESTING THROUGH MENTORING

Mentoring is defined by Stanley and Clinton as follows: "Mentoring is a relational process in which a mentor, who knows or has experienced something, transfers that something (resources of wisdom, information, experience, confidence, insight, relationships, status, etc.) to a mentoree, at an appropriate time and manner, so that it facilitates development or empowerment."[15]

Or put more simply, mentoring is a relational experience in which one person empowers another by sharing God-given resources. It is a relational exchange between two people with varying levels of involvement and degrees of intensity. Stanley and Clinton understand not only the various levels of involvement people have with one another, but also different mentoring functions. This empowers leaders (mentors) to use a number of different types of relationships to accomplish the goal of equipping God's people. This is pictured in the charts following as diverse investing.

DIVERSE INVESTING

One of the exciting aspects of this model is that God uses various people through various relationships to accomplish His purpose in the lives of believers. Leaders do not need to be everything to everyone.

It is through employing these relationships that leaders can broaden and deepen their influence of others. It is through these roles that leaders have the greatest impact on others. Leaders must be intentional about developing relationships that influence others and help them succeed in whatever God has called them to do and be.

Mentoring Type / Central Thrust of Empowerment:

Intensive

> **Discipler**—Enablement in basics of following Christ.
> **Spiritual Guide**—Accountability, direction, and insight for questions, commitments, and decisions affecting spirituality and maturity.
> **Coach**—Motivation, skills, and application needed to meet a task, challenge.

Occasional

> **Counselor**—Timely advice and correct perspectives on viewing self, others, circumstances, and ministry.
> **Teacher**—Knowledge and understanding of a particular subject.
> **Sponsor**—Career guidance and protection as leader moves within an organization.[16]

No matter which type of mentoring opportunity you are given, the key is building a relationship with the person you desire to impact. At the end of their book, Stanley and Clinton suggest "ten commandments" of mentoring. The first commandment is "Relationship." They state, "The stronger the relationship, the greater the empowerment.... It is important to keep in mind that you need to continue to develop the relationship." [17] In all of the different types of mentoring, relationships are essential.

As we consider what this means for missional leadership, especially for MTW, I believe it demands a heightened and intentional effort of mentoring younger missionaries and emerging leaders.

Bobb Biehl uses the illustration of a linchpin, which connects the doodlebug with the trailer for mentoring the next generation.[18]

Biehl explains this connection.

> *"I believe that mentoring is the linchpin in Christian leadership ... The linchpin of Christian leadership development is the mentoring process. Our current generation of Christian leadership could easily forget the linchpin and leave the potential of the next generation behind. But through mentoring, we can groom the next generation of leaders, and they can do more than we dared to dream."* [19]

FOCUSING ON THE NEXT GENERATIONS (GEN X, MILLENNIALS AND GEN Z)

Where will the leaders of the future come from? How are we going to prepare the leaders of the future? Knowing the general traits of Generation Next (those following the Baby Boomers and born between 1964-1977) is essential if we are to lead them effectively and bring them along as future leaders. [20]

Hans Finzel describes Generation Next as the "Paradox Generation" because they display unique characteristics, some of which stand in contrast to each other. Then he lists these "Gen X-er" characteristics by Jeff Bantz, who himself is a Gen X-er:

- Very individualistic, and yet highly value relationships.
- Don't respect authority, yet long to receive instruction.
- Skeptical, yet pragmatic.
- Have an extended adolescence, and yet they grew up too soon.
- Slow to commit, and passionately dedicated.
- A challenge to manage, but are excellent workers.
- Apathetic, and yet care deeply.

- Relativistic and searching for meaning.
- Disillusioned, yet they are not giving up.
- A hazy sense of their own identity.
- Cynical, hopeless.[21]

While these conflicts might exist, Generation X-ers seek to make a difference in the world, and to affect change. They might be unconventional and seek other ways to affect change, but that might be needed. And while "Generation Xers want to do things their own way, they still want and need support from today's leaders. They want role models who can inspire them to work toward their full potential. They want mentors to teach them the skills of leadership and help them overcome hurdles in their path." [22]

To empower young missionaries to lead for the future, the following suggestions are adapted from *The Future of Leadership*:

- Develop a new definition of leadership that includes young missionaries.
- Create a new conception of young missionaries that includes leadership.
- Offer young missionaries meaningful opportunities to become leaders.
- Recognize emerging leaders as valuable and active members with decision-making power.
- Be a mentor and a manager—not a teacher or a leader—of youth ministries initiatives.
- Trust the emerging leader-led process.[23]

Millennials' (born roughly between 1980 and 1995) characteristics and potentiality should be taken into consideration. Every mission leader should read "Missions and Millennials: Moblizing and preparing the Next Generations of Missionaries and Leaders," which addresses some of the unique characteristics and obstacles for mobilizing this generation. The authors mention characteristics that can be used to challenge them for world missions, even though they see needs right around them.

"American Christian millennials come with a missional spirit that is different from previous generations. They generally have a greater concern for social issues, justice, and for local missions rather than

international missions. Generally millennials want to make a difference, they desire to be mentored, and want to be trusted with leadership responsibilities. "[24]

This report expands on seven themes concerning millennials:

1. Millennials have a perception problem when it comes to international missions.
2. Millennials do not understand and define long-term commitments that same way MTW understands and defines long-term commitments.
3. Millennials (and generations following them) communicate differently from other generations.
4. Millennials consider money issues and fundraising as significant obstacles to serving as international missionaries.
5. Millennials function as a social tribe, and their values reflect this.
6. Millennials are looking for specific values and practices in the work place and in organizations they support.
7. Millennials have real fears hindering them from pursuing international missions.

The MTW report on millennials was written "to aid MTW as we work to more meaningfully engage future generations for international missions."[25]

Will the current leadership just write off these generations? Or will we prayerfully consider how to spur them on toward love and good deeds in the arena of world missions? The Lord of the Harvest is faithful and will call a new generation of missionaries from Gen X-ers and Millennials and the generations to follow. Present leaders must touch on their desire to make a difference while recruiting and mentoring them as they develop future leaders.

CONCLUSION AND RECOMMENDATIONS

I hope this paper has shown the importance of investing in future and emerging leaders. We looked at Paul's model of ministry through a network of people. Then we established that investing in people is to be accomplished through mentoring relationships. Finally, as the target group of emerging leaders comes from the Gen X-ers and Millennials, their unique generational characteristics should be considered in developing a plan for investing in young leaders.

Current mission leadership, and in particular my concern for MTW's leadership, must intentionally and purposefully embrace the task of mentoring the next generation of missionaries and emerging leaders. What should be our goals and plans to develop new mission leaders?

- Revise the description of an MTW Team Leader, Country Leader, and Regional Leader to reflect the high priority of mentoring missionaries as an essential part of their role.
- Provide mentoring training through Global Training & Development.
- Provide information on how to identify emerging leaders.
- Through current leadership, establish a list of emerging leaders for mentoring and development.
- Take current and emerging leaders through Gospel Coach by Scott Thomas and Tom Wood.
- Follow this document up with a paper on "Development Best Practices."

As we pursue God's design for investing in people intentionally and purposefully, we will be better prepared to fill leadership positions in the office and on the field.

Rich serves as MTW's Regional Director for Central America and the Caribbean since 2003. Rich is involved in numerous ministries in this region. Rich and his wife first served as MTW missionaries in the Philippines. Rich was responsible for training and mentoring Filipino church planters and served as the team leader during their last two years in Manila.

---

1   Hans Finzel, *Empowered Leaders* (Nashville: Word Publishing, 1998), 128.

2   Hans Finzel, *The Top Ten Mistakes Leaders Make* (Colorado Springs: Victor Books, 2000), 161.

3   John C. Maxwell, *The 21 Irrefutable Laws of Leadership* (Nashville: Thomas Nelson Publishers, 1998), 139.

4   Leighton Ford, *Transforming Leadership* (Downers Grove: InterVarsity Press, 1991), 161.

5   John MacArthur, *Called to Lead* (Nashville: Thomas Nelson, 2004), 184-185.

6   Ibid. 184.

7   Henry and Richard Blackaby, *Spiritual Leadership* (Nashville: Broadman and Holman Publishers, 2001), 20.

8   Robert Clinton, *The Making of a Leader* (Colorado Springs: NavPress, 1988), 245.

9   Aubrey Malphurs, *Being Leaders* (Grand Rapids: Baker Books, 2003), 10.

10   John Maxwell, *The 21 Irrefutable Laws of Leadership* (Nashville: Thomas Nelson, Inc, 1998), 101.

11   Leith Anderson, *Leadership That Works* (Minneapolis: Bethany House Publishers, 1999), 144.

12   Hans Finzel, *The Top Ten Mistakes Leaders Make* (Colorado Springs: Cook Communications, 2000), 40.

13   John Maxwell,*The 21 Indispensable Qualities of a Leader* (Nashville: Thomas Nelson, Inc, 1999), 106-108.

14   Carson Pue, *Mentoring Leaders* (Grand Rapids: Baker Books, 2005), 262.

15   Paul D. Stanley and J. Robert Clinton, *Connecting: The Mentoring Relationships You Need to Succeed in Life* (Colorado Springs: NavPress, 1992), 40.

16   Ibid, 41.

17   Ibid, 42.

18   Bobb Biehl, *Mentoring: Confidence in Finding a Mentor and Becoming One* (Nashville: Broadman & Holman Publishing, 1996), 143.

19   Ibid, 143-144.

20   Hans Finzel, *Empowered Leaders* (1998), 134.

21   Ibid, 134.

22   Bennis, Warren, Spreitzer, Gretchen, and Cummins, Thomas, eds. *The Future of Leadership* (San Francisco: Jossey-Bass, 2001), 251-252.

23   Ibid, 224.

24   Carl Chaplin, Kendra Jeffreys, and Aubra Whitten. *Missions and Millennials: Mobilizing and Preparing the Next Generations of Missionaries and Leaders* (Mission to the World: April 22, 2015), 3.

25   Ibid, 18.

18

Developing Flawed Servants into Thriving Leaders

by Bill Goodman
(written by Mellissa Kelley based on interviews with the author)

How should a Christian organization choose its leaders? In the early years of MTW, we often promoted people to leadership positions based on time served. But that proved to be an unreliable method, and multiple teams fractured due to leadership issues. We began to see that there must be a higher criteria for leadership than simply seniority. Over the years, we have become more intentional about choosing leaders because we understand how high the stakes are.

The truth is that leaders have enormous influence over the organizations they serve. There's a dear price to pay for poor leadership, and much benefit to reap from good leadership. Poor leaders can cause serious damage to a ministry, followers' lives, and the name of Christ. But it's amazing how profoundly God can work through an effective leader to advance the kingdom.

So, what should we look for to choose our leaders? If not seniority, what else? Many would say that personal integrity and honesty are essential in strong leadership and that character counts above all else.

Certainly, we want to choose leaders with good character traits, who can withstand the temptations of power, who can make tough decisions amidst adversity and uncertainty, who treat all with kindness and respect regardless of their standing. But if we look to the Bible for examples of the leaders God chose, we might be surprised. Look at Moses, who lied and struggled with anger; David, an adulterer and murderer; Saul, a zealous oppressor of Christ followers; Peter, a spineless hothead.

These biblical leaders, and many more, had significant character issues and at times made poor decisions, yet God specifically chose them and then used them mightily.

It's easy to assume that assessing character is a binary process: that either you have it or you don't. But perhaps not. Perhaps character flaws are a part of our fallen state. And instead of choosing leaders with a squeaky clean moral resume, we should acknowledge that all of us, in our fallen state, are flawed and in need of God's gracious restoration.

Taking the time to honestly assess our areas of weakness, and then creating a plan to mitigate them, is the best approach to creating stable, enduring leadership that yields great kingdom rewards.

It is impossible to find leaders without areas of weakness or personal failures. In fact, many leaders chosen for their "goodness" are placed on a pedestal and inevitably fall and disappoint those around them. This isolating process of elevating leaders above all others and expecting their perfection may actually speed their demise.

Instead of impeccable character, our litmus test for leadership should be leaders who are willing to confront and address their flaws through the glorious riches we have in Christ Jesus. All through Scripture, we see that God delights to address our flaws as we walk alongside Him in a posture of dependence and contrition (Psalm 51:17).

We can only do this by creating an atmosphere of transparency and openness, where we can acknowledge our sin and humbly ask for help. Though this process is not intuitive, taking the time to honestly assess our areas of weakness, and then creating a plan to mitigate them, is the best approach to creating stable, enduring leadership that yields great kingdom rewards.

OWNING OUR FLAWS

Most of us avoid acknowledging our character flaws, or at most we minimize them. It is much easier to move forward in familiar behavioral patterns than to confront the realities of our limitations and weaknesses and then to proactively address them. No one wants to be found lacking. Sometimes, in our attempt to keep these issues buried deep within us, we end up projecting them out onto others. As Matthew 7:4 says, "How can you say to your brother, 'Let me take the speck out of your eye,' when there is a log in your own eye?"

Though we may not be aware of them, our character issues are apparent to others and, left unchecked, have the potential to undermine our relationships, ministry, and leadership. Frequently, these flaws are most evident under stress or when we are being criticized. And interestingly, they are often related to our areas of strength; in fact, our biggest strength can become our biggest weakness.

I frequently struggle with competitiveness and needing to be right, and though I've always been aware of those besetting sins, it's only recently that I've become aware of another area of struggle. I frequently use humor to defuse a situation or quickly establish relationships with others. But I'm realizing that though my sense of humor can be one of my strengths it also can be a way that I avoid conflict and distance myself from others, particularly those who need my listening ear. Learning this about myself, that my sense of humor can be used for good or ill, gives me more awareness of how to monitor my interactions with others moving forward.

So, why do leaders, myself included, frequently struggle to see ourselves as we really are? Why do we regularly showcase our strengths to deflect attention from our flaws?

Frequently, we place our worth in ourselves and our accomplishments rather than in what Christ has done for us. The Apostle Paul's testimony in the book of Philippians testifies to this. Philippians 3:12-14 reads, "Not that I have already obtained this or am already perfect, but I press on to make it my own, because Christ Jesus has made me his own. Brothers, I do not consider that I have made it my own. But one thing I do: forgetting what lies behind and straining forward to what lies ahead, I press on toward the goal for the prize of the upward call of God in Christ Jesus."

Many of us also use our leadership roles as a way to fill up the emptiness inside. In Philippians 2:3-4, Paul says, "Do nothing out of selfish ambition or vain conceit. Rather, in humility value others above yourselves, not looking to your own interests but each of you to the interests of others." Here, Paul is instructing us to be "glory empty." We must have an attitude of humility like Christ or we'll never be willing to see what's holding us back. We must see ourselves as a child of God, so we have the freedom to look at our flaws. When we see the world through this lens we realize that we don't ultimately get our value from our role as a leader, but instead from who we are in Christ.

As you view leadership in the Bible you can't help but see the flaws of those God selected to lead His work. This can comfort us: If God can use flawed men like David and Saul He can use anyone, including me.

WORKING THROUGH CHARACTER ISSUES

Once we embrace what Christ has done for us, and the freedom we have in Christ, we can begin the process of evaluating our flaws, understanding them, and putting a plan in place to address them.

In his book *Leadership and Spirit*, Russ Moxley identifies several common character flaws many Christians in leadership exhibit: anger and emotional volatility, fear and insecurity, and excessive need for approval, recognition, or affirmation. Underneath these flaws is a common theme—they all stem from trying to validate ourselves apart from Christ.

Persisting in these ruts creates baggage. We have probably all experienced leadership where we've had to walk on eggshells to avoid an emotional reaction from one of our leaders. And we've seen leaders place so much value on their role that they become territorial and restrict channels of communication. We've also seen leaders who covet affirmation become defensive and angry when they don't get it. As an observer, it's easy to spot the dysfunction when a leader is performing poorly.

But how can we proactively address these propensities in ourselves before they begin to undermine our ministry? The answer, according to Moxley, is to pursue self-awareness. This is certainly an age-old process: As Socrates said, "An unexamined life is not worth living."

How can we take specific steps toward awareness? Fortunately, there are a number of excellent tools available for leaders. Here are several we are successfully using at MTW as we develop team leaders, regional directors, and country directors:

- **Hogan inventory**—a personality tool that identifies strengths, weaknesses, and "derailers"
- **EQi**—an emotional intelligence test
- **Myers Briggs**—a personality test that determines how people make

decisions and act under stress
- **RightPath**—a behavioral assessment that predicts worker/workplace fit

In addition to these tools, MTW's leadership assessment process offers role playing, interviews, and targeted feedback to provide a framework for leader growth. We see many leaders benefit from these tools, including the stories of these two men.

Several years ago, a man in our organization had substantial leadership potential but used humor inappropriately and had off-putting body language, and these things kept him from being taken seriously. We gave him feedback through the leadership assessment process, and he took it seriously. In time, he changed his appearance and became more intentional about his body language and humor. We saw so much growth in this man. He got a handle on the things that were hampering his leadership, and his ministry improved dramatically as a result.

Surround yourself with people you trust who have permission to speak truth into your life. We must invite others into our lives to help us see our blind spots.

Another person leading a cross-cultural team was frequently frustrated with team issues that he thought stemmed from his host culture. But after using several of the tools above, he began to realize that his own leadership choices were provoking problem behaviors in his team. Once he saw that and began to adjust, his team's dynamics improved.

One of the most important suggestions Moxley offers in his book is to surround yourself with people you trust who have permission to speak truth into your life. This includes godly friends who are willing to tell you, "Hey, you're being a jerk." We must invite others into our lives to help us see our blind spots.

The best tool I have used to address blind spots is a 360 review, which involves soliciting feedback from people in every aspect of your professional life: colleagues, superiors, and direct reports. The goal is to evaluate feedback from all sources to find patterns of behavior that can be improved. Each respondent is asked to answer the same questions: What do people say are your areas of strength? What do people say you need to do to be more effective? What are people afraid to tell you?

I learned some surprising information from my 360. Though I am generally good at thinking quickly on my feet, an overconfidence in this area sometimes leads to me to underprepare for a task. And this can become a weakness when I spend more energy thinking about what I'm going to say next instead of listening well. Now, I try to prepare in advance and take a beat to listen rather than rush in with a quick response. This knowledge has led me to meditate on James 1:19, "Everyone should be quick to listen, slow to speak, and slow to become angry."

It is essential to truly accept the feedback of others. And to humbly realize that there is sometimes a disconnect between what we intend through our actions, and the actual effect of our actions. Executive coach Cobie Langerak makes the distinction between intent and impact. We think intent is important, she says, but actually impact is the true measure of success. "People will say, 'Oh, I didn't mean it that way,'" said Langerak, but you must ask, "How did that action or decision impact my team?" That is the measure of success.

These tools are loaded with potential. It is amazing what God will show us about ourselves when we use tools like the 360 review in good faith and humbly ask for guidance. But we must commit to long-term plans to implement the changes we begin to make. I highly recommend meeting with a coach or accountability partner at regular intervals to check progress and set goals.

BECOMING A LEVEL 5 LEADER

In 2001, business consultant Jim Collins wrote the landmark book *From Good to Great* that revealed the key to highly successful companies. It turned out that what made leaders great, and by extension companies great, wasn't courage or business acumen or expertise or intelligence. It was, instead, profound humility coupled with intense determination. He termed those who reached these pinnacles of leadership success as "Level 5 leaders."

What can we do in our spheres of ministry to become a Level 5 leader for Christ? Collins seems to have stumbled onto biblical truth here—that the way up is the way down, that the way out is the way in, and that the path to greatness is the path of humility.

Let us be encouraged as we begin the lifelong process of honest self-assessment, mutual accountability, and humble leadership. We can do all things through Christ who strengthens us. Though we are flawed we have much hope, because God has provided all we need to thrive in the leadership roles He's entrusted to us.

Bill served for 25 years in Mexico with MTW before helping to start and lead MTW's Global Training and Development (GTD). He has served as Assistant Coordinator of MTW for three years.

SECTION 4

Discipleship and Evangelism

19

A Daily Death, Opening Our Lives to Make Disciples

by Dave Culmer

"That guy, Stefan . . . he is great. He takes initiative in our friendship and wants to hang out. He's excited and wants to learn and grow." Petko couldn't help but feel excited about this young believer who has been coming to our church plant. Stefan has quickly involved himself in serving and helping cook our communal post-service dinners, and he has been hungrily devouring each of the Christian books that our team has translated into Bulgarian. We have seen the evidence of Stefan's changed heart for ourselves, so we all nod happily with Petko.

What Petko doesn't realize is that the same can be said for his own heart and life. When I first started hanging out with Petko, he had only been a believer for a year. And he was so stoic and rigid that other new believers asked why I spent time with him. They found him unapproachable and unlikable. But he clearly wanted to spend time with me. Over time, through talks about God and sharing our vulnerabilities and need of the gospel, we became friends. I can mark the day that something changed in Petko. While we were walking and talking one day, I felt a rush of brotherly affection for him and said: "Petko, I want you to know that, as your friend, I love you." It was as though those words suddenly gave him the freedom to move from stoicism to loving others in freedom and grace. And he changed.

WHAT IS DISCIPLESHIP?
There is a part of me that cringes at the word discipleship because it conjures up an image of a closed circle of elite graduates of some sort of "spiritual boot camp" who condescend to gather with the rest of us

lowly sinners on Sunday mornings. For others, it may be this amorphous cloud of "something that I should be doing, but I don't know how ... or even exactly what it is." For these reasons, I find it most helpful to think about discipleship in terms of broad concepts that we see in Scripture, concepts that are actually universal throughout the Old and New Testaments.

To put some flesh to the concept, maybe it's helpful to come back to the essence of the gospel. We were once separated from God because of our sin and God sent His Son to break down the dividing walls of hostility, as expressed in Ephesians 2, that existed between God and us, and us and our fellow human beings. The essence of the gospel is restoration and reconciliation—a new, vibrant relationship with the One True God.

People need to become Christians and people need to be taught how to think and feel and act as a Christian. That is, a disciple, a follower of Jesus, one who embraces Him as Lord and Savior and Treasure.

As with any relationship, this is a process. Our relationships with others reflect, somewhat, our relationship with God in their quality and character. No one meets a person and instantly becomes deeply intimate with him in relationship. And I would propose that this is mirrored in every believer's relationship with God. If we are truly in relationship with Him, it is a lifelong process, akin to marriage or a deep and abiding friendship where we are constantly learning new things about one another, seeing one another in a new light, changing and growing together (except that with God, He does not change but we see more of who He is with time and growth and experience). As we grow in this relationship, we better understand who we are in relationship to Him and how we are to live in light of that relationship. That is discipleship. To quote John Piper: "[It] is a very long process. [It] is a lifetime of process ... I think what is important is not the terminology, but the reality. People need to become Christians and people need to be taught how to think and feel and act as a Christian. That is, a disciple, a follower of Jesus, one who embraces Him as Lord and Savior and Treasure."

So, how do we do this? Well, God has made us His ambassadors of the Good News. What is an ambassador but a representative of the Sovereign who has sent them. We are to represent Him in every way—not just with words, but with acts and in our character and disposition. The popular terminology is incarnational ministry and relationship. As Jesus became incarnate and lived life as a Jew of His time and circumstances, but without compromising His character and disposition, so are we to live. This means that we have the responsibility and the freedom to discern the principles of discipleship from Scripture and apply them to our particular context. Following are a number of principles I have identified that pertain to discipleship in all contexts:

1. Teaching/learning how to learn from God. (Deuteronomy 6:4-9) Being in relationship with God means allowing ourselves to be molded into His image and likeness by His gentle, loving, creative hands, and exhorting others toward the same.

2. Allowing ourselves to be fully human in relationship with others. In order for the first principle to happen, we must be honest about our humanity and brokenness and our need of the gospel and His people. We must acknowledge that we need His Church as much as the Church needs each of us. This is particularly challenging for our victorious American mentality, which equates vulnerability and brokenness and need of a Savior (and others) with something shameful.

3. Being available (this can be the risky and scary part). We must move out of isolation (whether we isolate ourselves individually or gather in isolation with our families) and into active involvement and relationship with others. We must be ready to commit ourselves to a life of openness, actively pursuing relationship with others, just as God actively pursued us. He didn't wait for us with His castle door open . . . He left the castle and came seeking after us. We must do the same.

4. Having the heart of the Father for others. This is the Father of the Prodigal Son and his elder brother, Who sees past the brokenness of one's "children" in faith and recognizes them as children who need to experience the love of the Father. This happens only as we recognize our own brokenness and need of the same sort of love, and recognize that we are the recipients of such amazing love.

5. Having an "end game" in view. As I become more and more cognizant of my own mortality, I recognize that I want to equip others in a manner that echoes Christ Himself, that those who come after me may surpass me and do much greater things than I could ever hope to do.

We must be ready to commit ourselves to a life of openness, actively pursuing relationship with others, just as God actively pursued us.

WHY DISCIPLESHIP?

Discipling relationships can be profound and life-enriching. One of my favorite of Boyan's attributes is that he is unafraid to ask me questions. He trusts me, and we can share pretty much anything with each other. Vlado doesn't ask questions the same way, but we also share those high levels of trust. They would gladly lay down whatever to help me in times of need, to be with me and speak truth to me when I need to hear it—either as comfort or as rebuke or as exhortation—and they have done so. I have had at least one of these men at my side when walking through the deepest and darkest moments of my life.

When asking the question of why should I be engaged in discipleship, the answer is at once obvious and urgent. It is obvious because it's what Jesus told us to do. Jesus told us that we must be His disciples, and then that we are to make disciples in His name. It's also obvious because all of us are in the process of discipleship right now. It started before we even became Christians and will continue until the end of our lives. And it is urgent because, quite simply, if we don't do it then who will? I know that God will one day take me away from those I love and serve alongside in my context in Eastern Europe. I want to shepherd them well while I'm here so they will in turn become shepherds themselves.

MODELS IN DISCIPLESHIP

Discipleship forms a huge part of my lived experience as a believer. Collin, the classmate who shared the gospel with me exactly when I was ready to hear it, had already experienced it himself on some level and imparted this knowledge to me even before I became a believer. We had been deskmates in chemistry class, and as I explored the truths of Christianity, we met weekly to discuss the questions that arose as I read through the Gospel of John. After I became a Christian, I lived with several believers in the same dorm and we shared our lives together and with the students around us. In this spiritual incubator, I was able to wrestle through questions of how to live a life in Christ. My brothers were patient with me during this time. I asked a lot of foolish and, at times, offensive questions and had lots of opportunities to practice the principles about which we so casually speak when we gather on Sunday mornings and in Bible studies. These were the natural out-workings of our relationship with God and others around us.

Then I transferred to Covenant College and became a resident advisor, and it became my responsibility to consider the spiritual well-being of everyone on my floor. As I came under the shepherding care of the resident director I learned how to submit to authority and to love this authority as I saw his wisdom and care in our relationship. He was patient with my independent and sometimes rebellious and distrustful spirit in ways that I only grew to appreciate toward the end of serving together. And he did it well. He frequently combined mentoring me with errands and activities where we could talk while we tended to the business of life together.

Certainly, my best model for discipleship is Jesus. Jesus is at the center of all of these relationships that have come into my life. He provided each person who has mentored me, so that I might learn to come and meet directly with Him and learn from Him—the One who offers true food and the water of life. And He is the perfect model—one who both loved and mentored at all times. He never neglected one in favor of the other when it came to His disciples' lives and His relationship with them. Doing this as He did, in a perfectly harmonious way, is difficult for us in our human state. But it's certainly what He has called us to do and is an example worth emulating.

OPPORTUNITIES AND CHALLENGES: BALANCING IN TENSION

In addition to the positive discipleship stories mentioned above, I have also had some bad experiences of discipleship. To be honest, my experiences sweep the spectrum from stilted and relationally-challenged once-a-week Bible studies, to a cult-like crowd that always had to be together. I want to highlight certain pitfalls that I have witnessed in my own life and ministry and in the life and service of others.

As with many things in the Christian life, we find ourselves trying to harmonize two seemingly opposite and incompatible extremes of a pendulum. On either end of the discipleship pendulum exist these possibilities: disciples or friends. Do I want those whom God has put in my life to be my disciples or my friends? I have swung to both of these extremes. For a time, I was involved in a university ministry whose servants can sometimes err on the "disciples" side. Though well-intentioned in their missional vigor, at times, servants in this ministry have short-sightedly seen disciples as projects and cast aside anyone in the community not perceived as fully on board with their mission. And I have to admit that I, too, in youthful vigor and zeal and with an "elder brother" attitude have been guilty of my part in inflicting such wounds.

Another inherent danger to this posture is the need always to be "on your game" with others. When I see myself primarily as someone's "discipler/mentor," I tend toward certain unhealthy attitudes that I have seen played out in almost every ministry context. First, I will tend to view those disciples as mine. So, when they start gravitating toward someone else, or even another ministry/body altogether, I will be tempted to respond jealously and territorially rather than trusting that they are the Lord's, and He will be faithful to complete the good work that He has started in their hearts. My proper response ought, rather, to be one of joy that they are truly seeking the Father and that they might see more of the Father through others than they do just through me.

Secondly, this sets someone up for the impossible balancing act between pride and shame. When I have "produced" so many disciples who are committed to our ministry and who are pursuing what I have laid out as their mission, I take pride in my handiwork. But I also have to be perfect. I always have to be the strong one who is forging ahead and showing others how it's done. I am unable to allow others to see that I am broken and in need of their support and encouragement and friendship and exhortation.

The other side of the discipleship pendulum is friendship for friendship's sake. I have seen in American culture a recent trend toward wanting to celebrate and rediscover true, meaningful friendship. As a single American now living in a culture that values friendship more deeply, I celebrate this trend. However, I also see a tendency to pursue friendship for its own sake without a direction, and I find that disconcerting. C.S. Lewis, in remarking on what true friendship looks like in *The Four Loves*, takes pains to carefully differentiate between mere companionship and true friendship. There must be some common pursuit that gives rise to the friendship. Put another way, companionship versus friendship is the difference between two friends who are simply facing one another on the road versus two friends who are walking along the path, side by side, enjoying the journey as their gaze is set forward in parallel toward a common goal.

C.S. Lewis speaks not only to directionless friendship but also to the jealous tug of mentoring when he talks about how true friendship is open to others joining in: "In each of my friends there is something that only some other friend can fully bring out. By myself I am not large enough to call the whole man into activity; I want other lights than my own to show all his facets .... Hence true Friendship is the least jealous of the loves. Two friends delight to be joined by a third." In like manner, I want my attitude to be, "Lord willing, He will preserve our friendship, and my friend's involvement with this other ministry will only serve to enrich all of our lives together."

Jesus imparted to His disciples truths about the kingdom of God as they walked along the way as friends <u>and</u> disciples. He did not stay aloof and speak truth to them from behind a lectern. He entered into life with these men so that they could get on-the-job training.

In Scripture, Jesus is both an absolutely committed friend and a faithfully visionary rabbi. Jesus somehow managed perfectly to make His disciples know that they were fully, 100 percent His friends. He laughed with them, was vulnerable with them, taught and led, allowed them to serve Him in ways, and invited them into His heart. The Creator of the universe opened up His own heart and soul and burdens and zeal to His friends. Just as C.S. Lewis says of Friendship as one of the Loves: "Eros will have naked bodies; Friendship naked personalities." Such was the case between Jesus and His disciples, and especially Peter, James, and John.

I can understand how Jesus could have loved even Judas. As their story together plays out, Jesus demonstrates a key principle of friendship in the context of discipleship. He loves every one of His disciples to the end, including the one who would betray Him. Am I ready to accept that it is worthwhile in my relationship with God, as well as for others whom I would shepherd, that one or some of those around us would eventually betray and walk away?

But Jesus was also on a mission with these men. He loved them, but He did not love them only. And He knew that His time on the earth was limited. So, He had a mission for them, and they were fully, 100 percent His disciples and would come to be known as His apostles ("sent ones"). So He took the time to teach them. He bore with their foolishness and shortsightedness. He imparted to them truths about the kingdom of God as they walked along the way as friends and disciples. He did not stay aloof and speak truth to them from behind a lectern. He entered into life with these men so that they could get their on-the-job training, which they would need in order to apply the underlying principles and truths to other contexts more effectively.

So, where do we err? We tend to see people according to our own personal disposition. If we are more laid-back, we want them to be friends. If we are driven, we want to foster a passion and mission in the lives of others. So, it is incredibly nuanced, but I must remember that the same friends who know all of my weaknesses, the struggles of my heart, those areas of grief in my life, and who have shared my greatest joys, will also one day replace me as men who are loving others deeply and sacrificially, and mentoring those others to maturity and faith. This is what Jesus meant when He said that the disciples would do greater things than He. They would have others to whom they would carry the same message of reconciliation. I see in Jesus One who loved His friends deeply as friends. And I see in Him His recognition of His role as the Great Disciple-maker and they as His first of many disciples. He recognized that He must impart truth to them so that they could impart that same truth to others. My calling is the same, and I must embrace the challenge to do both simultaneously as well. I won't do it perfectly, and I must be vigilant. The fact is that one day I will be taken out of my position here, either by death or disability or relocation, voluntary or forced.

COSTS AND REWARDS

As if all this weren't intimidating enough, we must think about the costs of genuinely giving ourselves to discipleship. So, what will it cost? In short, it will cost your life. It may cost your life in a literal sense. Following God's calling to make disciples on the mission field in certain areas of the world will potentially expose you and your family to great risk.

But what I mean about it costing our lives, more figuratively, is that it will cost something which is heavier than we might want to pay. It will cost us time, as we make deliberate choices to forgo opportunities for ourselves including our own advancement, free time, and personal space. It will cost us financial resources, as we sometimes choose to sacrifice of ourselves for the benefit of all. Just as the first Church shared all things in common, my friends here know they can reach out to me in times of need and I will be there. Yet I can also say they are there for me when I am in need as well. It will cost me time with friends or family as I open my home to "outsiders." It will cost us our pride and independence as we choose to be vulnerable. In our moments of weakness, we will have to make the deliberate choice to allow others, whom we have been called to serve, to serve us—to walk with us through frustrations and disappointments, to show us the local way of doing things, to sit with us as we grieve in hard moments of loss. It will sanctify you, and that sanctification will lay raw the most vulnerable parts of your soul before your eyes, before God, and possibly—hopefully—before the watching witness of others.

Finally, it will cost us disappointment and heartache, as we will spend time and pour out our hearts caring for others around us who may walk away from Jesus and may walk away from us. For me, those are the most painful costs. My only comfort in those moments comes from seeing that my Savior had to walk His final path completely alone, abandoned by all His disciples and friends.

What is the reward? The reward is also my life! I have already spoken about some of the wonderful aspects of my relationships with my European friends. These friendships have not come without their own frustrations, miscommunications, disappointments, and reminders on both sides of our own brokenness and inability to save ourselves and one another. I have also known many disappointments as I have watched men that I have called brothers and friends walk away from Christ because of the delights the world offers.

But I would trade none of that. The riches of friendship and discipleship have been far too great a reward. I have had the privilege of being the best man or groomsman at my friends' weddings in two cultures, and I have had the privilege of walking with my married friends as they wrestle through what it means to follow Jesus as husbands and as parents. I have enjoyed walking the European streets for hours as I talk with my friends through all of their deepest struggles and doubts and fears and hopes and joys as they seek to follow Christ themselves, and as we walk in obedience to Christ together. Jim Elliot's famous quote, "He is no fool who gives what he cannot keep in order to gain what he cannot lose," encompasses much more than simply physical life itself, the act of breathing and blood flowing through our veins. The apparent loss of privacy, wealth, and opportunities to anesthetize ourselves against the problems of others is more than cancelled out by the reward of shared lives, shared hopes, shared visions, shared brokenness, and a shared understanding that we are truly brothers and sisters in Christ.

> *The apparent loss of privacy, wealth, and opportunities to anesthetize ourselves against the problems of others is more than cancelled out by the reward of shared lives, shared hopes, shared visions, shared brokenness, and a shared understanding that we are truly brothers and sisters in Christ.*

A DAILY DEATH

So, where do we start? How do we start building habits that will allow us to enter into each other's lives and then model this lifestyle to others? We must look at the example of Christ Who has shaped and will shape our lives through His friendship and discipling. It's a process that can seem daunting, but it begins with several simple steps. They are not easy steps, but they are simple:

1. Open your home. Whether single or married, we have many opportunities to invite others into our lives. As we open our homes, we invite others to see us with our hair down, so to speak. They get to see how we deal with the daily decisions of life—financial stewardship, child-rearing, caring for and honoring our spouse, and how we approach all the other decisions of daily life. Of course, this is going to shine a light on our own character, so we must be ready to hear things we don't want to hear as others ask questions or make innocent comments that sometimes have the unintended consequence of convicting us.

2. Open your mind. Read widely. This is extremely helpful for reminding us that we do not have the market cornered on truth, and it forces us to not so eagerly label and categorize others. By reading, we see that there are others who follow Christ who hold a different doctrinal position on some things, and yet have much to offer us. Then, when we have the opportunity to disciple others, we will more quickly see that *all* truth is God's truth, and God may be wanting to show us new truths through those with whom we are engaged in discipleship-friendship.

3. Stop (for the love of Christ) treating discipleship as a lecture series, and take on the model of Christ. Regard all of life as a classroom, where you can impart wisdom or hear your friend's testimony (and gain wisdom from them) while building a bookshelf together. Jesus is our model for this, but a principal model. We must be the ones who contextualize it to our local environment. And as we do so, we model for others in that environment so that they, too, can go out and make disciples for Christ more effectively.

4. Choose vulnerability. It is so hard for us to truly and honestly acknowledge our own brokenness and need of a Savior. How much more so to acknowledge our need of our brothers and sisters and, yes, even our not-yet-believing friends. Paul, our premier evangelist, regularly declared his need of help and comfort and encouragement from others. We need others to walk through hard moments with us too. We need others to speak His truth. We need others, when we are struggling with that same secret, shameful sin again and again, to be a tangible representation of the Father, the Father who comes running to embrace His broken and repentant child, offering His love and grace in those hard moments.

5. Be faithful. How many of your true friends have left you in the lurch because you chose a certain career path or settled on a different doctrinal viewpoint (hint: if all your friends share your doctrinal views, your circle of friends is way too small)? So why would we do such a thing? Friend-disciples may choose to go their own way because of doctrinal differences or their rejection of the King, but we are called to continue to love faithfully. May we faithfully love as He loved, all the way to the end.

Dave, by profession, is a physician trained in family medicine and does get to use his medical skills on the mission field. By vocation, Dave has been ministering for the past ten years with a church-planting team in Sofia, Bulgaria. As a part of that team, he is primarily engaged with evangelism, discipleship, and leadership development as part of their church-planting effort.

20

Experiencing the Story of God's Redeeming Love

by H. E.(name withheld)

M. whirred into the room and maneuvered his wheelchair into position in the circle. As the others finished preparing their cups of tea, M. couldn't wait to start. "Who could have imagined the Bible was so exciting? I couldn't help myself, I went ahead and read the entire book of John two times last week!" A few weeks later, he preached to us from John 6: "Jesus is not just someone to believe in as a philosophy. He is not just a good teacher. When I first read these verses, it looked like Jesus was advocating cannibalism. But no! He is saying He is God and He wants to feed us, and for us to taste and experience with all our senses His bread of life within us. God wants to live inside us and give us life." Then with his right hand raised into a fist, pumping it up and down in the air, M. declared, "Jesus is Lord!"

Who was M.? An 87-year-old man, living alone, carrying around the memories of a life under communism. A widower, father, grandfather, great-grandfather, former engineer, still the life of the party, with a fondness for debate. And until just five years before, a certain atheist.

Who was M.? According to some leading church planters, M. belonged to the "lost" generation in the former communist culture, one that most likely would never be open to the news of the gospel. They felt that it was strategically efficacious to prioritize our efforts as believers and church planters elsewhere.

Yet it seems Jesus did not heed that church-planting strategy, nor was He deterred by the cultural heritage of communism. Jesus was not confined by the overwhelming statistical unlikelihood that M. would hear

His voice beckoning during that English class for senior citizens in the local, government-funded community center.

What happened after that English class? Five years of verse and chorus, yes and no. A yes to the evangelism course invitation and a no, this is interesting to learn about but I do not believe in God. A yes to the small group invitation, a no to the possibility of Jesus as a personal savior and friend. A yes to conversations about life and God around M.'s dining table in his apartment. A yes to prayer through a surgical mask in the hospital room. A yes to "I think it's possible that God exists." A yes to the community of a church body, "Tell me more, but no, that makes no sense that Jesus is The Way." A yes to reading the book of John, then again, yes, I need to read that story of Jesus again right now! And tap, tap, tap, now the knocking was undeniably loud even with the hearing aids removed at night—the most amazing grace sweet sound ever heard. And suddenly there was only YES and Jesus placed His hand on the door to M.'s heart and came in to eat with him.

As much as you might feel that your neighbor is different from you, as much as you might sense that your neighbor or community is far away from God, if you are tempted to doubt—as I have—that God really is bigger than evil or governments or political systems or intrinsic racism, there is hope.

For the past two decades, we have been members of various church-planting teams in a former communist region in Europe. The cultural air we have breathed in and out, in and out, says that God is dead, that God does not exist. Although we live in relative proximity to Martin Luther's city of Wittenberg, the hub of the Reformation, the overwhelming majority of people in the neighborhoods we have called home have no recognized cultural connection to church or the Bible.

Enveloped in this environment, my teammates and I often felt desperately lonely, hopeless, and frustrated. Especially in the first years, the starkness of living day after day in a place where everyone living around me thought we were crazy for believing in God, where I saw little fruit or evidence of His power in ways I could recognize, I went through agonizing months of doubt. Was I making God up? Did He really exist? Was He just a crutch for weak people—like me?

How can we, with ears tuned to the voice of our Shepherd, Redeemer, and Friend, learn to be the people listening to these precious fellow image-bearers in the locations where God has placed them? To sit with our neighbor in the mess and say "I see you, and you matter"? For this is how the Lover of our souls pursues us. Jesus humbled Himself, put skin on, and moved from the perfectly ordered, clean, safe community of heaven to walk the messy impoverished streets where we humans live, in order to love us even when we had gone astray and turned—every one—to our own way. Two thousand years ago, few expected this kind of humble, painful, and unglamorous path for a savior and king. This kind of redeeming love of a triune God blew the minds of those living in Jesus' day and continues to blow our minds today.

In the place where God has placed our local church body, few would have expected 87-year-old M. to hear the voice of Christ. How did our church plant end up being able to witness that story of Jesus working in a location and person that many had written off before the story began? I don't know, but as a firsthand witness, I long to tell the story so that anyone who reads these words can hear: as much as you might feel that your neighbor is different from you, as much as you might sense that your neighbor or community is far away from God, if you are tempted to doubt—as I have—that God really is bigger than evil or governments or political systems or intrinsic racism, there is hope. You might not be able to see it yet in your situation, but hold on to radical hope, my sister and brother, based on the resurrection power of Christ's triumph over death. For Jesus is King. He is real. He is living. He is active. He is redeeming, healing, making whole. The story of M. is a real-life, skin-on picture proving that even in the places where it seems God has been far away, God is working out His redemptive plan and Jesus continues to invite us to participate in it with Him. Wherever you are as a disciple of Christ, there is the power of the Spirit that raised Christ from the dead, there is the mystery of Christ in you, the hope of glory, working in and through you.

WORKING IN A POST-CHRISTIAN CULTURE

We have been doing church planting in a place that has been labeled "post-Christian," "atheistic," "secular," or described as "plowing in concrete." During the first years of our life in this place, I experienced what was meant by these descriptors. Living as a believer there felt unsettling, like the rug had been pulled out from under me; I was flailing around and wasn't sure when I might land. At first, what I observed around me intimidated me or even affected what I thought was possible in this place where God had put us. However, the grace of God has taken us on an unexpected journey through failure and longing to learn what daily dependence on Christ looks like in the simple details of everyday life. As he has been teaching us this life-giving posture of dependence, he has been showing us practically, day by day, how to be witnesses and ambassadors in the not-post-Christian region where he has placed our feet.

In the overarching lesson of dependence, God has been teaching us a profound truth: how "loving the Lord our God with all our heart, soul, and mind; and loving our neighbor as our self" is tied to a daily need to listen to the Lord our God and listen to our neighbor.

Dietrich Bonhoeffer describes the interplay of listening to God and listening to each other in his book *Life Together*:

> *Just as love to God begins with listening to His Word, so the beginning of love for the brethren is learning to listen to them. It is God's love for us that He not only gives us His Word but also lends us His ear. So it is His work that we do for our brother when we learn to listen to him. Christians, especially ministers, so often think they must always contribute something when they are in the company of others, that this is the one service they have to render. They forget that listening can be a greater service than speaking.*
>
> *Many people are looking for an ear that will listen. They do not find it among Christians, because these Christians are talking where they should be listening. But he who can no longer listen to his brother will soon be no longer listening to God either; he will be doing nothing but prattle in the presence of God too.*
>
> *This is the beginning of the death of the spiritual life, and in the end there is nothing left but spiritual chatter and clerical condescension arrayed in pious words. One who cannot listen long and patiently will presently be talking beside the point and be never really speaking to*

others, albeit he be not conscious of it. Anyone who thinks that his
time is too valuable to spend keeping quiet will eventually have no time
for God and his brother, but only for himself and for his own follies.[1]

Learning to love and listen—and learning to plan and strategize as church leaders so our local body can listen to God and listen to our neighbors—has been an unanticipated theme of our story the past two decades. I share a bit of that story here with the hope that God will use this witness of His work in our local body to encourage you, to renew your hope in Him, or see fresh opportunities for learning to love and listen to Him and your neighbors in your context.

SIN AND REPENTANCE LEADING TO FRIENDSHIP

One morning in our first years in a new-to-us culture and country, I took the trash out. We lived on a busy urban street lined with rows of concrete apartment buildings towering over a series of inner courtyards. Our courtyard, like all the others, contained a long row of variously colored trash cans, each one the size of a compact car. On that spring morning, as I began to empty our trash into the various receptacles, one of our neighbors walked up behind me, tore a bag from my hands, and began to yell. "Why are you putting this bag in that container? Everyone knows it doesn't go there! You're a complete idiot!"

After a few months in the new city, I had learned that getting yelled at in public was a normal, everyday occurrence, as predictable as the sun rising in the east. "Being nice" was not a cultural value. However, just because I was used to getting yelled at regularly did not make the experience sting any less. And so, on that morning, at that trash can moment, I felt the fire of rage growing inside. I was so tired of being insulted, so tired of the meanness.

So what did I do? I yelled back at my neighbor. I'm not sure what I said (I was still learning the new language), but two things were clear: my neighbor knew I was angry, and my neighbor knew that I didn't care what she had to say to me. I shouted and threw my trash in whichever bin I pleased, and then escaped as quickly as possible behind the closed door of our ground floor apartment.

For a moment, it felt wonderful to release that anger. I felt completely justified in my actions. But slowly, the good feeling melted away as I realized that now I had to add something else to my to-do list each day:

---

1   Dietrich Bonhoeffer, *Life Together* (HarperOne, 2009).

"Avoid neighbor at all costs." I was terrified at the thought of having to face her again at the mailboxes, the tram stop, the bakery, in the stairway—or even at the trash cans. I began to peek out in the hallway and listen to make sure I heard no footsteps before I walked into the common staircase and courtyard. My sinful, looking-to-justify-myself thoughts spiraled and came up with amazing solutions to this need to hide, such as: "Well, since this neighborhood is obviously so hard, we should move to a new apartment building, somewhere easier! Oh yes, at the very least, we should plant a church in a different, more reachable neighborhood—God certainly can't want me to live here! Maybe this is a sign we should leave this city all together." Eventually I ended up at perhaps the darkest place in the downward spiral: "I'm just not sure there's any hope for these people."

Thankfully, the God of the Bible is a God who has, from the beginning of time, brought light into the darkness. For the purpose of His own glory, God keeps His promise to complete the good work He has started in us. Therefore, it wasn't long before the Holy Spirit began to show me not only the ugliness of what I had done, but also make me aware of the crazy logic I was using. What was my response to the meanness and darkness I'd experienced in the new city? My answer was to use the same tactics I had been suffering under: I yelled and did not seek to understand; I was judgmental; I was harsh.

So, if avoiding my neighbor wasn't the answer to the problem, what was? God's Word clearly told me what to do, but what it said was something that actually seemed even harder than continuing to hide from my neighbor or move our family to a new apartment. I needed to humble myself and ask my neighbor for forgiveness. This was God's cure for the hiding problem.

The thought of doing this made me nauseous; I wrestled with it for days. Wouldn't it make more sense to fix this in a different way? There must certainly be a more culturally-relevant way to handle this problem, right?

But over and over, God kept reminding me that His Word, His ways are the way to light, the way to life. Not my ways, His ways. Not my logic, His logic. And His Word clearly says that when we do wrong, we must repent, we must ask for forgiveness. There wasn't any alternative, there was no other way to bring light into the darkness of my sinful act against my neighbor.

So finally, one night I started the agonizing journey up the four flights of stairs to our neighbor's apartment. I pressed the buzzer outside her door with a shaking finger and thought I might pass out. She opened the door. I wanted to run away. But somehow, God enabled me to get the much-practiced, new language words across my lips, "Please forgive me for yelling at you at the trash cans. It was wrong of me to lose my temper. Thank you for trying to teach me how to throw the trash away correctly." The neighbor looked puzzled. After an awkward pause, I said, "That's all. I hope you have a nice evening."

While I had no idea what my neighbor was thinking, as I walked back down the stairs, I became aware of a new sense of freedom. I no longer had to hide; the shame and fear I had felt were gone! The next morning, I didn't need to cautiously open the front door to check if she was in the staircase. I no longer was tempted to avoid contact when I met her at the mailbox, but could instead look her in the eye and say, "Good morning." Eventually, she began to return the greeting.

When I was able to view the art through the lens of my neighbor's heart, by entering in and viewing it through this precious fellow image-bearer's soul instead of judging from the outside with my own eyes, the Holy Spirit allowed me to see what had been there all along and I knew what to say: our neighbor's art reminded me of the love of God.

A few months later, the doorbell to our apartment rang. When I opened the door, there stood our neighbor. In her extended hand, she held an invitation to the opening of her art exhibit in local gallery. With a smile and warm greeting, she told me she hoped we could come to her special night, her first-ever public exhibit in a new gallery.

A few weeks later, on a warm summer evening, my husband and I walked to the art exhibit and took in the scene. The high-ceilinged room was filled with neat rows of two-foot-tall sculptures, placed on separate podiums at eye level. What were the sculptures? Each one consisted entirely of repulsive refuse that had been littered on the city streets, piled up and glued together into mounded forms. Poured over the top of each mountain was melted red wax, partially covering over the debris. Each trash sculpture appeared to be soaking under ribbons of thick coagulated blood.

When I first placed my eyes on the art, it shocked and scared me. I hated it. I wanted to look away. I was then unsure how to interact with my neighbor. What would I say? How could I engage with her about this in a way that would build her up? When the line of admirers had slowed, we waited to congratulate her on her opening night. As we shook her hand, my husband thanked her for inviting us to her exhibit. Then he did something I wasn't expecting: instead of commenting on the work, he told her we would love to have more time with her to hear more about what she is communicating in her work, and invited our neighbor over for tea a few days later.

Soon after, the neighbor from whom I once hid was sitting on our couch. As we asked her to tell us more about her story, paging through the thick portfolio she had brought with her, the Holy Spirit opened up a window for us to begin to get to know her. As she spoke about her work, she revealed herself to us. I still found it hard to look at her art, but as I listened to her, the Holy Spirit began to help me see and understand. Our neighbor shared that the trash medium was intentionally ugly and repulsive. The idea of a mound of trash had inspired her as she was reflecting on a personal experience of violence that took place in our city. As a way of healing her wounds, as a form of lament, she would walk the streets in the dark of night, collecting tangible evidence of pain, loneliness, and disconnection left by others who had gone before her.

When I was able to view the art through the lens of my neighbor's heart, by entering in and viewing it through this precious fellow image-bearer's soul instead of judging from the outside with my own eyes, the Holy Spirit allowed me to see what had been there all along and I knew what to say: our neighbor's art reminded me of the love of God. "The love of God?" she asked. "How is that possible? Tell me more." With that invitation, we shared the overarching redemptive story of God, fitting her story snugly into the narrative: a repulsive "trash" mound of sin, death, and brokenness crying out in pain for healing only possible through the covering blood of a perfect Savior.

LOVING GOD AND LISTENING IN PRAYER: HOPE REPLACING HOPELESSNESS

As God used this story—my sin against my neighbor, His leading me to repentance, and His opening the door to a relationship because of it—our team saw the need for a radical shift in our own hearts and functional worldviews. We came to see that our functional beliefs about God and biblical anthropology were pointing away from the magnetic north on the compass of our hearts in Christ. Over time, God led us to several questions to interact with Him and each other in prayer on these issues.

The first was a challenge on where we were putting our trust: Are we primarily living like we believe that God is God—omnipotent, active, loving, redeeming, in charge? Or are we acting instead as though the culture or world around us is like God, with ultimate power over us and our neighbors? Are we living like there is no hope?

Those were the places in everyday life where we had tended to forget the perspective of God's real overarching story.

When we asked God that question, we realized that we had begun to believe a lie, a lie that the hopelessness of our task was more real and powerful than the hope of Christ. It is not hard to fall prey to this temptation when we are surrounded with the pain of life and the rejection of God by those we are living amongst. The teeth-clenching, white-knuckled hard work seems instead being able to hold on to hope. God's Word teaches us that it is a daily struggle to believe the gospel and not to be conformed to the world. It is a daily struggle to continue to love and extend grace to others just as we have been loved and given undeserving grace from Christ.

Therefore, when we as a core group of eight Christians gathered with the dream of seeing God raise up a church in the atheist neighborhood of 28,000 people where God had placed us, we knew this question of how to actively battle for hope vs. hopelessness was first on our priority list. Our number one strategy for the work of church planting, in that neighborhood where it seemed no one was interested in God, was to pray. We wanted to open the ears of our hearts, to spend time listening to God and each other, reminding each other of and proclaiming in prayer to one another the promises of God that are true today, even in the midst of an atheistic and hostile environment. We longed for the reality of God's promises in faith and His words of truth to be more real to us than what we could see in the world around us. We prayed in faith and hope that the Holy Spirit would allow our neighbors to know the reality of this truth as well. We walked together through the streets of our neighborhood, praying and asking God to rain His mercy down on these people in even greater measure than the copious amounts of annual rainfall, to open doors and show us how to engage with people who lived here as His kingdom was coming.

We began to tell each other this story intentionally in various ways through praying through Scripture and speaking about the Word together. And we needed to be reminded of this truth not only in a worship service, but as we went about mundane everyday life—in our kitchens, on the sidewalk in front of the grade school after that fight at breakfast, on the playground, at the grocery store, on the bike path after a hard day of work, via text message or during a phone call to discuss carpool logistics, after another week of unemployment, on the soccer field. Those were the places in everyday life where we had tended to forget the perspective of God's real overarching story.

And because I need to be reminded of this again today, for I am forgetful, and so are you—what is this story? Our amazing reality is that we worship a God who spoke creation into being. He is the God who has been pursuing His people with His mighty right hand and a Father's gracious love throughout the ages. He is a God who came to Earth to live in the form of a man, to live and suffer and die in order to defeat sin and redeem the people whom He so greatly loves. And this same God is reigning today, with all of creation placed under His feet. He is the Everlasting Father, Wonderful Counselor, Mighty God, Prince of Peace.

Yes, His ongoing story is true and relevant today. And although we do not deserve it, this amazing God not only saves and redeems, but in that process He makes us His children, and invites us into His family. We wear His robes of righteousness and are full heirs of His riches through Christ. Although it is a great mystery to us, He has also chosen to invite us to reign with Him now through Christ, to participate in His kingdom coming. Our God asks us to participate in the "going and making" of new disciples, to be a sort of midwife for new family members to whom He is giving birth, to be His ambassadors to work among the nations, to keep sharing and passing on our inheritance. And there is no need for sibling squabbles over the estate in this family, since each daughter or son has the full measure of wealth through Christ—and through generously giving this love and wealth to others around us, our own riches in Christ are never depleted. Our loving Father also does not leave us like orphans, but sends His power to us in the Holy Spirit, the same power that raised Christ from the dead. This amazing power lives in and leads us, testifying of the One to whom we belong, both individually and together in the church, and allows us to be His witnesses. We may feel few in number and powerless in our atheistic and secular community, but we are not powerless. We have been given the love and authority of Christ to love and serve our neighbors. Hallelujah and Amen!

LOVING OUR NEIGHBOR AND LISTENING IN PRAYER: OVERCOMING SIMILAR VS. DIFFERENT

Thus armed with the wind of this life-giving story so tangible it tousled our hair and made the leaves on the trees rustle, even in the midst of grieving in hard situations that did not suddenly disappear, we began to tackle the second "marrow-piercing" question, "Are we placing ourselves above our neighbor? Do we feel like we are so different from our neighbor that we struggle to know how to bridge the gulf between us?" In this question as well, the Spirit convicted us. At the heart of it, when we examined things we were saying or ways we responded to situations, we realized we were functionally believing that we were better than our neighbor. We all knew theologically this was not true—that no one deserves the grace of Christ—but we tended to think, "we are right, they are wrong," or, "if only they could be like us." We focused on differences or the gulf between us and our not-yet-believing neighbor, and generally felt like this distance might be insurmountable. The result of this was a hampered sense of freedom to engage those around us below surface-level conversation. Yes, we had some good motives. We longed for our neighbor to have the peace and joy we were able to know in Christ, but we still tended to emphasize the differences between us. Not only was this hurtful to our neighbor, but it revealed our own failure to see our daily need for Christ. We needed to confess this sin and ask forgiveness from God.

Each of us desperately needs His mercy and a life-giving connection to God through Christ each day in every moment, whether we already know Him or not. If we think this way about our neighbor, the imagined gulf between us quickly closes.

We began to ponder what it would look like if instead of emphasizing differences, we looked at what we have in common: each of us is a unique human being created in the image of God and each of us desperately needs His mercy and a life-giving connection to God through Christ each day in every moment, whether we already know Him or not. If we think this way about our neighbor, we realized the imagined gulf between us quickly closed. I began to experience an expectation of wonder at meeting any new image bearer, and even as an awkward introvert, I was not as tempted to be afraid of interacting with someone God placed near me.

RUN AFTER AND ... LISTEN

So, with a renewed perspective to emphasize "sameness" with our neighbor in a common daily need for Christ, resting on the base of the overarching redemptive story of God, our core group continued to ask God how we could follow His lead to see a church grow in our neighborhood. In Acts 8, God provides a practical strategy for listening:

> *Now an angel of the Lord said to Philip, 'Rise and go toward the south to the road that goes down from Jerusalem to Gaza.' This is a desert place. And he rose and went. And there was an Ethiopian, a eunuch, a court official of Candace, queen of the Ethiopians, who was in charge of all her treasure. He had come to Jerusalem to worship and was returning, seated in his chariot, and he was reading the prophet Isaiah. And the Spirit said to Philip, 'Go over and join this chariot.' So Philip ran to him . . . .* (Acts 8:26-30a)

In this passage, in the midst of a book of the Bible where we see the Holy Spirit doing miraculously crazy, otherworldly miracles that point so clearly to the power of God and cause people to follow Him, God works in this passage through Philip in a way that seems mundane by comparison. In this instance, God did not place Philip right in the chariot, as would seem to us the most efficacious use of his time. Instead God placed Philip on the dry desert road, and in order to reach the man to be able to speak with him about the gospel, Philip had to start running. Running! Philip had to physically exert himself in order to catch up to the chariot. The story continues in verse 30, "So Philip ran to him and heard him reading Isaiah the prophet . . . . "

Wait, what? After running down the road, Philip starts the conversation by—listening? Yes, the man whose role it was to preach the Good News first listened, and he listened long enough to hear what the man was thinking about. Then, when Philip did open his mouth to communicate with the eunuch, he does not begin by telling, but instead by asking a question. He first seeks to understand where the man is coming from. In the last part of verse 30, we hear Philip's question, "Do you understand what you are reading?"

In response, the eunuch said, "How can I, unless someone guides me?" And he invited Philip to come up and sit with him (Acts 30b-31). Philip not only first listened and sought to understand the eunuch, but he also waited for the man to invite him in before jumping into the carriage—even though the Holy Spirit had told him to join it.

The story continues:

> *Now the passage of the Scripture that he was reading was this: 'Like a sheep he was led to the slaughter and like a lamb before its shearer is silent, so he opens not his mouth. In his humiliation justice was denied him. Who can describe his generation? For his life is taken away from the earth.'*
>
> *And the eunuch said to Philip, 'About whom, I ask you, does the prophet say this, about himself or about someone else?' Then Philip opened his mouth, and beginning with this Scripture he told him the good news about Jesus. And as they were going along the road they came to some water, and the eunuch said, 'See, here is water! What prevents me from being baptized?' And he commanded the chariot to stop, and they both went down into the water, Philip and the eunuch, and he baptized him.* (Acts 8:32-38)

As we asked God how to work as a church body in our neighborhood, we sensed the Holy Spirit moving us the way He had led Philip. He was encouraging us, "Here is your strategy: run after your neighbors and listen to them! Go to the places where they are and walk with them on their terms, not yours."

Just as Philip went to the eunuch on the desert road, so could we go to the locations where our neighbors were traveling, so to speak. Our neighbors may not have been interested in coming to church, but we could "run" to meet them at the park, around the dining room table, at a birthday party, art gallery, grocery store, bank, school, sidewalk, playground, restaurant, theater, and on and on. The possibilities of where we could witness were too numerous to list. What a change of perspective—instead of focusing on not being able to meet our neighbors to love them with the love of Christ at the church building, we began to focus on the places where we could connect, as individuals and as a body, to walk with our not-yet-believing neighbors in our community.

PLANNING TO LOVE AND LISTEN

The plans and strategies of our current church plant have developed and changed over time as a result of these stories God has written on our lives. God is leading us to re-evaluate, to pray and ask Him what activities we should do for a particular season to be transformed by His love and so we can listen to our neighbors to love them well. Some seasons we see much growth, some seasons we do not. This is not surprising since we are not the Holy Spirit and cannot make life. But together as a body of believers, we are experiencing a culture that is more hopeful than ever before with more connections in our community as we continue to tell each other the stories of God, learning to recognize Him working in the mundane of every day, and learning to listen to and love our neighbors in the midst of real life. Our current church plant began with eight believers in 2011. Six years later, we have witnessed God bring at least 45 new disciples to faith and join the active community of believers, from children and teenagers to 87-year-olds and everything in between.

We thank God for doing immeasurably more than we could have asked or imagined, both in our hearts and in the hearts of our neighbors. We do not know what tomorrow will bring in terms of conversions or growth. We do not yet know the full range of needs of our community or what our neighbor will face in three months. We have to live in dependence, to run after and listen like Philip to find that out. We have so much still to learn about God's love, how to listen to Him and how to love and listen to our neighbors. What we are sure of today is that God is God, and until Jesus comes back, He will be leading us as His people to be His witnesses by transforming us in His love and bringing starving orphans to the family feast—in the place where He has placed us, and in the place where He has placed you.

The writer has been serving with MTW in Europe for almost two decades and writes as a witness of what God has been doing in Christ through the living together and co-laboring of MTW teammates, national brothers and sisters, and neighbors in the place where they serve. The author remains anonymous because this is not solely one person's story to tell and for privacy reasons in the community where they serve.

21

The Counterintuitive Use of God's Power

by Jud Lamos

According to Wikipedia, that ubiquitous repository of all human wisdom: ". . . a counter-intuitive proposition is one that does not seem likely to be true when assessed using intuition, common sense, or gut feelings."

Say it ain't so.

I really want my gut feelings to be right. So much of who I am and so much of what I do is a result of an unwritten, internal code that I often call common sense. It is the wellspring of all my unspoken assumptions and my finely honed biases.

The Bible is different. It is a precious revelation of God's wisdom. It is His sense. It is, quite literally, His Living Word. It isn't common at all. In fact, it is always counterintuitive when viewed from a human perspective.

This is never more evident than in situations where we want to make something happen. James refers to this natural desire to produce in his New Testament epistle:

> *Come now, you who say, "Today or tomorrow we will go into such and such a town and spend a year there and trade and make a profit"—yet you do not know what tomorrow will bring. What is your life? For you are a mist that appears for a little time and then vanishes. Instead you ought to say, "If the Lord wills, we will live and do this or that." As it is you boast in your arrogance. All such boasting is evil.* (James 4:13-16 ESV)

A parallel passage can be found in the gospel of Luke where he recorded this parable, taught by our Lord:

> *"The land of a rich man produced plentifully and he thought to himself, 'What shall I do, for I have nowhere to store my crops?' And he said, 'I will do this: I will tear down my barns and build larger ones, and there I will store all my grain and goods. And I will say to my soul, "Soul, you have ample goods laid up for many years; relax, eat, drink and be merry."' But God said to him, 'Fool! This night your soul is required of you, and the things you have prepared, whose will they be?' So is the one who lays up treasure for himself and is not rich toward God."* (Luke 12:18-21 ESV)

I believe there are two levels of human activity that are addressed by these passages of Scripture. One level is activity that is directed and controlled by and toward self. The second level is activity that is directed toward God but controlled by self.

In my mind I hear some young missionary candidate asking, "Is missions a place for the unambitious, the unfocused, those lacking motivation and those unconcerned with product?" No! Missions is not a place for the unambitious.

THE WORLDLY ALLURE OF MINISTRY SUCCESS

Recently Jan and I spent a month mentoring new missionaries at MTW's Cross Cultural Ministry Internship in Brussels, Belgium. One young couple had been called out of careers in corporate America. And the husband had worked closely with the U.S. Armed Services. They struggled, initially, with the pace of missionary "work."

Why? I would suggest that they were used to getting things done—and quickly. You don't last long in the corporate or military world if you can't produce and produce on schedule.

But in my mind, I hear some young missionary candidate asking, "Is missions, then, a place for the unambitious, the unfocused, those lacking motivation and those unconcerned with product?" No! Missions is not a place for the unambitious.

Christ's disciples were not an unambitious group, however unfocused they may have seemed at times. Much of their missionary internship was spent focusing and refocusing on kingdom truths that were counterintuitive to their natural senses—but also learning to do God's work in God's way and in God's time.

Peter is a prime example. He had what the corporate world would call a Type A personality. Peter was a businessman. He wasn't only a fisherman; he owned a boat. Although it may have been a family business, he was obviously a prime driver for that business. He was used to making executive decisions.

As we read the gospel accounts of Peter's tutelage under Christ's leadership, we see a person who starts ministry as an proud, impatient, driven, impulsive workaholic who hated delays and ambivalence. Over time, we see a transformation in Peter that produces a repentant, humble sinner devoted to and dependent on God.

I have news for our young corporate friends. Drive, self-reliance, impatience, and workaholism is not only endemic in the business world—it's a pernicious virus that infects the world of ministry as well.

Let's take a look at the Apostle Paul. Another Type-A personality. In this case, a religious professional. Just take a look at Paul's CV in Philippians 3:

> *If anyone else thinks he has reason for confidence in the flesh, I have more: circumcised on the eighth day; of the people of Israel; of the tribe of Benjamin; a Hebrew of the Hebrews; as to the law a Pharisee; as to zeal, a persecutor of the church; as to righteousness under the law, blameless.* (Philippians 3:4-6 ESV)

The first section of his ministry CV is related to his perfect religious heritage—but the second section relates to his drive to leverage that perfect religious heritage into perfect religious performance. How? According to Paul himself, "in the flesh." Drive, impatience, pride, work, work, work.

GOD'S CALL TO HUMBLE DEPENDENCE

In both cases, Peter's and Paul's, God did something gracious. He sovereignly intervened. He chipped away patiently and lovingly at the ungodly passions, drives, sensibilities, and self-made truths that kept

Peter and Paul—once they were focused on God's will—doing His will in His way.

He took their worldly ambitions and turned them into kingdom ambitions. He took their fleshly ability and self confidence and turned it into Spirit-filled dependence on, and Christ-like confidence in Him. He humbled them.

Paul, even after his dramatic conversion and Spirit-led growth in faith, was tempted to attach a sense of self-worth to ministry success. In 2 Corinthians 11, Paul indulges in foolish boasting in order to correct misperceptions in the Corinthian church. In a sense, this is his revised CV, listing the kinds of things that previously would have caused him to boast, were those boasts not worthless in light of God's real work in his life.

In speaking of the wonders of revelation he had experienced he wrote:

> *So to keep me from becoming conceited because of the surpassing of the revelations, a thorn was given me in the flesh, a messenger of Satan to harass me, to keep me from becoming conceited. Three times I pleaded with the Lord about this, that it should leave me. But he said to me, "My grace is sufficient for you for my power is made perfect in weakness." Therefore I will boast all the more gladly of my weaknesses, so that the power of Christ may rest upon me. For the sake of Christ, then, I am content with weaknesses, insults, hardships, persecutions and calamities. For when I am weak, then I am strong.* (2 Corinthians 12:7-10 ESV)

Peter's transition from extreme self-confidence to an abject emptying of self occurred during the arrest of Jesus our Lord. Impulsive, self-confident, get-it-done Peter starts this transformative journey in the Garden of Gethsemane when he cuts off the ear of the High Priest's servant. Evidently no one knows more about what needs to be done in this instance than Peter himself. Especially Christ.

Just prior to this, at a moment when Jesus predicts that all will desert him, Peter claims that he will never deny his Lord. "Never, no never. Not me, Lord." Peter's act of armed resistance seems to underline this loyal sentiment perfectly. Peter is willing to make his loyalty a matter of life and death.

Immediately, Peter's quickly formed military insurrection unravels. Let's look at the scriptural account in Mark:

And when they had sung a hymn, they went out to the Mount of Olives. And Jesus said to them, "You will all fall away, for it is written, 'I will strike the shepherd, and the sheep will be scattered.' But after I am raised up, I will go before you to Galilee." Peter said to him, "Even though they all fall away, I will not." And Jesus said to him, "Truly, I tell you, this very night, before the rooster crows twice, you will deny me three times." But he said emphatically, "If I must die with you, I will not deny you." And they all said the same.

And they went to a place called Gethsemane. And he said to his disciples, "Sit here while I pray." And he took with him Peter and James and John, and began to be greatly distressed and troubled. And he said to them, "My soul is very sorrowful, even to death. Remain here and watch." And going a little farther, he fell on the ground and prayed that, if it were possible, the hour might pass from him. And he said, "Abba, Father, all things are possible for you. Remove this cup from me. Yet not what I will, but what you will." And he came and found them sleeping, and he said to Peter, "Simon, are you asleep? Could you not watch one hour? Watch and pray that you may not enter into temptation. The spirit indeed is willing, but the flesh is weak." And again he went away and prayed, saying the same words. And again he came and found them sleeping, for their eyes were very heavy, and they did not know what to answer him. And he came the third time and said to them, "Are you still sleeping and taking your rest? It is enough; the hour has come. The Son of Man is betrayed into the hands of sinners. Rise, let us be going; see, my betrayer is at hand."

And immediately, while he was still speaking, Judas came, one of the twelve, and with him a crowd with swords and clubs, from the chief priests and the scribes and the elders. Now the betrayer had given them a sign, saying, "The one I will kiss is the man. Seize him and lead him away under guard." And when he came, he went up to him at once and said, "Rabbi!" And he kissed him. And they laid hands on him and seized him. But one of those who stood by drew his sword and struck the servant of the high priest and cut off his ear. And Jesus said to them, "Have you come out as against a robber, with swords and clubs to capture me? Day after day I was with you in the temple teaching, and you did not seize me. But let the Scriptures be fulfilled." And they all left him and fled.

And a young man followed him, with nothing but a linen cloth about his body. And they seized him, but he left the linen cloth and ran away naked.

And they led Jesus to the high priest. And all the chief priests and the elders and the scribes came together. And Peter had followed him at a distance, right into the courtyard of the high priest. And he was sitting with the guards and warming himself at the fire. Now the chief priests and the whole Council were seeking testimony against Jesus to put him to death, but they found none. For many bore false witness against him, but their testimony did not agree. And some stood up and bore false witness against him, saying, "We heard him say, 'I will destroy this temple that is made with hands, and in three days I will build another, not made with hands.'" Yet even about this their testimony did not agree. And the high priest stood up in the midst and asked Jesus, "Have you no answer to make? What is it that these men testify against you?" But he remained silent and made no answer. Again the high priest asked him, "Are you the Christ, the Son of the Blessed?" And Jesus said, "I am, and you will see the Son of Man seated at the right hand of Power, and coming with the clouds of heaven." And the high priest tore his garments and said, "What further witnesses do we need? You have heard his blasphemy. What is your decision?" And they all condemned him as deserving death. And some began to spit on him and to cover his face and to strike him, saying to him, "Prophesy!" And the guards received him with blows.

And as Peter was below in the courtyard, one of the servant girls of the high priest came, and seeing Peter warming himself, she looked at him and said, "You also were with the Nazarene, Jesus." But he denied it, saying, "I neither know nor understand what you mean." And he went out into the gateway and the rooster crowed. And the servant girl saw him and began again to say to the bystanders, "This man is one of them." But again he denied it. And after a little while the bystanders again said to Peter, "Certainly you are one of them, for you are a Galilean." But he began to invoke a curse on himself and to swear, "I do not know this man of whom you speak." And immediately the rooster crowed a second time. And Peter remembered how Jesus had said to him, "Before the rooster crows twice, you will deny me three times." And he broke down and wept. (Mark 14:27-72 ESV)

What was the difference between God's plan and Peter's? God's great, eternal kingdom was ushered in by a unique spiritual victory—a victory that was accomplished through suffering, weakness, and death—not health, wealth, and strength. Eternal death was conquered by temporal death. Eternal suffering was conquered by temporal suffering. Eternal strength was obtained through temporal weakness.

Christ predicted that this victory over weakness, suffering, and death would be ushered in by rejection. Peter's bitter weeping in verse 72, I believe, is his final acceptance of how totally contrary his plan is in relation to God's.

God's great, eternal kingdom was ushered in by a unique spiritual victory—a victory that was accomplished through suffering, weakness, and death— not health, wealth, and strength. Eternal death was conquered by temporal death. Eternal suffering was conquered by temporal suffering. Eternal strength was obtained through temporal weakness.

GOD'S POWER DISPLAYED IN OUR SUFFERING, WEAKNESS, AND DEATH

Shortly after our family moved from Turkey to Belgium in 2001, I began to participate in a prison ministry in Brussels. A significant proportion of the male prison population was made up of Muslim-background, immigrant men. These men represented the most disenfranchised segment of society that I could find.

One result, a minor one, of that ministry led to my speaking in a church in Holland that supported that prison ministry. After I spoke, a couple came up to me and asked me to pray that they would receive spiritual power. I don't know that there was any connection in their minds between prison ministry and their request, but I immediately saw one.

Jesus emptied Himself of His power and glory in order to conquer. He came to set prisoners free—not by breaking down prison walls but by becoming a prisoner Himself. He came to save the rejected by being rejected. He came to save the poor by being poor. He came to save the weak by being weak.

Our success in ministry is based on a biblically accurate, counterintuitive understanding of God's truth—that the means of success belong to God alone and that they are always exactly opposite to human-based effort.

I told the couple in Holland that it was my belief that they would gain true spiritual power if I prayed for them to be rejected, to be impoverished, to suffer illness, to be misunderstood, and through it all to serve those who rejected them with love and mercy. I asked them if that is how they wanted me to pray. They shook their heads no and walked away.

In 1 Peter, chapter 4, we see a very different Peter than the one we see in Mark, chapter 4:

> *Beloved, do not be surprised at the fiery trial when it comes upon you to test you, as though something strange were happening to you. But rejoice insofar as you share Christ's sufferings, that you may also rejoice and be glad when his glory is revealed. If you are insulted for the name of Christ, you are blessed, because the Spirit of glory and of God rests upon you. But let none of you suffer as a murderer or a thief or an evildoer or as a meddler. Yet if anyone suffers as a Christian, let him not be ashamed, but let him glorify God in that name. For it is time for judgment to begin at the household of God; and if it begins with us, what will be the outcome for those who do not obey the gospel of God? And "If the righteous is scarcely saved, what will become of the ungodly and the sinner?" Therefore let those who suffer according to God's will entrust their souls to a faithful Creator while doing good.*
> (1 Peter 4:12-19 ESV)

In Philippians 3:11, we see Paul seeking a better knowledge of Christ and His resurrection power through suffering:

> *But whatever gain I had, I counted as loss for the sake of Christ. Indeed, I count everything as loss because of the surpassing worth of knowing*

Christ Jesus my Lord. For his sake I have suffered the loss of all things and count them as rubbish, in order that I may gain Christ and be found in him, not having a righteousness of my own that comes from the law, but that which comes through faith in Christ, the righteousness from God that depends on faith—that I may know him and the power of his resurrection, and may share his sufferings, becoming like him in his death, that by any means possible I may attain the resurrection from the dead. (Philippians 3:7-11 ESV)

God's power, for us, is power to suffer and die. Our success in ministry is based on a biblically accurate, counterintuitive understanding of God's truth—that the means of success belong to God alone and that they are always exactly opposite to human-based effort. When we pray "Thy kingdom come, Thy will be done on earth as it is in heaven," we cannot insert our own measures of success or our own means of accomplishing that prayer.

Paul said, "For me to live is Christ and to die is gain." Dietrich Bonhoeffer said, "When Christ calls a man, he bids him come and die." What is our response?

After graduate school and working in industry for a number years, Jud and his wife, Jan, joined Operation Mobilization (OM). In 1990 they joined Mission to the World. Jud has a B.A in Writing from Houghton College, an MA in Political Theory from Temple University and studied in a cross-disciplinary Southwest Asia/ North African graduate program. Jud was the International Director for Restricted Access Countries for MTW for several years. He is The 18.26 Network Director, which is a new global vocational ministry.

22

That the Little Ones Would Hear The Gospel

by Susan Newkirk

It's a cold winter morning in Westlake, South Africa. April[1] turns over and wakes her sister in the one-room shack where they live. Migrants from Malawi, her family members live in a dwelling made of corrugated metal that doesn't keep the heat or the cold out. But April's parents are Christians who love their children.

Across Westlake in a cement-block house, Grace lives in a much different environment. She may have four solid walls, a bathroom in her home, and nice clothes, but she is an orphan who has been sexually abused. The relatives she lives with taunt her with comments about how she is just like her mother, but not in a good sense. She is South African, of mixed race descent.

These girls are two of the 18.6 million reasons that outreach to children in South Africa is not only necessary, but strategic. In a country with a population of 53 million, almost half of its inhabitants are under the age of 18. In 2013 South Africa had 3.7 million orphans, half of whom had lost one or both parents to AIDS. More shocking is the fact that more than 150,000 of these children are believed to be living in child-headed households.[2]

South Africa is not alone. One third of the world population today is under the age of 15. World Vision estimates that 80 percent of young people worldwide, 1.4 billion, are growing up in non-Christian homes.[3] This growing demographic has become known as the 4/14 window. Unlike its counterpart, the geographic 10/40 window, the 4/14 window is a demographic window, named by Dr. Luis Bush. On the 4to14window.com website, the 4/14 window represents the largest unreached people group in the 10/40 window—namely, children between the ages of 4 and 14. Author and Pastor Kenny Conley posted in 2011 that "only 15 percent of global missions giving goes toward efforts to reach children with the gospel," but "60-80 percent of all responses to the gospel are made by children."[4]

One third of the world population today is under the age of 15. World Vision estimates that 80 percent of young people worldwide, 1.4 billion, are growing up in non-Christian homes. This growing demographic has become known as the 4/14 window.

If asked whether children's ministry is important today, most would say it is, perhaps thinking of their own children when they respond. But how many churches have a full-time children's minister/worker on staff? How many MTW teams dedicated to planting churches have full-time team members devoted specifically to child evangelism and discipleship? As a long-term MTW missionary working full time in children's ministry, I confess that until the Lord very solidly pointed me in this direction, children's ministry was not on my radar. Statistics showing the need for children's ministry may be useful for sparking our interest, but the Word of God offers the better motivation for our involvement in reaching them for Christ.

CHILDREN'S MINISTRY: A BIBLICAL IMPERATIVE

Early on in the Bible we find a basis for ministering not only to adults, but also to children. Genesis 17:7 points to a covenant established by God and given to Abraham and his descendants for generations to come. The sign of the covenant was the circumcision of male children. This physical sign pointed to a spiritual circumcision of the hearts of His people, who would live in the land God gave them, under His blessing and rule. If the Israelites failed to circumcise their young, God commanded them to circumcise all the adult males (see Joshua 5:6-8). Male children were not only included in the covenant between God and His chosen people; they were the recipients of the sign of that covenant, usually as a child.

Deuteronomy 6 further proves that God's promises extend not just to adults, but also to children. Entire families were to participate in the learning and following of God's law. Parents were commanded in Deuteronomy 6:7-9 to "impress them [God's commandments] on your children. Talk about them when you sit at home and when you walk along the road, when you lie down and when you get up. Tie them as symbols on your hands and bind them on your foreheads. Write them on the doorframes of your houses and on your gates." Every member of a Jewish family learned the commandments given to Moses on Mount Sinai. There were no age restrictions or waiting until the children were tucked into bed to study God's law.

Children are not only validated in Matthew 19, they are pointed to as the example to follow because the kingdom of heaven belongs "to such as these."

While that was the model for Jewish families in their homes, it is by no means the only needed context for teaching God's Word to children. Susan Hunt, in her book *Heirs of the Covenant*, points out the necessity not just for this model of experiential teaching, but for formal instruction as well. "God's covenant had to be the reference point for their life experiences, or the experiences would become the reference point," she wrote.[5] Just before he died, "Moses wrote down this law and gave it to the priests . . . then Moses commanded them: 'Assemble the people—men, women and children, and the aliens living in your towns—so that they can listen and learn to fear the LORD your God and follow carefully all the words of this law. Their children, who do not know this law, must hear it and learn to fear the LORD your God . . . '" (Deuteronomy 31:9-13). Even those who weren't Israelites were included in this command. How much more then, this side of Jesus's death and resurrection, should we be bringing the gospel and Bible teaching to the "aliens" in our mission contexts today.

The command to teach children continues in the New Testament when Jesus addresses the subject very clearly. Sparked by His disciples shooing children away when they came to see Him in Matthew 19:13-15, Jesus rebukes them: "Let the little children come to me, and do not hinder them, for the kingdom of heaven belongs to such as these." One

255

could try to argue that the Deuteronomy passages only applied to Jewish families under the Old Covenant. But this passage proves otherwise. Children are not only validated in Matthew 19, they are pointed to as the example to follow because the kingdom of heaven belongs "to such as these." One chapter earlier, Jesus raised the stakes even more when He said that if anyone caused "one of these little ones who believe in me to sin, it would be better for him to have a large millstone hung around his neck and to be drowned in the depths of the sea." Verses like these not only make me sit up and take notice when I prepare a Bible lesson for children, they bring a proper sense of fear and trembling at the consequence of causing a child to stumble.

The subject must have been important to the Lord, or he would not have continued bringing up the topic so often. In Matthew 18:10-14, Jesus warns His audience, namely His disciples, to not look down on "one of these little ones" and compares them to a lost sheep. In the same way the shepherd would go after the missing little sheep, our "Father in heaven is not willing that any of these little ones should be lost." The fact that both the gospels of Mark (Mark 10:13-16) and Luke (Luke 18:15-17) include this same teaching points to its importance in the scope of Jesus' ministry. Jesus Himself stayed behind in the temple for three days asking questions of the teachers when he was 12 years old. If He Himself, the second person of the Trinity and God Incarnate, sets the example who are we to ignore it? Children not only need to hear the gospel, they need to be taught the Bible in child-appropriate ways. Unlike cultural beliefs that say that babies are not sinful by nature, or that children don't have souls until they're adults, we know that children are sinful from birth and are able to understand the gospel and come to faith at a young age.

There are plenty of other Bible references to support the value of children's ministry. In John 6, it is a little boy whose lunch was used to feed 5,000 men and their families. When Paul led the Philippian jailer and his family to belief in Christ, he baptized the entire family, which must have included children (Acts 16:31-34). Four times in these verses, the author Luke emphasizes that Paul reached out to the jailer and his "household" (v. 31), to "all the others in the house" (v. 32); that he baptized "[the jailer] and all his family" (v. 33), and as a result the Philippian jailer "had come to believe in God—he and his whole family" (v. 34).

REACHING CHILDREN THROUGH MISSIONS

So in the wake of biblical proof and eye-opening statistics pointing to the need to not only include but also prioritize children in our aim to reach the world for Christ, what do we do now? How does a mission organization, and specifically MTW, begin to adapt its philosophy of ministry to reach the most strategic demographic in the world? How do each of us in our specific contexts start reaching out to children with the gospel?

We begin with prayer, not as an end, but as the fuel for action. Then we look for a need and start planning how to meet it. Church-planting teams can look for ways to minister to parents and children in their communities. In the context of the church, children's ministry is aimed at serving families and helping parents teach their own kids about Christ. Here in South Africa, I see church volunteers teach the Bible as part of the curriculum in public and private schools, or at after-school Bible clubs in poor communities. Children's ministry workers meet with small groups of children or one on one to study the Bible. There are plenty of creative ways to engage the children in our ministry contexts.

The important issue is not laboring over how to bring all the bells and whistles of a children's ministry in the U.S. into a foreign context where we serve. Sometimes that can do more damage than good. The key is starting where we are, with what we have.

I work through a South African church (Tokai Community Church) of 350 members, which sees nearby Westlake Village as part of its "Jerusalem" mission field (Acts 1:8). Volunteers from within the ranks of the church help with Bible clubs for children, a soccer ministry, a feeding program, and a women's outreach. The church's prayer is for Westlake residents to one day lead these ministries. After four years, God has begun to answer that prayer by bringing Christine[6] to our church.

Christine is a 22-year-old Westlake resident who believes the Lord wants her to not only attend Tokai Community Church, but to be a part of reaching her community for Christ. However, the road to reaching this goal is not a straight one. She assisted with Bible clubs at the local school and was being discipled and trained to eventually teach the Bible to children in her community. However, the reality of needing to work full time and also deal with areas of sin in her life meant she had to walk a different road for a time. But the desire to reach her community for the Lord is still strong. As a resident, she understands the need better than anyone. Westlake began as the result of a redevelopment project to provide housing for 2,000 people squatting on a piece of property wanted by a developer. It has grown into a community of more than 8,000 people living in 650 houses and 850 shacks. More than 30 percent of the working age population is unemployed, and more than 30 percent are HIV positive. Christine seeks to participate in God's plan to bring hope to a community of darkness and dysfunction.

The important issue is not laboring over how to bring all the bells and whistles of a children's ministry in the U.S. into a foreign context where we serve. The key is starting where we are, with what we have.

Each of the mission contexts in which MTW missionaries serve probably has a "Christine" waiting to being raised up by God to serve her community. Children's ministry begins with relationships, not only with children, but with their parents. It is built through long hours of playing soccer with kids in a community, or drinking tea with their parents while listening to their life stories. For seven years, our church sent volunteers to lead a Bible club for girls in Westlake. It started with four girls and grew to more than 50. Other churches hosting events in the community attracted far more children than we did. We didn't give out food or have "hip" Christian music or games. We often asked ourselves why they came back each week, especially those who seemed bent on misbehaving. I believe the Lord was using those Tuesday afternoons of relationship-building through studying the Bible and praying together week after week to work in the hearts of those girls. Some came to faith in Christ, others did not. Some of the fruit of teaching God's Word to these girls we may never see.

IDENTIFYING RESOURCES
Teaching God's Word to children brings some challenges with it. Good resources that are contextual and have solid Bible content can be hard to find. I borrow curriculum and ideas from other children's ministry workers in the area and use materials from websites. One option for curriculum that is high quality while being cost effective is created by

St. Helen's Church in London. "Mustard Seeds"[7] (mustard-seeds.net) is a children's ministry resource that includes curriculum for toddlers and series of lesson units for ages 3-11. Mustard Seeds is also in the process of developing language packs to accompany each unit, providing children with take home material in their own languages. The beauty of these lessons is the adaptability of them to different age groups. Each lesson has teaching ideas for younger and older children. Application and examples tend to be from a British perspective, but games and activities are easily adaptable to any culture. No curriculum is perfect, and finding what works best for one specific context requires research. The trickiest part is finding visual aids that are suitable for the children in your mission context. One excellent resource for Bible story visual aids is "Ultimate Visual Aids," a CD-ROM set put out by Scripture Union.[8] It includes clip-art type illustrations that are true to the original Bible context. Images can be colored by hand, or colored with computer software and printed.

At the end of the day, it is the Lord Who will bring people to Himself. But being well-prepared, making prayer a focal point of the ministry, and keeping the Bible central in every teaching opportunity are vital components of outreach.

Child Evangelism Fellowship (CEF)[9] also offers curriculum for many cross-cultural contexts, including Africa. This organization focuses heavily on evangelism to children and sells useful props and gospel-telling materials. Every lesson has a gospel outline included in it, which can lead to children being desensitized to the message as they hear it week after week. However, CEF materials are effective, especially as they are created for use in different cultural contexts.

Most of the children with whom my church works in Westlake have little previous Bible knowledge. One of the tools we have found most effective in introducing the overall scope of the Bible is "The King, the Snake and the Promise," (also called "The Bible in 10 Easy Lessons").[10] This curriculum is written from an Australian perspective, but can be adapted to other cultural contexts. Missing from the lesson plans is the story of Moses and the Exodus, which the curriculum writers suggest doing as a Vacation Bible School or camp during the course of 10 weeks. The CD-ROM includes sheet music, vocal tracks for songs, craft and game ideas, and a word-for-word text for even the least-experienced teacher. The follow-up to this curriculum, "Meet the King,"[11] has lessons from the book of Mark, focusing on the kingship of Jesus. Its format is similar in style to its predecessor.

Good materials in themselves do not guarantee an effective children's program. At the end of the day, it is the Lord Who will bring people to Himself. But being well-prepared, making prayer a focal point of the ministry, and keeping the Bible central in every teaching opportunity are vital components of outreach. Building relationships is also key in reaching people, young or old.

Grace and April have heard the gospel, but so many still have not. What will we do with the 1.4 billion children under the age of 15 who are yet to be reached? Can we go on ignoring them or seeing them merely as a means to reach their parents? Our Father in heaven is not willing that any of these little ones should be lost. My prayer is that we won't either.

Susan Newkirk has served since 2008 with MTW, doing children's and women's ministry in a disadvantaged community in Cape Town, South Africa. Previously she was an MTW missionary in Madrid, Spain from 1994-1996. She came to Christ after hearing the gospel from her Sunday school teacher as a child. Susan enjoys traveling, especially going on safari game drives.

1   All names have been changed for child protection purposes.

2   Statistics South Africa (2003-2014), *General Household Survey 2002-2013*, (Pretoria, Cape Town: Statistics South Africa). Analysis by Katherine Hall and Winnie Sambu, Children's Institute, University of Cape Town. Posted on childrencount.ci.org.za.

3   Children's Ministries Institute, a Ministry of Child Evangelism Fellowship, cefcmi.com (Warrenton, Missouri: 2014).

4   Kenny Conley, "The 4-14 Window" (childrensministryonline.com, 2011).

5   Susan Hunt, *Heirs of the Covenant*, (Wheaton, Illinois: Crossway Books, 1998).

6   Name changed for confidentiality purposes.

7   Mustard-seeds.net, "Children's Ministry Resource" (London: TnT Ministries).

8   Pauline Adams and Judith Merrell, "Ultimate Visual Aids" (Scripture Union, 2008).

9   Child Evangelism Fellowship, cefonline.com (Warrenton, Missouri).

10 Phil and Louise Campbell, "The Bible in 10 Easy Lessons," also titled "The King, the Snake and the Promise," (Australia: Emu Music, 1998).

11 Phil Campbell, "Meet the King" (Australia: Emu Music, 2003). Available on Matthias Media website (matthiasmedia.com.au), which has online stores in the U.S. and Australia.

23

From Church Planting to "Human Planting"

by Turgay Üçal
(written by Mellissa Kelley based on interviews with the author)

When I was a recently converted Christian living in Istanbul, Turkey, in 1986, I had no idea how to grow in Christ to maturity, and even less of an idea of how my life would change as a result of my new faith.

In my early Christian walk I felt like a project, a canvas upon which a number of Christian ministries wanted to paint their goals and ideas, and this false friendship at times made me feel used. I was disillusioned with the competitive and impersonal evangelistic techniques and cookie-cutter methods of discipleship I experienced. There was an over-focus on numbers and results, and it nearly destroyed my spiritual life just as it was beginning.

I hungered for something more authentic, more honest, a true walk with Jesus that reflected who He really was. That path eventually led me to learn more about first-century Jesus and how to model His methods of teaching and discipleship in our current context. Approaching faith in this way has revitalized my walk with Christ and renewed my passion for reaching people who are hungry for a transforming relationship with God.

Now, pastoring the Istanbul Presbyterian Church more than 30 years later, I have learned much, grown much, and have more fully-formed opinions about how to share Christ authentically in a Muslim context.

The core concept, to me, is focusing on relationally-driven "human planting" instead of a programmatic focus on traditional church planting. To me, this is the difference between a duty-bound, self-propelled faith and a rich, fruitful life of love and joy in Christ.

HUMAN PLANTING VS. CHURCH PLANTING

Back in the 1980s, my Muslim parents and extended family were openly hostile about my conversion, with some of them even believing I was a spy for the Greek government. This type of pushback was devastating and it took many years of walking in faith to calm their fears, but these struggles were not surprising. I knew that Muslim and Turkish culture would not accept one of their own embracing Christ.

What I didn't expect was to effectively become a pawn within the small world of Christian missionaries and organizations in Istanbul at the time. As a new believer, I was pulled this way and that by multiple Christian ministries; I even attended "competing" Christian services in the same cathedral in downtown Istanbul—in the mornings a Latin mass with a Catholic congregation, and in the evenings an informal Protestant Armenian congregation strumming guitars.

I want to paint a picture of what a misguided missions strategy looks like from the viewpoint of nationals, and to cast a vision for a new, more authentic, more fruitful way of encouraging nationals to do ministry in their own backyard.

As one of very few Muslim-background believers openly living out my faith in Istanbul, I was highly sought by multiple Christians to become the poster child of their movement. Several of these believers pressed me into ministry before I had even been fully discipled myself. Unfortunately, this formative experience continues to color the way I view formula-driven ministry.

Why am I telling you all of this? To paint a picture of what a misguided missions strategy looks like from the viewpoint of nationals, and to cast a vision for a new, more authentic, more fruitful way of encouraging nationals to do ministry in their own backyard.

The core of this work is what I call "human planting." Spiritually and figuratively, this concept is a reaction against the kind of church planting that relies heavily on programs, methods, formulas, buildings, and money as a way of pushing ministry forward. That kind of church planting sees the big picture rather than the individual person, numbers over relationships, and opportunity over engagement.

In contrast, human planting is focused on lovingly hunting individual human beings and saving them from their basic animal level of egoism, with the hopes of restoring them to the beautiful image of God that He intended. It desires this transformation for the good of the other, friend to friend, not to fulfill quotas or to reach a program goal. I have faith that this approach will yield great kingdom rewards. For we know that if a person changes, nations change.

Human planting sees and values each human being—reaching one person at a time while giving him space to bring his own gifts and visions. We don't need more big plans and projects. We simply need relationships on the human level. Instead of putting people into our own boxes, we should encourage them to create their own boxes. Maybe we will discover new and better boxes by journeying with them in this way.

FIRST CENTURY EXPLORATION

Though I progressed in ministry for several decades after my conversion, and by all outward appearances that ministry seemed to be thriving, I continued to feel dissonance with the mission partners who shaped our church activities and plans to fit within their Western paradigm. There seemed to be an underlying assumption—America is a place of success, and as our partner you must be successful in your Christian faith and ministry also.

This intensified my perception that Christianity was a big, institutional entity to be reckoned with, rather than a personal, day-by-day relationship with Jesus. Under this colonial mentality, I found that I never attained Christianity as my own.

But a turning point came in 2008. I had an "a-ha moment": How could I, as a Turk wrestling with a Western form of Christianity, learn from first-century, Middle Eastern Jesus? What could I learn from Him about ministering to people in my context?

I decided to seek out a Jewish rabbi in Istanbul to learn more about the world in which Jesus lived. This rabbi led me through the Torah and encouraged me to reflect deeply on Jesus' lifestyle of simplicity and compassion, His Jewish mindset and practices, considering leadership and worship concepts from this perspective. God gave me a fresh understanding of the gospels and I felt I was really engaging with the Living Christ. It was transforming to hear Jesus' voice more directly and not only as He has been interpreted and handed down through the ages through various ethnic traditions, cultural interpretations and theological systems.

Suddenly, this changed the picture and brought me joy. The Bible became my own and wasn't just words on a page or concepts to be grasped and taught anymore. My spirituality was enriched and my perspective improved as I began to just sit at the feet of Jesus. As I spent more time reflecting on Jesus in His world, I envisioned a new way of relating in our context and in our church. Our worship styles, outreach and discipleship began to mesh with our goals of engaging and connecting more deeply with our surrounding community and culture in Istanbul.

We developed an authentic, honest approach to worship and discipleship and evangelism so that it still looked like our Middle Eastern culture. Our goal was less about religion and more about touching people on a human level, giving them a desire to know more about Christ Jesus.

This led me to create a common prayer booklet that explored an ancient way to glorify God. It includes prayers, liturgies, and hymns. I've found a new passion for hymn-writing since then and have penned more than 100 hymns pairing local music with ancient melodies. Heart language and music are powerful bonding agents. We regularly sing these hymns in our church and they speak deeply to our hearts. Sometimes people walk by and hear the music and enter because of it.

We also began to put hospitality front and center in our ministry and grew in our experience and ability of welcoming our neighbors into both our 'Messianic Center' and our worship services. We developed an authentic, honest approach to worship and discipleship and evangelism so that it still looked like our Middle Eastern culture. Our goal was less about religion (which people here emphatically do not want) and more about touching people on a human level, giving them a desire to know more about Christ Jesus.

In this process, we are the messengers of the Lord. Jesus fills us and we go and touch. We do not change people; we trust that only Jesus does that. But our primary aim is to be available to others, to meet them in their need. This is the reason we are here—to bring order to chaos. And I cannot do this in my own strength because my ego gets in the way. I can only do this by being empty. How does this look? We see the chaos dispelled in the simple act of coming together in homes to worship, the healed offering healing to others.

This approach works very well in our community and context. The Middle East is all about relationships. Many Americans have a non-relational attitude, preferring to impart knowledge intellectually rather than in the context of relationship. But most of the world has a strong cultural emphasis on relationships.

MINISTRY BACKBONE

So, what does this relational ministry look like in action? Let me paint a picture of the mix of ministry and relational activity that happens week in and week out. This is what ministry looks like at our church in Istanbul.

First, let us welcome you into our church lobby. Our church office used to look like any other office—computer monitors, receptionist, desks, chairs. But after my a-ha moment studying first-century Jesus and his world, we stripped everything down and got back to the basics, including our physical space at church and the office in the apartment building next to the sanctuary. In the office, that we now call the Messianic Center, we removed the desks and the computers and have added rugs, Ottoman style couches and decorations, and a table and chairs for meals. Most of the walls have built in shelves filled with several thousand books, of a wide variety. It now looks more like a library/home than a business office, and it allows us to focus on hospitality, sharing meals, daily worship and conversational teaching and discussions. Outside, we have a beautiful garden we've planted with dirt and plants donated by the city. We want our church space to be a warm, welcoming environment for members and newcomers alike.

Organizing our space this way equips us for highly relational ministry. People come to know our church as a place for spiritual inquiry and conversation—a place of sanctuary, a place to experience Christ's touch.

Something special is going on here. Typically, visitors feel like outsiders when they visit a new church. There are closed meetings reserved for leadership, there are church events they don't know about, and they don't meet key leaders right away. But openness is the key to our ministry in Istanbul. We have an open door policy with discipleship meetings, and it's easy for newcomers to join into the center of activity. People have told us they feel at home in this type of setting. Nothing is hidden, and there are no barriers to entry. One person, who comes from the community on Sunday afternoons to practice with the local municipality choir, commented in surprise on how there were literally no locked doors anywhere.

We have an open door policy with discipleship meetings, and it's easy for newcomers to join into the center of activity. People have told us they feel at home in this type of setting. Nothing is hidden, and there are no barriers to entry.

Instead of a rigid membership process, we allow for a process of becoming. It's a more gradual process, more natural, with an eye toward longevity.

In this context, we focus more on hospitality and caring for others than moving people through a formulaic assimilation process. For example, when talking with newcomers we don't refer to ourselves as full-time ministers, as this typically creates questions about money, and instead wait for their questions before talking about spirituality. We don't try to change people. We trust that Christ will do that as we move forward in friendship with those He has brought to us.

This natural approach even translates to how we train and disciple new believers. As newcomers spend time with us, they begin to notice mature followers all around them, and they begin to ask questions. And this circle of believers works together to answer those questions and build new disciples. In the past when we used more traditional Christian teaching methods, like paperwork and school lessons, people became very serious and reserved. But now that we just use the Bible and conversation, people open up and engage more readily. It is a fruitful way to impart knowledge but also focus on the heart.

After people are discipled and are ready to share that teaching with others, I encourage them to go enter into their part of our wider community and imitate what we're doing here. I tell them to use the Holy Scriptures and our common prayer booklet, and just spend time with people. That's how ordinary people come to bow down and glorify God within our body, which includes people from Orthodox, secular and Muslim backgrounds.

Here, our spirituality conveys the love of God, and it looks different for different people. A person can be a doctor or a professor or a nurse, but that doesn't matter. It's something like falling in love. God's transforming love permeates each part of our lives and is experienced by each individual in unique ways. So, too, our love for others should express itself in ways that are unique to the person with whom we are interacting.

LEADING WITH RELATIONSHIP: A CASE STUDY

Relationship continues to be the primary way we reach non-believers in Istanbul. We have many stories of lives changed through the gospel, but here are a few.

My wife and I became friends with our neighbor, the director of the museum across the street from our church in Istanbul. For two years we were normal friends—we would drink tea together and she would occasionally stop by the church. One day, she asked out of the blue, "Pastor, I want to be baptized now. Is it possible? Is there any reason I shouldn't be baptized?" I asked her, "Did you read Acts 8? About the Ethiopian eunuch?" These kind of "chance encounters" clearly demonstrate that this is the Lord's work. This woman went on to become the administrator of our church association, and now leads our official works.

Another story involves a local choir that practiced in our building. One choir member began interacting with church members and asked a lot of questions. We eventually asked her if she wanted to join our Monday small group. After attending group for some time, she came to our Ash Wednesday service, and said that was the ultimate turning point that "changed her life."

It's amazing how the Lord can use us even when we don't follow a step-by-step evangelistic plan. Several years ago, I asked two nonbelieving friends to help organize our Christmas Eve service. One year later, one of them came to faith and was baptized. They just felt at home with us at church, and it didn't seem strange to invite them into our events and services. They found themselves in the life of the church and started to ask questions.

If you give space in normal daily life, these things will happen. Evangelism opportunities come through discipleship, talking about life, and the deeper meanings behind and within the stories and teachings of Jesus.

Relaxed, conversational methods work well here in this very Eastern context. Some mission techniques create artificial situations: "Are they understanding everything? Are they learning what they need? Let's give them this book. Let's make sure they do this or that." But our goal is to simply welcome people well, to show sincere interest in them as a person, and to help them experience true worship.

Relaxed, conversational methods work well here in this very Eastern context. Some mission techniques create artificial situations ... but our goal is to simply welcome people well, to show sincere interest in them as a person, and to help them experience true worship.

When we invite people in, we're not selling anything. We just want to show them the love of Christ and to answer their questions about Him when they're ready. Others say, "We want you to come to our church," but they really want to make you a slave of their particular branch of religion. People become pawns and are told they can't do normal life anymore ("Stop hanging out with your old friends; instead, do this missions trip or that Bible study"). I've seen fledgling disciples here enter full-time ministry, then bicker about theology, lose their joy, and lose touch with normal life and interactions. Eventually, some even fall away from the faith. This stands in direct opposition to healthy life-on-life discipleship.

We want new disciples to see faith infuse their normal lives, not supplant it. We want them to be a channel of God's light wherever they are. Our goal is to help them become more responsive to other human beings, touching as many people as they can.

These are the stories of our work in Istanbul, where human planting is yielding great kingdom rewards. Though our context is not universal, we believe that authentic, relational ministry is essential to any Christian endeavor that seeks long-term impact. I had to return to Jesus in the first century to grasp these truths that, by God's grace, will carry us forward into a glorious future. To God be the glory.

Pastor Turgay is from a Turkish Muslim background, and has spent his whole ministry life in Turkey. Christ called him to himself in his late teens. In 1986, he started the first church in Istanbul of ethnic Turkish followers of Christ. In 1993, he founded Istanbul Presbyterian-All Saints Moda. He later started Leadership Development Initiative (LDI), while continuing as pastor of Istanbul Presbyterian. LDI serves the body of Christ to encourage, equip, consult and advise in matters of contextual church development and proactive Christ-centered engagement of our diverse neighbors.

SECTION 5

Mission Principles

24

Missional Interdependence

by R. Cartee Bales

"When the right hand washes the left hand, and the left hand washes the right hand, both hands become clean" (Nigerian Proverb)

Working together with others in the endeavor of cross-cultural ministry is difficult—on a good day. Even believers from my same country, age, family status, and background who labor together can think quite differently on aspects of mission or theology. Throw in the differences in culture and background of those host partners with whom we labor, and the degree of difficulty increases. As the difficulties increase, all too often the "community" finds itself functionally divided along lines of leadership, resources, and roles. These communities on mission begin to look like the one reported by Glen Schwartz, executive director emeritus of World Mission Associates, who wrote, "Some time ago the director of a funding agency with an office in East Africa was asked what the role of the receiving partners was in their partnership. His response was, 'We give the money, and they write the reports.'"[1] Clearly, something is wrong.

We apply labels like "partners" and "missional community" in attempts to describe the group assembled on mission. Given the difficulties that arise from the varying degrees of difference from one another, it is important to consider the fundamental relationship of the individuals in the group as they labor together. Is the description related in the story by Glen Schwartz effective and God-glorifying? Or is there another, deeper relationship that we should consider for our work together? I think there is.

DEFINING INTERDEPENDENCE

In 1877, the German botanist Albert Frank co-opted the then-modern word used for community, "symbiosis," to describe the mutual dependence of one organism on another for life: great white sharks and remora fish, clownfish and sea anemones, egrets and buffalos. This word, taken from the Greek, literally means "living together," in which a mutuality in life together is necessary for any success in life at all. These "living together" organisms are interdependent, meaning that they share a "dependence on each other, for one another," according to Webster's New World Dictionary. If one fails, all fail.

As helpful as Frank's description of community and the need for the "other" may be, however, the relationships he describes exist between completely different organisms. What do great white sharks and cows have to do with missions and human beings? Is there help for us in doing community, in living together in this unique endeavor of cross-cultural missions? Is this idea of interdependence in our missional communities helpful to us?

The search for understanding begins, of course, in God's Word, and a depiction of the missional relationships within the Godhead. While much can be and has been said of Jesus' high priestly prayer in John 17, in it we are given a glimpse of the interdependence of the persons of the Trinity:

> *"When Jesus had spoken these words, he lifted up his eyes to heaven, and said, 'Father, the hour has come; glorify your Son that the Son may glorify you . . . And now, Father, glorify me in your own presence with the glory that I had with you before the world existed. I have manifested your name to the people whom you gave me out of the world. Yours they were, and you gave them to me, and they have kept your word. Now they know that everything that you have given me is from you. For I have given them the words that you gave me, and they have received them and have come to know in truth that I came from you; and they have believed that you sent me. I am praying for them. I am not praying for the world but for those whom you have given me, for they are yours. All mine are yours, and yours are mine, and I am glorified in them. And I am no longer in the world, but they are in the world, and I am coming to you. Holy Father, keep them in your name, which you have given me, that they may be one, even as we are one.*
>
> *I have given them your word, and the world has hated them because they are not of the world, just as I am not of the world. As you sent*

me into the world, so I have sent them into the world. I do not ask for these only, but also for those who will believe in me through their word, that they may all be one, just as you, Father, are in me, and I in you, that they also may be in us, so that the world may believe that you have sent me. The glory that you have given me I have given to them, that they may be one even as we are one, I in them and you in me, that they may become perfectly one, so that the world may know that you sent me and loved them even as you loved me" (John 17:1-23) [edited for brevity].

So, how is this beautiful prayer by Jesus instructive about interdependence? First, in the Trinity we see that God is one (Deuteronomy 6:4). Despite the diversity in the persons, there exists no "yours, mine, and ours" of independence among them. There is not a mission that the Son engages without the Father, or the Father without the Son. Each plays a vital role in the whole mission of God, and is depended upon—relied on—by the other to fulfill His role, while—in turn—relying and depending upon the other ("Nevertheless, not my will, but yours be done" Luke 22:42b). There is a perfect harmony among the persons of the Trinity in their interdependence in mission and purpose, and in the resources for that mission.

INTERDEPENDENT IN MISSION

The Father gives His people to Jesus (v. 6) and Jesus gives them the Father's words (v. 8), so that they know the Father and believe in Jesus. Jesus prays for them that the Son might be glorified in them, and that they may have the same one-ness of the Father and the Son. Then the Son sends them into the world that others will believe through their word, and prays for them (us) as well, that they might become one, even as the Father and the Son are one. The Father and Son work interdependently in their respective roles in accomplishing the purposes of God: neither accomplishes the mission alone. Each person contributes to the role of that mission. And, lest we forget the Holy Spirit—who does not explicitly appear in this prayer—we know He equally participates in the mission in an interdependent way. Just one chapter earlier, Jesus says of the Spirit (John 16:13-15), "When the Spirit of truth comes, he will guide you into all the truth, for he will not speak on his own authority, but whatever he hears he will speak, and he will declare to you the things that are to come. He will glorify me, for he will take what is mine and declare it to you. All that the Father has is mine; therefore I said that he will take what is mine and declare it to you." The Holy Spirit participates in glorifying Jesus by taking what is His [Jesus'] and declaring it to His people. Each of these participative roles requires interdependence: a reliance on the role of another, and an action in harmony with a common mission. All work together for the success of the mission, and all are necessary.

INTERDEPENDENT IN RESOURCES

I use the word resources here to mean those things that are utilized in this common mission. The people given to Jesus are first given by the Father (v. 6) and have also been given the words of the Father (v. 8, 14), as well as the glory given by the Father to the Son (v. 22). But these resources are shared in the sense that the Father and Son share the word and glory for the purpose of the mission. In fact, it is by sharing this glory that the Son returns glory to the Father (v. 1). Glory, as a heavenly resource, is shared among the persons of the Trinity. It is also true of the words of the Father: they are not controlled by one, but shared and deployed by all. In this mission of God, the persons of the Godhead are interdependent in both mission roles and resources. Each plays a critical role without which the mission isn't possible, and the resources deployed are shared and directed by all.

Being one in community—interdependent—just as the Trinity, is not only descriptive, it is the communal relationship we are sent into.

I'm not God. So, what does the interdependence of the Trinity have to do with me, or with the mission community in which God has placed me? In the midst of this incredible passage, Jesus prays, "As you sent me into the world, so I have sent them into the world" (v. 19). Even as Jesus is describing His sending in the context of the interdependent working of that sending, He says, in essence, "I sent my people in the same way. The same 'one-ness' and interdependence we have in community is the same manner I have sent them to do mission." In case it seems this is an overstatement, notice that Jesus immediately follows by praying, "I ask . . . that [the purpose] they may all be one, *just as you, Father, are in me, and I in you*, that they also may be in us, so that the world may believe that you have sent me" (emphasis mine). It is the very context of the sending. Being one in community—interdependent—just as the Trinity, is not only descriptive, it is the communal relationship we are sent into.

If this is true, we would expect to see interdependence described and lived out in the New Testament community, wouldn't we? Of course. The church's interdependence in community is described in 1 Corinthians 12:1-27, that wonderful passage where Paul uses the metaphor of the human body to show the functioning of the various members of the community of believers. He points to the diversity of members, but clearly demonstrates the interdependence intended between them. "God arranged all the members in the body, each one of them, as He chose. If all were a single member, where would the body be? As it is, there are many parts, yet one body" (1 Corinthians 12:18-20). No member of the body, Paul points out, is replaceable by other body parts, and each depends upon the others for functioning as a body—they are interdependent members of the same whole. The hand doesn't say, "Hey, that's my blood you're using there, kidney," nor does one leg say, "Go north if you want; I'm heading west," to the other. Of this metaphor of the body, the New Dictionary of Theology writes: "Paul uses the body figure to describe the interdependence of Christians as members of Christ and of each other. Christ is united to his body, the church, as a husband to his wife."[2] Wayne Grudem, in his book *Systematic Theology*, writes on this passage: "The metaphor of the church as the body of Christ should increase our interdependence on one another and our appreciation of the diversity of gifts within the body."[3] Dr. Grudem further writes, "Even the diversity of gifts should lead to greater unity and interdependence in the church ... and this diversity in unity will itself be a foretaste of the unity that believers will have in heaven."[4] Christ's prayer for the way He has sent His disciples (in the same manner He is sent) is in view: that we would be one, interdependent.

Many other examples of interdependence could be cited from Scripture: the interdependence of a husband and a wife so that they could be called "one" (Genesis 2:24); the interdependent community of believers described in Acts 2, holding all things in common (cf. 2:42-47); the interdependence of the churches demonstrated through the work of Paul's collection for the relief of the church in Jerusalem;[5] the ministry of Pricilla and Aquila in Ephesus as they took time away from their ministry to work with Apollos, for a great future effect on the church (Acts 18:28).[6]

The church on mission in the world is sent as an interdependent body, exhibiting the relationships among the Godhead, where the diversity of roles and gifts exist but are organized in a way that creates beautiful unity as mission and resources are shared. Unfortunately, our independent selves often emerge in this mission, especially as difficulties increase. Whether for reasons of expedience or differences in philosophy of ministry or vision, or perhaps desired ownership of achievement and the accompanying acclamation, the heart's tendency toward independence rises. I want to do it my way; failing that, I'll take my ball and go play somewhere else.

THE ALLURE OF INDEPENDENCE

Here the core of independence is found: in me. I want things done the "right" way, which is my way, naturally. When there are accolades for success, I want to be the one receiving them. When there is a decision to be taken, I want the votes to line up behind my idea. If there is a misunderstanding, it's not my failing to understand the other or to communicate well. When values clash (i.e. individual vs. collective, indirect vs. direct communication styles, high or low power distance)[7] my way of looking at the world should prevail. As difficult as this is to admit, this harsh criticism exposes my, and maybe your, heart's bias toward independence. It forms barriers, "excludes and embraces"[8] based on its own self-seeking terms. And it makes interdependence impossible. Here, however, the core of interdependence is found: the gospel. It reminds me that I am a son of a King who has accepted me completely, based not on my work, but on the work and worth of Christ alone (Romans 8:15). It reminds me that He, and not me, is Lord of the Harvest (Matthew 9:38), and that my King is building His church (Matthew 16:18), even when I fail and get in the way through my independence. It reminds me that interdependence is possible as I value each co-laborer whom "he created in his own image . . . male and female" (Genesis 1:27), but that forgiveness for me is always extended when I crawl back to the cross from another failure (1 John 1:9). My journey to interdependence begins in the transformation of my own heart by the great news of the gospel.

How then do our teams begin to move from independence to interdependence? First, recognize that the move isn't achieved all at once. With the battle for independence at work in us, together with the real difficulties we will face in pursuing interdependence, the movement away from independence will require ongoing cycles of analysis and change.

Second, it will require a deep commitment by the community: first, to one another, and then to transforming our relationships.

PRACTICAL STEPS TOWARD INTERDEPENDENCE

Allow me to outline a broad, three-step process for moving in the direction of interdependence:

1. Review

In the ministry you now serve, does interdependence among the mission community (meaning *everyone* involved in the mission) exist? Are strategies, goals, and tasks determined by one person, or by one faction of the community, or do your partners also participate in the development of these things?

If you list the roles and tasks of the community, are there dependencies between them? In other words, does each have to succeed in order for everyone to succeed? Whom do you rely upon to accomplish your group's mission together, and who relies upon you?

Who directs the resources and makes decisions regarding their use in the mission? Are those resource utilization decisions shared by the community? Or do one or two people make that decision for the field? If you are able to take your ball and play somewhere else, there is not a high level of interdependence.

Do all members of the community have an opportunity to utilize their spiritual gifts, or do only one or a few do all of the public activity, while the others are relegated to positions in the back, despite their gifting?

Who receives the investment of training, retreats, sabbaticals? Are these resources shared? Does everyone get the advantage of them?

Yes, there is diversity in gifts. Yes, we commit to shared leadership. But if interdependence—this oneness in our missional community—is to be pursued, we must be honest with ourselves about divisions that spring from our hearts and rob us (and the church) of that oneness.

By the way: when reviewing or assessing where you are on the independence vs. interdependence continuum in your missional community, it will be necessary to seek the input of others. The effect of confirmation bias mixed with a need for affirmation will ordinarily lead us to seek assessment from those who likely think like us. Therefore, we must ask others—those outside your typical circle—to honestly assess these critical factors.

2. Repent

Jesus prays for our "one-ness" in John 17 and sends us in the same way He is sent, in which our one-ness is a sign and witness to the world that we are His. We are sent relying upon and being relied upon by others for the success of the mission. To the extent that I subvert His sending through my own proclivities toward independence and through my own brokenness, I must seek His forgiveness and healing. *Lord Jesus, forgive me for wanting to do things my way, or wanting to control outcomes, or even robbing others of the blessing of serving you in Your strength because of my actions. Make us one in relationship, even as you and the Father are one.*

3. Revise

Go back to the drawing board with your entire community (team, partners, etc.) to redesign work and resources and to begin the move from independence to interdependence. Using some of the questions from the "Review" section above, work together to recast how mission roles/tasks and ownership of resources for the mission will be shared. Particularly focus on:

- **Interdependent leadership.** We commit to a plurality of leaders, but do the leaders include those from the community who are unlike us (for example, our partners)? Are we carefully listening to each leader? Do all leaders have the ability to voice objections and discuss until a satisfactory conclusion is reached?
- **Interdependent roles/tasks.** We commit to a diversity in gifts. Is each member of the community serving in a role that maximizes the use of her gifts? Are these roles arranged so that each relies on the others for success? Or does one "send money" and the other "writes reports"?
- **Interdependent opportunities.** We commit to ongoing education and rest. Does each member of the community have the opportunity to attend the same retreats and training that others do?
- **Interdependent resources.** We commit to stewardship of the resources God has given us for mission. Interdependence suggests that no one person (or group) should own all of the resources, nor make decisions about their use. How can decisions be made together for the use of resources? And, how can resources be held commonly in a way that someone can't "take their ball to another playing field"?

Imagine the potential outcomes of a process like this if used in the East African partnership in the opening story. Instead of one side giving the money and the other side writing reports, what if strategies were agreed on together, and the funding requirements that flowed from those strategies were also determined together? What if the money was given to a common bank account for which one member of each side of the partnership had signing authority, and for amounts exceeding some level both members were required to sign? And then the expenditures were presented and reviewed each month by the entire team, along with successes (and discouragements) on the strategic plan, followed by prayer together to give thanks for the successes and to ask for the Lord's help in the discouragements? What if each member of the partnership rotated the responsibility and privilege of writing the reports each month? This begins to move the East African work in this story from independence to interdependence.

The world will know we are one, even as God is One, if we value the dignity of each member of our missional communities.

Glen Schwartz recounts another story he heard about a congregation in the south of England, who had been told of a country in North Africa in which the church suffered persecution and even martyrdom even though God's Spirit had started many new churches in that same country. Wanting to help their brothers in Africa, the people in England wrote, "What can we do to help you?" The African congregation questioned back, "First, tell us what we can do to help you?" The congregation in England replied, "We don't have any needs with which you can help," to which the congregation in Africa responded, "If we can't help you, then you can't help us." [9]

Interdependence is not easy, nor is it comfortable. I grew up in America, the land of the free and independent. I breathed the air of, "Pick yourself up by your bootstraps," and swam in the ocean of, "If you want something done right, do it yourself." My heart has a strong tendency toward independence (Genesis 3 is a good reminder). Honestly, it's often easier and faster and less difficult to just "do it myself." But the world will know we are one, even as God is One, if we value the dignity of each member of our missional communities. If we will stare in the face of the folly of independence and, like our African brothers and sisters above, we will seek interdependence in our mission communities. To His glory.

Rev. Cartee Bales began a career in technology management and consulting, and was eventually redirected into vocational Gospel ministry through his passion for cross-cultural missions. This passion carried him to Asia. Through this journey, God has merged and used Cartee's leadership and business experience with his ministry training, and matched it with a passion for the nations. He and his wife Colleen have lived in South Asia seven years, where Cartee now oversees and encourages the work of MTW throughout Asia Pacific as the MTW International Director for the region.

1   Gary Parker and Glenn Schwartz, "Self-Reliance or Interdependence," *New Horizons in Missions* (Sept.-Dec. 1998): accessed June 2016, http://www.missionfrontiers.org/issue/article/self-reliance-or-interdependence.

2   *New Dictionary of Theology* (University of Colleges and Christian Fellowship: 1988), 141. Electronic Edition: Oak Tree Software, Inc., v 1.3.

3   Wayne Grudem, *Systematic Theology* (Grand Rapids: Zondervan Publishing House, 1994), 859. Electronic Edition: Bits and Bytes, 2008.

4   Grudem, *Systematic Theology*, 1019.

5   *New Dictionary of Biblical Theology* (Downer's Grove: Intervarsity Press, 2000), 201. Electronic Edition: Oak Tree Software, Inc., v 2.1.

6   David Peterson, *The Acts of the Apostles*, Pillar New Testament Commentary (Grand Rapids: Wm. B. Eerdman's 2009), 524. Electronic Edition: Oak Tree Software, Inc., v 1.3.

7   Sherwood Lingenfelter, *Ministering Cross Culturally* (Baker Academic, 2016). This book provides a helpful understanding of cultural dimensions and an online assessment in gauging one's own cultural competence.

8   Miroslav Volf, *Exclusion and Embrace: A Theological Exploration of Identity, Otherness, and Reconciliation* (Abington Press, 2010).

9   Gary Parker and Glenn Schwartz, "Self-Reliance or Interdependence," *New Horizons in Missions* (Sept.-Dec. 1998): accessed June 2016, http://www.missionfrontiers.org/issue/article/self-reliance-or-interdependence.

25

Mutual Accountability and the Gospel of Grace

by Brian Deringer

The church-planting expert from America strode through our city with confidence, energy, and focus. He wore a blue short-sleeve shirt and khaki pants, carried nothing in his hands, and looked often at his watch. I had to walk quickly to stay close enough to answer his questions, provide demographic information, and report on our progress as a church-planting team. Offering his services to us as a consultant, he said, "I am here in part carrying out my church's accountability tour of ministry sites we support." At the end of the second day, he asked to meet with the whole team.

The next day, with everyone present, he proceeded to lay out for us a church-planting strategy that he had drawn up over the last two days. This in itself was a difficult conversation to navigate, hearing from someone who had never planted a church internationally, never crossed cultures, didn't speak a foreign language, and didn't really know us. It was excruciating to receive his criticism of our work. He talked about how little we'd accomplished over the last four years. Sensing our lack of enthusiasm, he went on to tell us that in America if a church plant has not taken off in two years, it's over.

He returned home, his church withdrew its support, and we never heard from him again.

He had held us accountable.

This story, albeit dated, a little embellished, and intentionally vague on details, is drawn from truth. It represents the worst-case scenario of a visit by what Steve Brown calls a "well-intentioned dragon," but serves to illustrate one reason why missionaries can be skeptical of churches that want to hold them accountable. Now, for a moment, allow yourself to imagine the same scenario taking place as an American missionary exercising the due diligence of accountability might visit a national brother or sister. This we have also seen.

ACCOUNTABILITY: THE GRACE OF CARING

It is not difficult to understand why healthy accountability doesn't always take place and often isn't welcome on the mission field. As a result, we see ministries continue for years without a significant assessment, positive or negative. Some labor without encouragement. They might even attempt to communicate, to get feedback, and hear nothing. Problems continue to simmer without attention, to the detriment of kingdom growth. It feels like it is far enough away that we can ignore it, that we can let it go on because it's not hurting anything. Once I visited a field where one of the members of the team was cutting himself. The wounds were in full view of anyone who would care to look! And yet, no one did.

Accountability is not power over others; it is the grace of caring. One cannot live an unaccountable life or conduct ministry without accountability and think that he will escape the consequences, whether one is a Western missionary or a national leader.

The concept of mutual accountability is present all through Scripture. We are called to be accountable to leadership in the church (Hebrews 13:17), and to stir one another up to love and good works (Hebrews 10:24-25). Why then is it so easy for us to look the other way?

In the following pages, we will look at the reasons why people avoid accountability, the difference between wholesome accountability and destructive accountability, and the need for the gospel of grace in order to make constructive mutual accountability possible. We will also suggest some practical ways to bring accountability into our relationships, especially our cross-cultural relationships.

WHY WE AVOID ACCOUNTABILITY

Love cares enough to lean into the pain and messiness of accountability, and the gospel of grace creates the healing freedom necessary for us to be transparent with one another. Since in the gospel we have nothing to prove and nothing to lose, it is possible to invite others to truly know us.

Not long ago, I was dealing with a complex medical situation. One physician had diagnosed the problem early on, but I was not confident in his assessment. Nevertheless, I accepted the course of treatment and went on my way. Later, I sought a second opinion. The second physician saw the situation differently and was perplexed as to why I did not voice my concerns the first time I was seen. "I suppose," I said, "that I did not want to offend him." The second physician said, "It is always appropriate to ask for a second opinion. Anyone who would be offended by that is in the wrong vocation." Why this reticence to speak? From the other side, why do we give off vibes that we don't want to hear it? Even at the risk of one's own health, or the health of one's ministry, we will often prefer to be closed off or silent.

Fear of uninvited and undue criticism, or the risk of offense as in the above stories aren't the only reasons why we shun accountability. Sometimes we are in fact attempting to escape reality, to avoid the consequences of our actions. Deep down, we know that we have fallen prey to ministry without faith and have given in to fear. We have surrounded ourselves with just enough reportable progress that it seems to be reasonable success to most onlookers. Secretly, we feel like an imposter, a leech sucking from the money bags of the church. We have no confidence that what we are doing makes a difference. The idea of being exposed is . . . frightening. So why would we invite anyone to look more closely?

On one occasion, an American missionary had created an easy lifestyle for himself. His home was spacious, his activities were much more extravagant than what might be afforded by the people he served, and frankly he wasn't working very hard. One day, national leadership confronted him. Thus exposed, the American missionary left the field never to return. Fear of exposure is another cause for shunning accountability. One must also wonder about the spirit of the intervention and the relationship between the missionary and the national leadership.

Another time, a new pastor was moderating a session meeting and a motion was made to excommunicate a member of the church. The new pastor was unfamiliar with the situation. The concerns surrounding this person were indeed grave, but before proceeding he asked the elders who had been shepherding this person. No one spoke. Who recently had contact with him? Silence. Have we even attempted to contact him? Blank stares. Wisely, the session stopped the discipline process until there had been a serious effort to reach out in grace-filled love and lean into the messiness of the situation.

I once visited a ministry site where I was impressed by a remarkable level of activity by a brother, but uneasy about the lack openness in our communication. He was unwilling to discuss with me where all the resources were coming from. I started asking some questions and soon discovered that there were a number of parties giving financially to the same project. However, they were unaware of each other's contributions. I called a meeting of the principals and we openly discussed in the presence of the leader what each of us was doing. The meeting revealed that there was overlap, that the leader had been raising more money than was needed, and was able to do so by keeping his partners in the dark about one another.

If we are to be in a position of mutual accountability, it must begin with the integrity of being open to receive from others, and a realization that no one has all the answers.

OVERCOMING OBSTACLES TO ACCOUNTABILITY

In 1 Peter 5:1-3, Peter writes, "So I exhort the elders among you, as a fellow elder and a witness of the sufferings of Christ, as well as a partaker in the glory that is going to be revealed: shepherd the flock of God that is among you, exercising oversight, not under compulsion, but willingly, as God would have you; not for shameful gain, but eagerly; *not domineering over those in your charge, but being examples to the flock."*

One of the key elements of successfully accountable relationships is the attitude of the heart, which is essentially a gospel issue. The more we understand about accountability through humility and brokenness, we understand that there is no place to be domineering. If we are to be in a position of mutual accountability, it must begin with the integrity of being open to receive from others, and a realization that no one has all the answers.

We will mistrust accountability if it is one way only. When in authority, we will often demand transparency from others, while not so much as tipping our own hat. We will sometimes lord our authority over others, rather than approach the relationship from the perspective of service, sacrifice, and humility. One-way demands for transparency are often taken as an indictment or a threat rather than a mutual commitment.

We find other rationalizations for avoiding accountability. We might say that a culture of grace will not require an accounting. It seems antithetical to preach grace and then ask for evidence. Sometimes fear of conflict will prevent us from going down that road. We resort to peace-faking as a substitute for openness and true peace. We will sometimes hide behind a respect for the privacy of another person. Or we might flippantly call it the providence of God. What need is there to practice accountability if the results are in God's hands anyway? And yet the consequences of avoiding accountability are also worrisome.

What builds trust? This is an important question for building cross cultural relationships. One thing that builds trust is appropriate levels of transparency, a key ingredient of effective accountability. Without it, two people might work together, but never develop a relationship of mutual trust. Such was the case in one situation where missionaries and nationals were trying to work together planting churches, the national brothers refused to report on the use of funds. The missionary refused to talk about the resources at his disposal, or to fully vest in the project. A lack of willing mutual accountability led to destroyed trust, broken relationships, and failure.

HEALTHY VS. UNHEALTHY ACCOUNTABILITY

The consequences for being unwilling to be held accountable can be damaging to the extreme. We are therefore tempted to mitigate against that damage by implementing structures designed to prevent abuse. However, trust that is based solely on consistent observance of policy, iron-clad work processes, requirements, and agreements will not solve the problems by themselves. They are nothing without trusting people.

This is complicated because we know that theologically and experientially we can't and shouldn't blindly trust people. Refusing to see is not what is meant by grace. We live in the now and not yet. In Christ, our salvation is secure. However, in the plan of redemption our journey is not over. Paul saw this dynamic at work in his life. Romans 6-8 engages the dilemma that while we know what is right, and even in Christ desire what is right, we still often do not do the things we ought to do, and the things we know we should not do we do anyway. Biblical relationships of trust are not Pollyanna. It is about two humble, contrite people who are each aware of their own vulnerability to sin and are willing to hear and speak truth to one another in love. It will not always go well.

That is why the ability to enter such a relationship is less about trust in people and more about the work of the Holy Spirit, the promises of God the Father, and the presence of the Lord. People are flawed and sinful, no matter what kind of track record a person has, and the only one ultimately worthy of our trust is the Lord.

2 Thessalonians 3:4, "We have confidence in the Lord that you are doing and will continue to do the things we command."

Not practicing accountability allows wrong things to continue. That might seem obvious, but it is amazing how long one can live with an elephant in the room. How is it possible that a dysfunctional team, a failing church plant, misappropriation of funds, bad missiology, debilitating depression, infidelity, or abuse continue for years? And yet it often does! Without the will to hold one another accountable, little change is possible.

The ability to enter such a relationship is less about trust in people and more about the work of the Holy Spirit, the promises of God the Father, and the presence of the Lord.

In one situation, a brother was strongly suspected of misappropriation of funds. It was felt that even investigating this would cause a major blow-up. It was difficult to discern how one might approach it. As a result, the brother got a pass. On the surface, this felt to some like a win because the conflict "went away." I believe we have yet to fully understand the consequences we will reap because of this decision.

In fleshing these things out, a sinking feeling falls over me. Accountability, while important, can also be a relationally destructive force when misapplied. In order for this paper to be meaningful, it is important to drill down and provide evocative examples and evidence. Yet in doing so, it seems in itself a violation of trust. Even if the details are shrouded, I know the sources. A lack of accountability in my own life on many levels humbles me as I write about various situations. That is probably a heathy thing.

It is always dangerous to talk about topics like abortion, infidelity, and addictions. It is dangerous because it is not theory. If one preaches on one of these topics, he must be well aware that there are many people in the audience for whom this strikes a very personal, sensitive nerve. The topic of accountability can have the same effect. It can be threatening. When you start talking to a person about accountability, not just as a topic for discussion, but as a something one hopes to mutually practice, it's suddenly very personal.

I remember when I first went to the field as a missionary. I had to write down on a weekly basis how many times I shared the gospel and how many people came to Christ. Our team set unreasonable goals for evangelism in the context where we served, and this accountability actually caused or furthered the exact behavior it was intended to prevent—not practicing evangelism. We threw our hands up in discouragement.

GRACE FUELS ACCOUNTABILITY
Love doesn't turn away.

We hesitate to get involved with someone because their problems seem too complicated, threatening, or even scary. But Jesus reached out to the demon possessed (Luke 4:31-37). He even mixed it up with leaders in the synagogue who He knew would seek to silence Him (Luke 4:14-30). When someone has done something against us, we will often find ourselves shrinking away. We might try to justify it by saying, "I just need to forgive this person." And certainly that might be true sometimes. But often what is in one's heart sounds more like, "I'm mad at you. You're not worth it. I'm fine." Peter betrayed Jesus. And Jesus could have walked away. But He leaned into Peter's pain to restore him (John 21:15-25). Jesus sought out the paralyzed, the poor, the rich, the self-righteous, soldiers and widows, prostitutes and adulterers, the hungry and the faithless, tax collectors and religious leaders, thieves, murderers, and even those who would betray Him. In fact, the entire story of redemption is about God seeking out those who are not seeking Him. It is about God seeking out those who know the truth, who know the right thing to do, but who hold it back as if they were holding back a strong spring.

Love doesn't turn away from people with messy lives. Love proactively engages and moves toward others, even at great cost.

As a parent, I have experienced many challenges as I've watched my children grow up. At times it is exhausting. At times I have had no idea what to do. One thing I know, however, is that if I see my son or daughter struggling and I turn my face away, that is not love. In any relationship, if we care, we will turn our face toward our brother. Not away. That is why Matthew 18:15ff, the well-worn passage on resolving conflict, is really a passage about love. When you ask someone the purpose of church discipline, he will often say, "To protect the purity of the church." While this is true, it is not the main reason we practice church discipline. Through church discipline, properly lived out, we are saying that rather than turning one's face away while someone drifts from the household of faith, we are to seek them out. We care enough to get involved. Love sees. Ours is the God who sees. God sees me; we must see others. Genesis 16:13 says, "She gave this name to the Lord who spoke to her: 'You are the God who sees me,' for she said, 'I have now seen the One who sees me.'"

Love doesn't turn away from people with messy lives. Love proactively engages and moves toward others, even at great cost.

God loves us this way. By the presence of His Spirit He holds us accountable for our thoughts and deeds. Our victory is in Christ, but we have yet to be conformed perfectly to His image. And yet His love will not let us go. He is the God who sees. He sees us in our distress and in our joys. Our lives are never too messy for Him to get involved. He has put away our shame and guilt in order that we might know Him better. In the Trinity, the three persons are one. He invites us into that kind of fellowship, a fellowship of being one in Christ. It is a fellowship of grace, of caring.

Bad things happen when we try to substitute policy, work processes, and reports for a fellowship of grace. Institutional accountability will never make us open with one another like a family. Using technology, forms, and processes to hold people accountable doesn't help either. The church is a family before it is a building, a program, a service, or a system of courts. It is a family. When it ceases to be a family, it will quickly turn cold and bureaucratic. Yet, when we submit to one another out of reverence for Christ, then honesty bathed in love will draw us together and forward. Our confidence in one another will bring joy to our work and relationships (Ephesians 5:21ff). In fact, our submission to one another is a vivid picture of the gospel, whether it happens in the context of marriage, the church, or our missional relationships.

In fact, there are nearly 100 passages in the Scriptures containing the word combination "one another." Some of them are negative examples, but the large majority of the passages concern the positive ways that we are called to account: reminding of the faithfulness of God and His truth; encouraging; caring and giving; showing justice, mercy, and compassion; showing the way; washing feet; honoring; forgiving; accepting; serving; being humble, gentle, patient, and forbearing; admonishing; and spurring on toward love and good deeds.

It all comes down to loving one another.

John 13:34-35 says, "A new command I give you: Love one another. As I have loved you, so you must love one another. By this everyone will know that you are my disciples, if you love one another."

Work processes and reports may be helpful in streamlining some communication processes, but if these are not founded on trusting, grace-filled relationships then the tools become useless. A contract is only as useful as the integrity of those who sign it. In the same way, external accountability constraints will be ignored, disrespected, and circumvented if they are not an expression of mutual appreciation, relationship, and trust.

ACTIONS STEPS TOWARD ACCOUNTABILITY

So, practically speaking what is to be done?

First, MTW must continue to propagate a theology of the ongoing ministry of the gospel of grace. It should characterize our training, our HR activities, our worldwide preaching, our staff, our missionary and international relationships, and most importantly our individual walk with Christ. If we want wholesome accountable relationships we must start with ourselves. From the coordinator to every missionary in the organization, we should be appropriately transparent, enabled to do so because of the inward work of grace. The gospel should create a culture of openness rather than defensiveness. It should develop missionaries who have nothing to prove and nothing to lose. Power and reputation will diminish in their influence. Mutual appreciation and trust will naturally grow. We will know this is taking place when there is a culture of building one another up as opposed to policing one another. Grace is the prior question.

Second, MTW must have a culture of loving one another. Accountability is sometimes painful, but our commitment is to love one another no matter what. It is a commitment to let go of past offenses and look to the future. Only in this type of culture will fear recede. In fact, people who are harboring secret shame and doubt are already in pain. Bringing truth into the light, and then loving one another through it, should bring healing and relief.

"Therefore, confess your sins to one another and pray for one another, that you may be healed. The prayer of a righteous person has great power as it is working" (James 5:16).

Third, we must not turn away. James 4:17 says, "to know good and not do it is sin." There are so many reasons this is true, not least of which is a concern over the well-being of those we serve. Someone who is not accountable is vulnerable and alone. They are at risk of continuing down a damaging pathway. Certainly there might be times when it is not within our sphere of relationships to get involved. But insomuch as God has put us together, love will insist that we see one another. We must make it a habit of leaning into pain, and we can only do so because of the power of the gospel.

A culture of openness and safety, brought about by a common experience of a grace-filled life, will naturally create honesty which will enable us to address needed areas of accountability, and love one another through it.

Fourth, we must continue to grow in our appreciation of what this might look like in other cultures. The American, straightforward approach to things will not work everywhere. Too often, we seek to impose our way of doing things with little emotional intelligence. The principle remains the same that grace leads to relationship, transparency, trust, and iron sharpening iron (Proverbs 27:17). However, the culture and form of it will necessarily be shaped by each people group. In an American setting, one might ask a question directly, whereas in another culture it is appropriate to ask a question through a third party. Is that wrong, or simply different? What does it mean when a national brother resists our attempts at developing an accountability relationship? Is he not mature in Christ? Is he fearful of being exposed? Or is there a cross-culture gap, a failure of communication that has thrown up an unnecessary relational barrier? It is hard enough to practice this in our own culture. It requires additional layers of understanding to do it in another. But love covers a multitude of sins, and love communicates in every culture.

Last, MTW must be willing to be held accountable by our international partners and friends. So often accountability in missional relationships is one way. We demand transparency from our national brothers, but we are not willing to do the same. We seek to mentor others, but we are often the ones in need of teaching. We will break off a relationship because a national brother is not forthcoming regarding the management of his resources, but we are unwilling to tell him much about the resources we have or what we do with them. We examine the lives of nationals, but there is often an unspoken understanding that it is rude for the reverse to happen. We like to think that colonial stereotypes are a thing of the past, but despite many areas of progress, the deeper and more subtle distinctions of privilege remain. In Christ there is neither Jew nor Greek, but accountability is most often a one-way street.

If we find ourselves eager to set up systems of accountability, that eagerness might actually be a flag that something is wrong. What is the motivation? Do we believe that we can improve performance through inspection of behavior? That might be true on the surface and for a time, but at what cost? We cannot force people to do this, to live this way. A culture of openness and safety, brought about by a common experience of a grace-filled life, will naturally create honesty which will enable us to address needed areas of accountability, and love one another through it.

Brian Deringer and his family served as long term missionaries in Paris, France where an MTW team was able to plant a church that still continues today. He has served as Sr. Pastor of Friendly Hills Church, International Director for Europe, International Director for Global Support Ministries, and currently a leader in Member Care and Development.

26

Toward a Self-Supported Khmer Church

by Dr. Lloyd Kim

This chapter addresses the question, "Why is the Khmer church not self-supported?" This was the question posed by the conference leadership[1] to those teaching at Phnom Penh Bible School (PPBS).[2] The results outlined in this paper come from short interviews and discussions with different lecturers at PPBS. Those interviewed come from different cultural backgrounds and experiences—both Khmer and foreign. However, this paper does not necessarily represent the views of PPBS as an institution.

The goal of this paper is to contribute to the ongoing discussion of how best to serve the Cambodian church. We come with an attitude of humility that recognizes the complexities of the situation and the fact that there are no easy answers. We hope, however, that the insights gained from this work will lead to further prayer, discussion, and dependence upon our heavenly Father for the benefit of the Khmer Church to the glory of God.

DEFINING INTERDEPENDENCE

The first thought that comes to mind is, "Are we asking the right question?" And what do we mean when we say "self-supporting"? The generally-accepted goal of the missions community has been to help establish self-propagating, self-governing, self-supporting, and more recently, self-theologizing churches. Often we speak of helping to establish "independent" churches, primarily meaning independent from foreign money and control. However, we should be careful with the language of independence. Do we want Khmer churches to come up with their own theology independent from the larger Christian community? Do we want the Khmer church to be independent in their association with the larger Christian community?

> *If we value the idea of working together—giving and receiving from one another as the body of Christ—then we should also support financial interdependence rather than independence.*

We need further clarification. Some have acknowledged this problem and speak not of "independence," but "interdependence." The idea is that both the Khmer church and foreign churches need each other. We give and take from each other, and depend on each other. This picture more closely follows the analogy of the Apostle Paul of the church as a body (Ephesians 4:4, 15-16, Romans 12:4-8, 1 Corinthians 12:12-31). When it comes to theology, propagation, and perhaps even governance the idea of interdependence is welcomed. For instance, foreign churches and Khmer churches can gain much as we dialogue together regarding theological issues. Furthermore, the Khmer church would not want to be independent of historical Christian creeds and confessions. One PPBS lecturer stated he believed the local church should be interdependent even in terms of their governance. He meant that though the local church would have the final say in how to run their church, they should listen to the larger Christian community for advice, direction, and guidance. I would add that the local Khmer church should also be involved in giving advice and direction to other church bodies outside of Cambodia. Interdependence, in relation to propagation, would mean a more collaborative effort in evangelism and church planting, building on the strengths of the different Christian ethnic communities.

However, there seems to be a reluctance to speak of interdependency in relation to financial support. There is a strong push for financial independence—perhaps a backlash to years of unhealthy dependence in certain parts of the missions world. Yet this seems inconsistent with the general philosophy of seeking interdependence among the church of God. If we value the idea of working together—giving and receiving from one another as the body of Christ—then we should also support financial interdependence rather than independence. So what does healthy financial interdependence look like in the context of the larger interdependence relationship?

The term "self-supporting" can evoke different images for different people. The general definition would be for the local church to be able to support its own pastor, ministry expenses, and general maintenance expenses independent from foreign groups or individuals. But how far do we go with the idea of independence? A typical approach to missions with the goal of independence would be to bar giving monetary support to local churches. Some would argue that the local church should not get used to receiving funds from the outside, because once they do they will have no motivation to support themselves. But even a financially-independent church would then have a philosophy of ministry that supports itself, but refuses to give to other ministries—simply modeling the approach it has experienced. An approach to missions that has interdependence in mind is different. The goal for the local church is not simply survival or maintaining the financial obligations of the local congregation, but giving for the expansion of the kingdom beyond the borders of Cambodia.

CHALLENGES TO A SELF-SUPPORTING CHURCH

Practices of Foreign Missionaries and Groups

When asked the question, "Why is the Khmer church not self-supporting?," the most common answer is because foreign mission groups or individuals are willing to support the Khmer church. In other words, many of the local Khmer churches have been taught from the beginning that they don't need to give, because wealthy foreign Christians will give for them. It has become a culture in the church to expect to receive rather than to give. And the people primarily to blame are the mission groups or individuals, who often times give with good motives but end up creating an unhealthy dependency.

One PPBS lecturer commented that even if many groups agree that they should not give to local Khmer churches, there will always be some other groups that are willing to give freely; therefore, the problem will continue. Local churches simply change allegiances and are drawn to those who give freely, while breaking ties with those that do not give. He also mentioned that some groups start out with the ideology not to financially support local Khmer churches, but in the end do so anyway.

We cannot underestimate the pressure for mission groups to give money to local churches or to local pastors. There is often an undeniable need to give in the context of rural Cambodia, where the lines of giving to alleviate poverty and giving to support a pastor are blurred. What further exacerbates the problem is the fact that these mission groups often feel a great deal of pressure to "show the results" of their labors. And the truth of the matter is that giving money does produce quick results, but often at a larger long-term cost. One lecturer shared that many Cambodian pastors can't help but compare themselves with other Cambodian pastors. Those who have lots of monetary resources to fund many programs tend to grow much faster than those without. It is such a discouragement to those without funds that quite often they give up the ministry altogether. At the same time, those ministries that tend to grow quickly because of large financial resources tend to shrink just as quickly when the financial resources are all used up.

The goal for the local church is not simply survival or maintaining the financial obligations of the local congregation, but giving for the expansion of the kingdom beyond the borders of Cambodia.

What is assumed in all these responses is that foreign groups should resist the temptation of giving any financial assistance to local Khmer churches. But is there room for financial giving that does produce long-term benefit? As discussed above, perhaps a healthier way of looking at the situation is to ask, "What would be the best way to financially support the local Khmer church?" Financial giving can be done to inspire local giving, encourage self-supporting churches, and/or provide a model of giving that can be reproduced by the local church.

Lack of Training

One explanation for the Khmer Church's lack of financial self-sufficiency is its tendency to overemphasize evangelism over the nurture and growth of local believers. Frequently, local pastors give all their attention to the conversion of non-Christians. Therefore their sermons are very simple gospel messages or apologetic messages outlining the differences between Buddhism and Christianity. However, the people who remain in the church are not fed or trained to maturity. The general trend is for the pastors to focus on newcomers and new believers to the neglect of older believers. As a result, those in the church have never been taught how to give, or to serve, or to grow in their personal walk with the Lord. Local pastors justify this by assuming that those who have been in the church for a long time are mature enough to continue on by themselves. Furthermore, the training that local pastors receive is not sufficient to take care of the flock. They may be trained in evangelism but not so much in pastoral care. What seems lacking is a healthy understanding of the church.

Financial giving can be done to inspire local giving, encourage self-supporting churches, and/or provide a model of giving that can be reproduced by the local church.

One lecturer noted that the concept of giving an offering is different in the context of the church and in the context of Buddhism. In Buddhism, giving is a religious act. When Buddhists give, they think about the benefit they will receive in the future, the next life. In the church, they think very practically. They believe the church has enough money because it is supported by foreigners. Giving an offering is not seen as devotion to God or worship. Rather, they believe the pastor is wealthier than them, so they don't feel like they should give. They don't see this necessarily as a religious act of love or act of worship. The prevailing thought is that there is no need to give to the church because they have enough money as it is.

Also contributing to the lack of giving is the idea that it is the leaders' job to find support from outsiders. Though it is unlikely that this idea is taught verbally to the church members, it is communicated nonetheless. Perhaps it follows from the idea that the pastor is a community leader and advocate. Many non-governmental organizations (NGOs) came pouring into the country in the early '90s and 2000s, offering free services and development projects. Local leaders who were able to secure these services were highly esteemed in their communities. It was part of their job to look after the best interests of their community and secure much-needed help. Perhaps this same idea has spilled over into the realm of the local Khmer church. The pastor, as the leader and advocate of the local church community, is to secure outside resources for the community.

Part of the problem is that local pastors are not getting sufficient training in how to grow a church to maturity. Even at the Phnom Penh Bible School, there is a recognized gap in training future pastors in the area of encouraging their congregation to financial self-sufficiency. In addition, there is a need for training in how to set up clear, accountable financial systems within the church with regular reports to the congregation. Some churches teach about offering, but not about supporting the church. Money is used for evangelism and outreaches, not for caring for the community or supporting the pastor.

Anecdotally, one PPBS lecturer shared how many graduates of the school began as pastors, but then dropped out. Or else they start their own businesses with the intention of supporting the ministry. Those who do start businesses support the church, but only for a short time. Then they stop. He also noted that some church leaders serve only to get money. Perhaps they come into ministry because they do not have a job. If their support stops, then they will stop serving.

Lack of Sustainable Ministry Structures

In order to understand why the Khmer Church in Phnom Penh—generally speaking—is not self-supported, we need to look at the ministry structures of the local churches. Many of the local churches have not effectively reached the middle and upper classes. They are either focused on the poor or students. Several city churches have begun with outreaches to slums and poorer areas or have begun by ministering to orphans. Often times, an orphanage or woman's shelter finds that it needs to provide some sort of church life for its clients. Therefore, a church is started at the orphanage or woman's shelter. But of course, this church ministry structure is not financially sustainable and will inevitably be dependent on outside resources.

Another approach is to start an English center or college dormitory. The English centers tend to attract young students, who often lack financial resources to support a local church. Furthermore, in their particular life stage, students tend to be less committed to a particular local church and often float between different ministries and churches. These churches, because of the demographics, tend to be less financially stable. Dormitory ministries allow large numbers of college students to be gathered for Sunday worship. These captive audiences are often grateful for free or almost free lodging and food to help them through their university years. But we have noticed that after they graduate and get jobs, they rarely stay and serve in the "dorm" church. Again, this ministry structure is not inherently sustainable.

Perhaps contributing to the lack of financial self-sufficiency in rural churches is the tendency to import a model of the church that would be more contextually fitting in the city. When it comes to supporting a local pastor in the rural context, it might make more sense to talk about meeting physical needs such as food and lodging rather than in terms of cash. One lecturer suggested that in the rural context, offerings do not have to be cash, but can be food, grain, rice, or animals. There seems to be a professional mentality toward ministry that views the office of pastor as a good job to have rather than a calling from God. The problem comes into play when the local rural pastor sees a mission agency as his employer and himself as an employee. Mission agencies must do a better job thinking through these issues and setting up ministry structures that lend themselves toward a self-supporting Khmer church.

What seems clear from the discussion above is the fact that there are problems on both sides: the mission groups and the local Khmer leaders. The fact that the Khmer church is a young church should not be underestimated. It will take generations for Khmer leadership to develop and effectively lead the Khmer church into maturity. However, what does seem clear is the need for comprehensive training in the areas of practical theology and ecclesiology.

A WAY FORWARD

We have discussed several challenges the Khmer church faces as it moves toward supporting itself. Is there a way forward? I suggest the Khmer churches and missionaries need to focus on four particular significant matters to help improve the situations described.

1. There needs to be more active discussions on best practices in missions giving to local ministries. We must wrestle with this as a community—not just missionaries, but also local Khmer leadership. We all must come to the table and ask ourselves, "What is best way we can support the Khmer church?" We must invest in forums and conferences that help build understanding on both sides.

2. Offer more training to those preparing for church ministry. We must invest in equipping Khmer pastors to develop accountable, financial systems for their local churches and to encourage their congregations to support their local church. We must change the perception that the local church is only a place to receive and not a place to give. We also must change the perception that the pastorate is simply a job rather than a calling.

3. We must invest in churches that seek to reach all levels of society. If churches can reach middle and upper class Cambodians, then a potential pool of resources will be available to reach the whole nation. As mission groups, we should think through ministry models that can become self-supporting rather than continuing models that breed dependency. This is not to say that college dorm ministries or orphan ministries should be neglected. But can we link these ministries with others that are perhaps more comprehensive in scope? For example, encouraging local Khmer churches to support and sponsor these types of mercy ministries, rather than having mercy ministries start churches.

4. Finally, we would be wise to bathe all these discussions, plans, and actions in prayer, seeking the direction and wisdom that comes from above. At the same time, we should also rejoice in the work of God that has been done in Cambodia. As much as there is to criticize about mission groups serving in Cambodia as well as local Khmer churches, there is just as much for which to thank and praise God. We need patience and steadfastness in our labors.

GROWING IN WISDOM

As mentioned in the beginning, this paper seeks to contribute to the ongoing discussion of how best to serve the Cambodian church. We ask ourselves difficult questions, probing questions, not to discourage us from the task, but to motivate us to strive for excellence to the glory of God and in dependence upon His Holy Spirit. There are indeed many areas in which we as mission groups can improve. There are also many areas in which the local Khmer church can grow.

As the discussion on the Khmer church's financial self-sufficiency continues, it is our hope that we will continue to wrestle with how the idea of interdependence works itself out in all areas of the Khmer church's relationship to the larger body of Christ. We pray that through these types of discussions and forums, much wisdom can be gained for the benefit of the Khmer church. "Where there is no guidance, a people falls, but in an abundance of counselors there is safety" (Proverbs 11:14).

Lloyd Kim became coordinator (director) of Mission to the World (MTW) in 2014. He was associate pastor with New Life Mission Church (PCA) in Fullerton, Calif. Lloyd and his wife served as missionaries with MTW beginning in 2004 in the Philippines and then in Cambodia, where they initiated a new church-planting work which has grown to five sites and four church plants. Lloyd served as MTW's international director of the Asia-Pacific region before becoming coordinator of MTW.

---

1   This article was published and read for a conference in Self-sustaining church plants in Indochina region: Thailand, Myanmar, Vietnam, Laos, and Cambodia, in 2009 in Phnom Penh, Cambodia. Published as Kim, L. (2011). *Toward a Self-supported Khmer Church* by Indochina Korean Missionary Association Theological Research Department, Phnom Penh: Salt & Light Publishing. 296-303.

2   Established in 1992. The school is non-denominational and evangelical.

27

Sustainable Livelihood for National Pastors

by Tina Shim

In Cambodia, despite having only two percent of the population profess Christianity as their religion, there are seven formal Bible schools and many more informal Bible teaching programs.[1] Many of the church leaders or pastors have a genuine heart for the Lord and their people. This is good news given the fact that the genocide of the 1970s left so few Christians in Cambodia and that today the average Cambodian church leader is only 38 years old and has been a Christian for just eight years.[2]

Are there challenges to encouraging and training up a new generation of pastors and Christians in this environment? Absolutely. There is opposition from family members for whom a rejection of Buddhism is seen not merely as a rejection of a personal religion, but as a complete rejection of their family and cultural identity as a Cambodian. Cambodian Christians often face the risk of suddenly finding themselves cast out of their family, the only community they have ever known.

Cambodian pastors are inspiring in their zeal for the gospel as they overcome the challenges of family rejection. Their joy for the Good News is infectious and they want everyone to know about it. They desire to plant churches to minister to whole communities, not just individual Christians. They love their "jobs."

The sad reality is that this kind of job often doesn't pay much, if at all. As these Cambodian pastors marry and start families, they feel a huge pinch in their wallets as they try to provide for their spouse and children. Remember, in many cases, they've been cast out of their extended family because of their faith so they do not have the benefit of resources that a normal Cambodian in the community would have. They bear the weight of responsibility alone as they face the challenge of bringing in enough income to provide for their family without giving up the pastoral job they love.

A CHALLENGE FOR THE DEVELOPING WORLD

This story is not unique to Cambodia. It plays itself out with some variations throughout the developing world. In fact, the idea of a professional pastor who can be supported solely through the tithes of the church is only considered "normal" because it is an American cultural norm. In contrast, in countries where the average worker is just above the poverty line, the idea that tithes alone could support the salary of a pastor is almost preposterous.

While many financial models and solutions to these pastors' problems have been debated and attempted, this article will focus on income-generating ideas that center on business. "Business as mission" is a broad field and while there is room to debate its precise definition, most people would agree that at its heart is a desire to use fundamental business principles, most importantly profit generation, in order that others would benefit from experiencing the gospel. The exact manner in which they experience the gospel can vary from the way in which the business itself is run and treats people to explicitly evangelizing employees or people in the community around them. The use of the profits can serve to support kingdom building by funding ministry activities of the business itself or funding ministers of the gospel outside of the business.

THE BUMPY ROAD FOR SMALL BUSINESSES
OWNED BY NATIONAL PASTORS

The main idea we will explore here is the notion of enabling sufficient income for pastors through their own small business. In this case, the primary purpose of the business is simply to generate enough profit to supplement whatever financial shortfall the pastor has for daily living expenses. The business itself may not be an explicit ministry, although the manner in which the pastor treats his customers and employees should demonstrate Christ's attitude toward people with love, grace, honesty, and dignity.

There are advantages and disadvantages to starting and running a business in the developing world. Capital requirements to start a new business are lower than in the developed world, so if the pastor can receive an infusion of cash to start his work, the amount of cash needed to start a business is not necessarily prohibitive. The business landscape is often not overly complex or crowded with competitors, so there is usually more room for new business ideas.

On the flip side, the business infrastructure in developing countries is often unreliable and incomplete. For example, supply chains are infamously inconsistent as the provision of materials or finished goods is dependent on unreliable road conditions, poor vehicle conditions, and corrupt customs or transportation officials requiring unknown amounts of bribes to permit the passage of each truck. Electricity and water supply can also be inconsistent in developing countries, and if a new business idea relies on electricity or water to produce a product or deliver a service to customers, then there will likely be some dissatisfied customers in the course of a normal business day.

We have observed a few keys to success for pastors who are able to become self-sufficient through their own small business. These keys to success boil down to one critical factor: the pastors' recognition of their need for help.

In addition to the typical difficulties facing a business owner in the developing world, pastors face the challenge of meeting two goals with one business: running a profitable business and freeing up enough time to actually serve as a pastor. The challenge of a pastor starting and running a business without acquiring the necessary business knowledge can often result in the early failure of the business and loss of capital investment funds. Even if the pastor is able to keep the business running, being involved in the day-to-day operations in a world without online ordering and bill-pay, working postal mail, reliable employees, or easy transportation on clearly marked streets usually means that nearly all of the pastor's time is taken up with the business, leaving very little time for the job he loves, pastoring.

KEYS TO SUCCESS

We have observed a few keys to success for pastors who are able to become self-sufficient through their own small business. These keys to success boil down to one critical factor: the pastors' recognition of their need for help. They ask for help and they willingly delegate authority and responsibilities so that together with these helpers they can achieve the greater objective—running a profitable business so that they have the income necessary to continue spending most of their personal time in ministry. In some ways it is a real-life reflection of the Apostle Paul's example of the many body parts working together with Christ as the head. Many helpers with different roles, who are working together toward the ultimate goal of enabling gospel proclamation.

Some specific ways in which pastors recruit helpers include:

- Identifying a business manager.
- Identifying and educating a business helper.
- Recruiting church leaders to assist with the work of the church.

IDENTIFYING A BUSINESS MANAGER

Pastors who have a trustworthy family member, often their spouse, who can serve as the responsible manager of the small business tend to see more success in their business endeavor. They are able to continue with their pastoral duties while still benefiting from a business that can generate income to support their family. The family member managing the business should have decision-making authority and should have an incentive for profitable business performance. In the case of a spouse, this incentive is built in: the family can only eat, pay rent, and send the kids to school if the business generates a profit. If this kind of authority is given to a sibling or even a non-family member, the pastor and/or spouse should consider other ways to ensure that the business is managed ethically. Surprise check-ins, surprise cash counts, good systems for tracking inventory and cash, and even security cameras are proven methods of enabling truthfulness in business operations.

IDENTIFYING A BUSINESS HELPER

In addition to recruiting able-bodied helpers to manage the business, pastors with successful businesses also invite in business expertise from able-minded individuals. They humbly acknowledge that they may not have expertise in the area of business and they seek out helpers to either train in-house employees or to whom they can outsource some aspects of their business. These business helpers should be nationals with proven business experience in the country or expatriates with proven business experience and a firm understanding of how to conduct business within the country and its cultural context. While fundamental business principles will be the same no matter what country the business operates in, the manner in which the business operates and is managed is steeped in culture and local business norms that can have a significant impact on daily business operations and the decisions made to improve profitability.

ASSESSING THE BUSINESS

With existing businesses, business helpers often first conduct an assessment of the business operations and then offer training in specific areas with high potential. Once they have suggested some areas for improvement, discussed their ideas with the pastor and the business manager, and come to an agreement on areas of focus, the business helper can set up coaching sessions and timeline-based goals. For new business ideas, the business helper can first assess and ensure that the appropriate structure is in place to meet profit goals and then suggest some next steps, including estimated timing, budget, and required manpower, to help the pastor fully understand what investing in the business venture will require.

Setting up measurable goals is important because it will help both the business helper and the pastor track whether or not the training and new ideas for change are making a difference. Business helpers will typically check on the status as frequently as possible to ensure that valuable resources and money are being used as efficiently as possible.

EDUCATING THE BUSINESS MANAGER IN COUNTRY

The manner and length of the business training can vary extensively and is highly dependent on the needs of the pastor's individual business and the existing skills of the business manager. One other important element that this article does not have the space to adequately address is the baseline level of education the pastor and business manager have. In countries where the base education is less advanced, but the business opportunity is fairly simple, effective business training may be conducted without formal classes or degrees from educational institutions. Instead, basic training in core business concepts like product or service differentiation and profitable operations (revenues exceeding total costs) with close coaching from the business helper should be enough to ensure that the pastor is running the business using sound business principles. At times, non-business training in subjects such as language and math can also prove to be impactful, enabling the pastor or the business manager to better understand any additional business training.

As an example, in Cambodia, the average education level of a pastor is Grade 8 and the public educational system is very mediocre. By Grade 8, they will have learned enough to have basic reading, writing, and math skills, but will not be exposed to basic problem solving, critical thinking, and logic skills. Outside of the pastor population, we have found some local business owners do not understand mathematic concepts such as multiplication, thereby making it difficult to understand systems of inventory management or purchasing items at quantity discounts. Therefore, training in non-business subjects can go hand in hand with regular business subjects to help maximize the improvement potential of both the business helper and the business.

In some cases, the pastor and the business manager have a relatively high level of education already. The business helper can recommend training on specific business topics after assessing the current business operations or future business idea. Training can be formal and held through programs at available local universities or informal through coaching by the business helper. In most cases, a combination of formal business education and informal coaching puts the business in the best position for success.

EDUCATING THE BUSINESS MANAGER
THROUGH SHORT-TERM TEAMS

If there is no business helper available or the business helper does not have the expertise needed to coach the pastor or the business manager, and attending formal classes at a nearby school is not possible, the missions team may bring in short-term experts to provide specific training. These short-term experts may be other nationals who have technical business expertise or practical experience with overcoming a specific issue in the country. They may also be expatriates who have technical business expertise and are willing to come for a short-term trip.

While we have seen some self-identified business experts come to the field for multi-month or one-year internships, these individuals have typically been young college graduates with gracious and humble hearts, but unfortunately, not much actual business experience. While their service is greatly appreciated, the local business owners and managers need business helpers who have enough years of experience to be able to help them steer the business toward long-term profitability in varying situations and circumstances.

Prior to bringing in any short-term expatriate experts, the long-term missionaries and the business manager should first assess the business and its key needs, assuming that they have the necessary knowledge to conduct the business assessment. Once they have identified the areas needing assistance, they can then request the right kind of expertise. In many cases, general business expertise is sufficient to provide adequate training for general strategy, costing, profit generation, and basic operations. However, in other cases, due to the specific industry type or the competitive environment, more specialized expertise could be very helpful to the business manager.

For example, some church members who started a construction business in Cambodia had great experience with actual construction, but little experience with developing contracts and a pricing scheme that would allow them to make a sustainable profit in the long run. While a general business expert could be helpful in identifying and reaching the right target market and identifying costs and expenses in their existing construction operations, finding a business helper with specific expertise in construction contracts and the actual construction industry would be much more helpful. Since the industry in Cambodia traditionally has fairly low profit margins, having inside industry experience could be the difference between a company operating at a loss or making a profit.

Upon arriving on the field, short-term business experts typically offer seminars on specific topics of interest to several business managers at once and make time for one-on-one coaching sessions to better understand and advise on each business manager's business. It would be advisable for the pastor to also be present at these meetings because as the business owner, he may need to be involved in providing information or making decisions related to the overall business strategy. In addition, the benefit of the training provided by these short-term experts is usually maximized when any long-term missionaries can first brief them on cultural do's and don'ts before they interact with the nationals.

RECRUITING CHURCH LEADERS

In addition to identifying managers and helpers for their business, pastors who are successful at balancing both business and church responsibilities also recruit and empower church leaders. The biblical model of identifying lay leaders and entrusting responsibility with them also makes good business sense. Too often we see examples of pastors who are overworked and burned out even without the additional responsibility of owning and running a business. For those pastors who are responsible for the church and their own business, following the example of the early church and finding other leaders to lead, teach, and care for the growing congregation is a necessity.

Church leaders will likely include both ordained (or studying to be ordained) pastors as well as lay leaders. As with any organization, one key to success is the clear communication of roles and responsibilities. Without a clear understanding of what they are supposed to do, who they are meant to care for, and what decisions they have authority over, church leaders will either act too dependently or too independently. If they are too dependent, then their role is ineffective and redundant, as they will constantly be asking the national pastor for further help and assistance. They may turn out to be more of a hindrance than help! If they are too independent, then they may make decisions or take action in ways that are inconsistent with biblical teaching or denominational convictions.

In an economic sense, sustainable businesses offer helpful services to the community and employment to locals. Locals who know that Christians operate the local businesses can also consider the spiritual claims of Christianity in a more credible light.

At one of our Cambodian church plants, the head national pastor also owns several businesses with his wife. God has graciously brought him two pastors who are studying toward ordination. One assistant pastor has city church planting and ministry responsibilities and the other assistant pastor has village church planting and ministry responsibilities. The senior pastor is still involved in key decisions, but he is now able to focus on teaching, other presbytery-wide concerns, overall church strategy, and, of course, running his businesses with the help of his business manager. The profits from these businesses help sustain the church building rent and an additional dormitory that was set up for local university students.

IMPACTING THE LOCAL COMMUNITY

In success stories of pastors who are able to sustainably operate both church and business, we also find a positive impact to the local community. In an economic sense, sustainable businesses offer helpful services to the community and employment to locals. Locals who know that Christians operate the local businesses can also consider the spiritual claims of Christianity in a more credible light. They see how the manner in which they treat employees, customers, and suppliers is different from other local businesses. They see how the spiritual realm can directly impact their everyday living in a positive way.

Tina Shim served in Phnom Penh, Cambodia with her husband Albert and their three elementary aged daughters from 2012-2016 with MTW. Prior to leaving for the field, she worked for more than 12 years in business with large corporations such as Ernst & Young and Johnson & Johnson as well as with her home church of Pacific Crossroads Church in Los Angeles, California. While serving in the field, she supported individual pastors, local churches, non-governmental organizations, and schools with relevant business advice and training.

---

1   Steve Hyde, *Portrait of the Body of Christ in Cambodia* (Phnom Penh, Cambodia: Words of Life Ministries, 2012), 19.

2   Hyde, *Portrait of the Body of Christ in Cambodia*, 15.

28

Missions, God is the Beginning, the Center, and the End

by Addison Soltau

After assessing the second half of the previous century, one professor of mission history wrote this conclusion, "The historical context in which we engage in missions has changed radically," and then adds, "I believe we have now entered its most creative and productive period of the missionary movement."[1] This is significant, as his positive assessment follows his review of the growth of the church on the three continents of Africa, Asia, and Latin America. The amazing harvest of new believers continues across these three continents while by contrast, the church grows slowly or even declines in the rest of the world. Much of the growth that has taken place has come, not primarily because of Western missionary involvement, but through the work of the Holy Spirit.

Much of the growth that has taken place has come, not primarily because of Western missionary involvement, but through the work of the Holy Spirit.

A BRIEF LOOK AT MISSION HISTORY

We may well ask, do we find such a pattern in the past 2,000 years of mission history? As students of mission history, we note the following:

- The church as an institution has not been the primary instigator of its mission outreach to the world. Too often it has been one of the obstacles.
- When missionary impulses/movements have arisen, in the majority of cases they were the result of individuals or small groups who have been at the center (see Pietist movement, et al), not the church.
- The institutions most responsible for preparing people for mission work in the U.S. have been Bible institutes or Bible colleges, not theological seminaries.
- Recently, the sending agencies of those who have volunteered for mission service have been "faith missions," not church- or denomination-related mission societies.
- Many of those who have volunteered for mission service have had little status in the church. In fact, in many cases, these people were of the opinion that missions could be conducted best not by the church itself, but through special mission societies created for that purpose. On both philosophical and pragmatic grounds, the church was perceived as uninvolved, unresponsive, and unwieldy for the cause of missions.

All these evidences cited above, and there are more, point to the ministry of the Holy Spirit who, through the years, has moved often in unpredictable and unforeseen ways in the hearts of people when the church has not, to bring His gospel to the lost.

What does this say to those in Reformed churches who hold a high view of the church, insist on formal theological preparation for the ministry, and follow confessional standards that have little to say about the missionary nature of the church? Can we agree with Paul Pierson's suggestion that the church is about to enter or has entered its most creative and productive period in missions history? Can this be said about our churches, and is it to this we are looking, hoping, and praying? Are we asking the Holy Spirit to start a new work in our churches in light of the 4.7 billion people who do not yet know the Lord? If the history of missions bears testimony of God's continuous wrestling with His church, as J. H. Bavinck suggests, we may well wonder if God will have to continue wrestling or will the church be more responsive to the task still before it?[2]

A FRESH HERMENEUTIC NEEDED

This is a matter which calls for serious consideration and which in turn suggests the title of this paper, "The Bible's Grand Narrative." The title comes out of reading Christopher J. H. Wright's *The Mission of God* the sub-title being "Unlocking the Bible's Grand Narrative."[3] Published nine years ago, the seeds of this 500+ page book started when the author, raised in a missionary family, made the observation that there seemed to be too little connection between theology and mission. Theology was all about God, he understood, what God is like, what God said, and what mostly dead people had speculated about all three. Mission, on the other hand, is all about us, the living, and what we have been doing since the time of William Carey.

A few years later, this same writer was asked to teach a course titled "The Biblical Basis of Mission" at All Souls Christian College in England. He found no difficulty finding biblical texts that supported the topic of missions. But as he taught the course he concluded the course could better be named not "The Biblical Basis of Mission" but "The Missional Basis of the Bible." He wanted his students to grasp the fact that the Bible itself is a missional phenomenon. "The Bible renders to us," he argues, "the story of God's mission through God's people in their engagement with God's world for the sake of the whole of God's creation."[4] For the next 500 pages Dr. Wright makes this point well.

It is not the purpose of this brief paper to reproduce the full and impressive treatment of his thesis, but only to try and document some of his basic points while at the same time suggesting that a reading of this book is important for serious students of the mission of the church. The thrust of this paper therefore is that in light of the past history of the church and its involvement in mission or lack thereof, plus the time of history in which we find ourselves (i.e., a radically changed and changing world), it will only be through reading our Bibles with a fresh hermeneutic that the church may discover what has been missed before so that the future can be a truly creative and productive period.

Where do we find such a hermeneutic? The original title of this chapter was, "The Bible's Grand Narrative," which may sound somewhat presumptuous. After all, haven't we been reading the Bible all these years, and if so, what has Dr. Wright discovered in his study of Scripture that would make a fresh reading of the Bible necessary if indeed the church is to respond to the challenges of this day?

BACK TO THE BIBLE AND HISTORY AGAIN

What does the history of missions reveal? For one thing it tells how the Protestant Church has only engaged seriously in its mission outreach to other nations and cultures in the last 200 years or so. It was only as recent as 1793 that William Carey, much against the will of his wife and his church, sailed to India as the first missionary in the modern-day missionary movement. Where and how did Carey develop such a great burden for un-evangelized people in foreign lands? It appears to have come from neither the preaching he heard nor from his church leaders. In fact, the story is that one of the elders present at a gathering told Carey God would save the heathen without his help or anyone else's for that matter. Is this another illustration of what led J. H. Bavinck to suggest that throughout history God had to wrestle with His church to get it to have a concern for the lost?[5]

It will only be through reading our Bibles with a fresh hermeneutic that the church may discover what has been missed before so that the future can be a truly creative and productive period.

The book of Acts teaches that the church was extremely slow and even unwilling to engage in missions even though the command of Christ was still fresh in its ears. There were, of course, major obstacles which had to be faced and overcome. There was fear of the unknown as well as spiritual blindness (the way the Bible was read and understood), and most telling, what Bavinck saw as the inclination of the church to keep the status quo, to remain undisturbed, a tendency he believes has always plagued the church. "The church loves to be occupied with itself and its own problems," Bavinck writes, "It loves peace and calm and is deathly afraid of anything that would shake it up and bring unrest."[6]

Have these and other factors been present all these years? Are what Bavinck describes as major difficulties the church faced in its early history still obstacles the church faces today? Could this be one of the reasons why many Reformed theological seminaries require only one course on the mission of the church in the entire seminary curriculum, and why presbyteries too rarely ask those seeking ordination for their understanding and convictions regarding the church's mission?

Dr. Wright believes the church hasn't read the Bible correctly, that the Bible too rarely has been understood as a missionary book with God and His mission forming the Bible's grand narrative.

There are doubtless some who disagree with this thesis but he makes his case cogently and persuasively.

THE BIBLE'S MISSIONAL CHARACTER

The missional character of the Bible begins, he argues, with the Bible's very existence. It is missional in that it witnesses to the movement of God from the beginning toward His creation of the world as well as the human beings He made in His image. Early on, the biblical story highlights Adam and Eve's rebellion against God's grand purpose for His creation and how God refused to forsake His rebellious fallen creation and people. Instead, He determined to redeem and restore the fallen creation to His original design, never forgetting or forsaking His original purpose. The Old Testament tells its story as The Story, as part of the ultimate and universal story that will embrace the whole of creation, time, and humanity within its scope. The biblical story, this grand narrative, narrates the story of God's journey on a long road of redemption. It is the story of His continuing to work out His redemptive purposes in subsequent human history finishing the story with the hope of His new creation. The Scriptures are clear that God has had this goal or mission since the beginning, a mission that He has promised to accomplish by the power of His Word. This is the mission of the biblical God portrayed in Scripture.

But it isn't simply the narrative of Scripture that tells this story. The biblical texts themselves speak of God's people in their confrontation with controversy or threat from their surrounding neighbors, threats they needed to address in the context of their mission. The Old Testament historical books document their mission. Many of these Old Testament texts speak of Israel's engagement with the surrounding world, telling what they believed God had done and was doing in their world. These same texts tell of Israel's struggle with the religion of Canaan while the prophets document their capitulation, which ended in captivity and exile.

The New Testament also is essentially a missionary document. The New Testament tells the story of this mission with special emphasis on the message proclaimed by the missionaries. The Gospels were written to explain the significance of the good news about Jesus Christ, essential to the missionary task of the early church. Paul also writes as a missionary in the midst of his missionary work.

It is this missiological thrust that gives theological coherence to the Bible, unifying both Old and New Testaments. "In short," Wright says, "a missionary hermeneutic proceeds from the assumption that the whole Bible renders to us the story of God's mission through God's people in their engagement with God's world for the sake of the whole of God's creation."[7]

THE IMPORTANCE OF THE RIGHT STARTING POINT
This, he says, is the starting point of how the Scriptures are to be read. There is much more, of course, but this is the starting point; to recognize that by starting with a missiological approach to the Bible, we are led to think first of the grand purpose for which the Bible exists: the missional God portrayed in the Bible and the story the Bible tells about God, His people, and about the whole world and its future. One writer argues that it is "this missionary dimension, so often neglected in modern theological interpretation, that which unifies both Old and New Testaments and coordinates their various themes into a single motif."[8]

A missional hermeneutic of the Bible begins with the mission of God and "traces the flow of all other dimensions of mission as they affect human history from that center and starting point."[9] From the mission of God, or God with a mission, we next find humanity with a mission, the mandate to fill the earth, subdue it, and to rule over creation. To be human, therefore, is to have a purposeful role in God's creation.

Following this, the Scriptures tell of the mission of God's people, the Israelites. Israel came into existence as a people with a mission given to them for the sake of God's wider purpose of blessing the nations.

To this people, Jesus comes with His own mission. His mission was both to restore Israel but also for them to be the agent of reaching the ends of the world with the message of God's salvation. God's mission determined Jesus' mission. It is interesting to see this in the story of Jesus when He appeared to the disciples following His resurrection from the dead. He opened their minds, we are told, so they could understand the Scriptures. What the Scriptures said was that Christ would suffer and rise from the dead . . . and repentance and forgiveness of sins would be preached to all nations beginning at Jerusalem (Luke 24:45-47). Jesus' mission to all nations was to flow out of His resurrection. "The full meaning of recognizing Jesus as Messiah lies in recognizing also his role in relation to God's mission for Israel for the blessing of the nations." [10]

Finally, the Bible story includes the church with a mission. Jesus entrusted to the church a mission related to the crucified and risen Jesus. "You are my witnesses," Jesus told His disciples, and as the ones who walked with Jesus during His earthly ministry they were entrusted with the role of witnesses of their Lord and His work, to take that message to the ends of the earth (Acts 1:8).

Unless the church is brought face to face with the fact that it is missionary through and through, that it is missionary by its very nature and that the missionary task belongs to the entire body, missionary work can quickly become the activity of specialists carried on in unknown places of no great interest to the main body.

WHAT THIS MEANS FOR UNDERSTANDING THE CHURCH'S NATURE

Setting the marks of the church clearly and decisively within the context of mission serves as an important corrective to the church's longstanding problem of introversion, that of seeking its own good even to the point of forgetting its nature. Everything the church is and does must be seen in the context of mission. If this is the case, the church carries out the basic and continuing tasks of worship, fellowship, nurture, and service, each having a missionary *dimension* although not necessarily a missionary *intention*.

The doxological task is so central and all-controlling that it should constitute the very core of the life of the church. But history shows that even with the best of intentions, when the missionary dimension is forgotten or lacking, worship can quickly turn in upon itself and begin to lose its meaning.

The church is not only called to praise God; it is also called to be concerned with itself. It makes the Word of God known to each generation;

it perseveres in the service of God and exercises loving care of the souls belonging to it. Fellowship and nurture lie at the heart of the church's existence but, along with worship, it too must be seen in the context of mission. The missionary dimension of the body of Christ means that fellowship and nurture exercised within the body may not happen at the expense of those outside the body.

The missionary dimension of the church is primary. Unless the church is brought face to face with the fact that it is missionary through and through, that it is missionary by its very nature and that the missionary task belongs to the entire body, missionary work can quickly become the activity of specialists carried on in unknown places of no great interest to the main body.

David Bosch writes, "Missiology should provoke theology as a whole to discover anew that mission is not simply a more or less neglected department of the church's life which only enters the picture when a specialist from the outside appears on the scene or when a collection is taken. Missiology is not simply yet another subject, but a dimension of theology as a whole, an indispensable dimension which must preserve the church from parochialism and provincialism."[11]

HOW MIGHT THIS AFFECT THEOLOGICAL EDUCATION?

As a dimension of theology, missiology is interested in all the disciplines of theological education, the way the courses are taught, how worship is conducted, even in student and faculty conversation in the lunchroom. It is there to confront provincialism wherever it is discovered, to help people gain a greater vision of the world, to point them to the Scriptures again for a fresh understanding of God's concern for the peoples of the world. If the marks of the church are seen in the context of mission, if the nature of the church is truly mission oriented, the critical function of missiology should serve to keep this before the Christian community, especially in theological education. The seminary student must not be allowed to forget that the early Christian mission was the progenitor of theology; that the church was by circumstances forced to theologize; that theology, biblically understood, exists to accompany the church on its mission to the world. In the words of Martin Kahler, "Theology is a companion of the Christian mission."[12] For a fuller discussion on this topic read *Reaching the Unreached, The Old-New Challenge*, edited by Harvie M. Conn.[13]

CONCLUDING THOUGHTS

Wright concludes his book with words well worth including at this point. "Here is The Story," he writes, "the grand universal narrative that stretches from creation to new creation, and accounts for everything in between. This is The Story that tells us where we have come from, how we got to be here, who we are, why the world is in the mess it is, how it can be changed and has been changed, and where we are ultimately going. And the whole story is predicated on the reality of this God and the mission of this God. He is the originator of the story, the teller of the story, the prime actor in the story, the planner and guide of the story's plot, the meaning of the story and its ultimate completion. He is its beginning, end and center. It is the story of the mission of God, of this God and no other."[14]

Sometimes we may wrestle with the question of how we can make the gospel relevant to the world. But in this story, God is about the business of transforming the world to fit the shape of the gospel.

We may also wonder how the care of creation might fit into our concept and practice of mission. This story asks whether our lives, lived on God's earth and under God's sight, are aligned with God's mission that stretches from creation to cosmic transformation and the arrival of a new heaven and new earth.

We may argue about what can legitimately be included in the mission that God expects from the church, when we should be asking what kind of church God expects for His mission in all its fullness.

The only concept of mission into which God fits is the one of which He is the beginning, the center, and the end, and the only access that we have to that mission of God is given to us in the Bible. This is the grand narrative that we find when we read all the Scriptures in the light of the mission of God.

Born of missionary parents in Korea, Dr. Addison P. Soltau is nearing the completion of sixty-four years of ministry in 2016. He began his ministry in Japan where he taught at the Japan Christian Theological Seminary (Tokyo) and pastored two Japanese churches (also in Tokyo) over the course of seventeen years. Later, his ministry in the US followed a similar pattern, teaching at Reformed Bible College (now Kuyper College) Grand Rapids, Michigan, at Covenant Theological Seminary (St. Louis, Missouri), and Knox Theological Seminary (Ft. Lauderdale, Forida) and as pastor of Teaching and Missions at Coral Ridge PCA and First Presbyterian PCA of Coral Springs.

1   Paul E. Pierson, *The Dynamics of Christian Mission: History through a Missiological Perspective*, (William Carey International University Press, 2009), 352.

2   J. H. Bavinck, *An Introduction to the Science of Missions* (Philadelphia: Presbyterian and Reformed Publishing Company, 1960), 275.

3   Christopher J. H. Wright, *The Mission of God: Unlocking the Bible's Grand Narrative* (Downers Grove, Illinois: InterVarsity Press, 2006)

4   Wright, *The Mission of God*, 22.

5   Bavinck, *An Introduction to the Science of Missions*

6   Bavinck, *An Introduction to the Science of Missions*, 276.

7   Wright, *The Mission of God*, 51.

8   David Filbeck, *Yes, God of the Gentiles Too: The Missionary Message of the Old Testament* (Wheaton: Billy Graham Center, 1994), 10.

9   Wright, *The Mission of God*, 62.

10 Wright, *The Mission of God*, 31.

11 David Bosch, *Theological Education in Missionary Perspective* (Missiology, January 10, 1982) 26.

12 Bosch, *Theological Education in Missionary Perspective*, 27.

13 Harvie M. Conn, editor, *Reaching the Unreached, The Old-New Challenge* (New Jersey: Presbyterian and Reformed Publishing Company, 1984), 155.

14 Wright, *The Mission of God*, 533.

Conclusion

by Dr. Lloyd Kim, Coordinator of Mission to the World

In a certain sense, missions is the same as it was when Jesus gave His disciples the great commission. His followers are still going to all the nations baptizing in the name of the Father, Son, and Holy Ghost, teaching them to observe all that Jesus commanded" (Matt 28:19-20). And yet, in another sense, missions is so very different than it was even a generation ago. We are seeing a need for greater collaboration across ethnic and national boundaries for missions. We are seeing a need for more in depth training and discipleship. We are seeing a need for a more healthy integration of word and deed ministries. And we are seeing a need for greater trust and respect among an increasingly diverse missions community.

What is represented in these chapters is a mosaic of perspectives on some very difficult questions. You may not agree with all that was written; but hopefully these articles have led to greater reflection, discussion, and engagement with issues that are relevant to all who take the Great Commission seriously.

But note well that the articles contained in this book are more than academic musings on global mission issues. Interwoven in each chapter is the life experience of practitioners who speak from the trenches. They are a collection of battle stories, war time tactics, and insights from those on the front lines. They represent the blood, sweat, and tears of many years of faithful labors. More than filling our heads with knowledge, these stories are to inspire us, sharpen us, and challenge us to engage with them in kingdom advancement.

Therefore, it is our prayer that this book will result in greater kingdom prayer, kingdom giving, and kingdom advancement in the sending of many labors into the harvest field (Matt 9:38). Indeed the fields are ripe for harvest! But above all, our greatest desire is that our King Jesus would be honored and glorified in this humble attempt to exalt Him in our reflections on His Great Commission. *Soli Deo Gloria!*